MATERIALISM AND
THE TASK OF ANTHROPOSOPHY

MATERIALISM AND THE TASK OF ANTHROPOSOPHY

Seventeen lectures given in Dornach
between April 2 and June 5, 1921

RUDOLF STEINER

The Anthroposophic Press
Hudson, N.Y.

Rudolf Steiner Press
London

The seventeen lectures presented here were given in Dornach, Switzerland, between April 2 and June 5, 1921. In the Collected Edition of Rudolf Steiner's works in German, the volume containing the original texts is entitled *Perspektiven der Menschheitsentwicklung* (Vol. 204 in the Bibliographic Survey). They were translated from the German by Maria St. Goar.

Distributed in the U.S. by Anthroposophic Press, Bell's Pond, Star Route, Hudson, N.Y. 12534.
Distributed in the U.K. by Rudolf Steiner Press, 38 Museum Street, London, WC1.

Library of Congress Cataloging-in-Publication Data
Steiner, Rudolf, 1861-1925
    Materialism and the Task of Anthroposophy

    Translation of: Perspektiven der Menschheitsentwicklung.
    1. Anthroposophy.   2. Materialism.   I. Title.
BP595.S894P4413   1987   299'.935   87-1171

ISBN 0-88010-177-6
     0-88010-176-8 (pbk.) Anthroposophic Press
     85440-105-9
     85440-095-8 (pbk.) Rudolf Steiner Press

Cover design by Van James

Printed in the United States of America

CONTENTS

Lecture I, Dornach, April 2, 1921   1
Materialism was justified in the nineteenth
century; clinging to it generates catastrophes.
Knowledge of the material world remains, theoretical materialism must cease. The latter is a
reflection of developments in the nineteenth
century when the physical body, particularly
brain and nervous system, had evolved into
perfect replicas of soul and spirit, while the
etheric, dream producing force in man had
diminished. Moritz Benedikt and thinking
that is completely immersed in the physical.
Shorthand. Today, physical, structural perfection has passed its zenith.

Lecture II, April 3, 1921   21
Errors in mere thinking and errors rooted in
actuality. The latter, for example theoretical
materialism, can have a beneficial side for
mankind. Structural forces of the head are recognized by imagination; those of rhythmic
system by inspiration, those of metabolic system by intuition. The nature of imagination;
essence of reflective thinking; objective perception. Knowledge and death.

Lecture III, April 9, 1921   37
Prior to Aristotle, process of acquiring speech
was still comprehended; hence, instinctive
awareness that the soul-spiritual element
resounding in the word is identical with the
one that, having created nature in the world,

has become silent; also insight into preexistence, still earlier, into reincarnation. Path leading from fading out of ancient word-comprehension to abstract spirituality of logic and concept: logic of Aristotle; "nous" of Anaxagoras; "idea" of Plato; Logos teaching of Gnosticism; Logos and Christianity; Gospel of John. Fourth century A.D. final loss of Logos knowledge. Conscious reattainment through anthroposophy.

Lecture IV, April 15, 1921   53

Until the fourth century A.D., a form of Oriental astronomy and medicine prevailed, acquired from a cosmic wisdom that instinctively understood the etheric domain. This wisdom also flowed into cultic life. Image of the Mithras cult; Christianity. Dionysius the Areopagite; further advance of ancient wisdom reaching to Basilius Valentinus, Jacob Boehme and Paracelsus. Since Constantine and Justinian the Egypto-Roman "principle of determination" penetrates association between truth and the word; it cuts off any comprehension of Christianity based on pre-Christian wisdom.

Lecture V, April 16, 1921   73

Transition in the fourth century A.D. Nature of Greek culture, its tragedy. The Occident pushes the wisdom of ancient Greece and the Mithras cult back into the Orient. For the religious life of the northern nations, factual narration of the events of Palestine remains, also dogmas of the ecumenical councils necessary for strengthening of *I*. The wisdom of the Orient penetrates Europe in Arabism only as an intellectual culture. In some European souls, the mystery of bread and wine is revived and with it that of ancient astronomy and medicine. Its reality, concentrated in the Grail Mystery, hovers over Western world turned materialistic; it can only be discovered through inner questioning by the individual. Titurel. External crusades to Jerusalem are renewed materialistic distortion of this search.

Lecture VI, April 17, 1921   89

The Oriental mind dwelt in spiritual world and based on it had to comprehend material realm. Europeans live in material world and based on it must seek to understand spiritual domain. Transition from one to the other in Greek culture. Gnosticism's problem to comprehend Christ in Jesus. Suspension of this struggle due to nationalized Roman Christianity. "Humanization" of Christianity in Europe. The *Heliand* epic. Insensibility regarding higher wisdom. Search for the Grail. Danger of being caught up in materialism since fifteenth century. Soloviev's call for Christianized state. Forces that hinder path of spiritual activation; love of evil.

Lecture VII, April 22, 1921   109

Friedrich Nietzsche's philosophical development and tragedy as struggle against forces of decline and a symptom of degree of spirit alienation during last third of nineteenth century. Image of man, meaning of earth life and nature of Christianity cannot be grasped any longer even by Nietzsche; their distortion in the concept of "superman," the "eternal return of the same" and the "Antichrist."

Lecture VIII, April 23, 1921 127

Measure,number, weight: examples of the loss of self and reality in a humanity on the way to abstraction. Well into the second post-Atlantean epoch, numbers were still experienced as qualities possessing living being, received from cosmic totality by the astral body and imprinted into etheric body. In third post-Atlantean epoch, measure was experienced as the force proceeding from etheric body that forms the physical body according to cosmic relationships; until the first, weight was sensed as primal experience between *I* and astral body, perceptible to mankind as condition of balance between being fettered to earth and soaring upward. Last remaining aftereffects of these qualities only in art.

Lecture IX, April 24, 1921 151

The nineteenth century as culmination in history of abstract spirituality and materialism since fourth century. Dogma and ritual. Formerly: life in the *body* that thus experienced cosmic spirituality; today: life in the *spirit* that turns to matter and fails to recognize itself. Different in Leibnitz's case. The power of comprehending spiritual scientific concepts that the modern intellect can create out of itself as possibility for transforming and enlivening of rigid and inwardly indolent intelligence. The three forms of indolence: neo-Catholicism, which preserves the old content in dogmas, Protestantism with its compromise between tradition and intellect, and enlightened intellectualism without spiritual content. Future polarization into Catholic traditionalism and spiritually awakening intellectuality.

Lecture X, April 29, 1921   173
Necessity of reaching the goal of each given level of evolution in individual life as well as that of humanity. Goal of the fourth epoch was development of intellectual soul; on basis of etheric body's activity, man awakened from cosmic sensing to cosmic reason. Since fifteenth century, etheric activity has completely impressed itself into physical body, thinking turned into human, subjective shadow images, causing separation into merely logical thinking and a will left to its own devices and bound to desires and instinct. Overcoming of this separation, for example, in Jesuitism. Necessity in the twentieth century of bringing reality into shadowy thinking by way of the human *I* so that it can dwell in transforming manner in the social and economic world that has turned chaotic.

Lecture XI, April 30, 1921   191
Significance of the year 1840 as point in time of

actual dawning of consciousness soul. In the various cultures, this dawning encountered different older forms of consciousness: in England, a state of mind resembling ancient Homeric Greece; in France, a partial legacy of the Latin intellectual soul culture; in Italy, a portion of the ancient sentient soul culture; in central Europe, a legacy from the fourth century A.D. In Eastern Europe, this process has largely been slept through. Oswald Spengler's *Prussianism and Socialism*.

Lecture XII, May 1, 1921   211
The two main streams of nineteenth century: formally juristic Roman Catholicism on the part of the Latin nations with their spiritual and ideological struggles and, arising out of social and industrial practices, the economic mode of thinking of the Anglo-Saxons with their problems of power. Both streams are ultimately rooted in Persian culture, Catholicism in the Ormuzd worship, the Anglo-Saxon element in Ahrimanic initiations. Joseph de Maistre, the knowledgeable and brilliant representative of ancient Catholicism; his battle against the spirit coming into vogue since fifteenth century. The necessary counterbalance and renewal through a free spiritual life. Goethe's insight concerning this; his reaction to debate between Cuviers and Geoffroy Saint-Hilaire.

Lecture XIII, May 5, 1921   235
Earthly man's connection with the planetary

forces. As late as the fourth post-Atlantean epoch, awareness of the ego development's link with sun; necessity today to regain this insight. Polarity of sun and moon forces in structure of earthly man. Differentiation of forces as noted through the process of eating: effects of earthly forces, the circumference, moon, and sun forces. Further differentiation of planetary influences in astral body: besides the sun, Saturn, Jupiter, and Mars are effective in "upper" man; in "lower" man, besides the moon, Mercury and Venus. Constellation and earthly birth.

Lecture XIV, May 13, 1921   255

Materialistic science and spiritual science as spiritual-cosmic events between moon's exit and return. The spirit of natural science could give rise to a new kingdom of nature between mineral and plant in the form of shadowy, living spider beings that cover the earth in weblike fashion during the latter's reunification with moon and lunar life. Humanity would thereby be cut off from world's life and spirituality. Cultivation of spiritual science facilitates arrival from other planets of spiritual beings who are striving to come to earth since the end of the nineteenth century; their activity becomes possible only by way of a thinking that grasps living, ensouled elements. Path to this transformation: unification of clear thinking with artistic perception in a science that simultaneously will become art. Goethe's teaching of morphology; his "Hymn to Nature"; Nietzsche's picture of the valley of death.

Lecture XV, June 2, 1921   273

John Scotus Erigena's thinking, an expression
of a developmental metamorphosis between
ancient visionary and intellectual thinking.
The aftereffects of "negative theology" by
Dionysius the Areopagite and Origen on the
age of Scotus. The four parts of the book *De
divisione naturae*: the doctrine of God, doctrine
of the hierarchies, spirit doctrine of nature
and man, eschatology; no thoughts as yet on a
social doctrine. Erigena's thinking: still spiritual reality, already abstract concepts. Mirror-
ing of the knowledge of earlier cultural epochs
in first three parts of the book but not in chro-
nological sequence; the fourth part: striving of
intellect at that time to comprehend Christianity and future of humanity. Since fifteenth
century this flows into the groundwork of natural science. The contradiction of our age that
actually dwells in refined spirit but as to its
contents has become increasingly materialistic.

Lecture XVI, June 3, 1921   299

World decline and world dawn. Erigena
between old and new thinking. The Gospel of
John as testimony that Christ, the Logos, is
creator of earthly realm. In antiquity, the
"Father principle" held sway: man experienced himself in body and blood as the image
of the divine Father as represented in the tribal
father of the generations; God and Spirit held
sway in earth and moon forces. First three
parts of Erigena's book tie in with this. Early
Christian knowledge concerning the nature of

Father forces and Christ force. The Gospel of John. Transition from pre-Christian blood sacrifices to offering of bread and wine. The end of the world as decline of ancient, body-bound spirit force took place in the fourth century. By degrees, it always appears again in human consciousness; the mood of the crusades; Alfred Suess; Oswald Spengler. Possibility of renewal based on real spirit perception.

Lecture XVII, June 5, 1921   321
Transition in the fourth century from the viewpoint of the changing life of the body; illness and healing. Egypt: the body as part of earth's totality; necessity of maintaining the body in harmonious relationship with earth's four elements; its shape, the work of art by the *I* that is independent of birth and death. Greece: the corporeal life as expression of the soul-spiritual on this side which was experienced as being almost identical with the living, sculpturing system of fluids; the four kinds of fluids in the human being. Rome: soul feels itself bound up in earthly existence. The reflection of these transformations in development of the seven sciences, from living revelation to abstraction. Entry of Christianity. Julian the Apostate. Constantine. Justinian. Displacement of living knowledge to East (Gondishapur). Battle of consciousness between Avicenna and Averroes to comprehend the *I* based on Aristotelianism as opposed to Germanic direction. The task of anthroposophy.

Notes   341

It was in the middle and second half of the nineteenth century that materialism had its period of greatest development. In today's lecture we will center our interest more on the *theoretical side* of this materialistic evolution. A great deal of what I shall have to say about the theoretical aspect can also be said in almost the same words of the more practical aspect of materialism. For the moment, however, we will leave that aside and turn our attention more to the materialistic world conception that was prevalent in the civilized world in the middle and second half of the nineteenth century.

We shall find that we are here concerned with a two-fold task. First, we have to gain a clear perception of the extent to which this materialistic world view is to be opposed, of how we must be armed with all the concepts and ideas enabling us to refute the materialistic world view as such. But in addition to being armed with the necessary conceptions, we find that from the point of view of spiritual science we are required at the same time to do something more, namely, to understand this materialistic world view. First of all, we must understand it in its content; secondly, we must also understand how it came about that such an extreme materialistic world view was ever able to enter human evolution.

It may sound contradictory to say that it is required of man on the one hand to be able to fight the materialistic world view, and on the other hand to be able to understand it. But those who base themselves on spiritual science will not find any contradiction here; it is merely an apparent one. For the case is rather like this. In the course of the evolution of mankind moments must needs come when human beings are in a sense pulled down, brought below a certain level, in order that they may later by their own efforts lift themselves up again. And it would really be of no help to mankind at all if by some divine decree or the like it could be protected from having to undergo these low levels of existence. In order for human beings to attain to full use of their powers of freedom, it is absolutely necessary that they descend to the low levels in their world conception as well as in their life. The danger does not lie in the fact that something like this appears at the proper time, and for theoretical materialism this was the middle of the nineteenth century. The danger consists in the fact that if something like this has happened in the course of normal evolution, people then continue to adhere to it, so that an experience that was necessary for one particular point in time is carried over into later times. If it is correct to say that in the middle of the nineteenth century materialism was in a certain sense a test mankind had to undergo, it is equally correct to say that the persistent adherence to materialism is bound to work terrible harm now, and that all the catastrophes befalling the world and humanity that we have to experience are due to the fact that a great majority of people still tries to cling to materialism.

What does theoretical materialism really signify? It signifies the view regarding the human being primarily as the sum of the material processes of his physical body. Theoretical materialism has studied all the processes of the physical, sensory body, and although what has been attained in this study is still more or less in its first beginnings, final conclusions have nevertheless already been drawn from it in regard to a world view. Man has been explained as the confluence of these physical forces; his soul nature is declared to be merely something that is produced through the workings of these physical forces. It is theoretical materialism, however, that initiated investigation of the physical nature of the human being, and it is this, the extensive examination of man's physical nature, that must remain. On the other hand, what the nineteenth century drew as a conclusion from this physical research is something that must not be allowed to figure as more than a passing phenomenon in human evolution. And as a passing phenomenon, let us now proceed to understand it.

What is really involved here? When we look back in the evolution of mankind—and with the help of what I have given in *Occult Science*[1] we are able to look back rather far—we can see that the human being has passed through the greatest variety of different stages. Even if we limit our observation to what has taken place in the course of earth evolution, we are bound to conclude that this human being started with a form that was quite primitive in comparison to its present form, and that this form then underwent gradual change, approaching ever nearer to the form the human being possesses today. As long as we focus on the rough outline of the human form, the differences will not appear to be so great in the course of human history. When we compare with the means at the disposal of external history, the form of an ancient Egyptian or even an ancient Indian with the form of a man of present-day European civilization, we will discover only relatively small differences, as long as we stay with the rough outlines or superficial aspects of observation. For such a rough viewpoint, the great differences in regard to the primitive forms of development emerge only in early man in prehistoric ages.

When we refine our observation, however, when we begin to study what is hidden from outer view, then what I have said no longer holds good. For then we are obliged to admit that a great and significant difference exists between the organism of a civilized man of the present and the organism of an ancient Egyptian, or even an ancient Greek or Roman. And although the change has come about in a much more subtle and delicate manner in historical times, there has most assuredly been such change in regard to all the finer forming and shaping of the human organism. This subtle change reached a certain culmination in the middle of the nineteenth century. Paradoxical as it may sound, it is nevertheless a fact that in regard to his inner structure, in regard to what the human organism can possibly attain, man had reached perfection at about the middle of the nineteenth century. Since then, a kind of decadence has set in. Since that time, the human organism has been involved in retrogression. Therefore, also in the middle of the nineteenth century, the organs that serve as the physical organs of human intellectual activity had reached perfection in their development.

What we call the intellect of man requires, of course, physical organs. In earlier ages, these physical organs were far less developed than they were in the middle of the nineteenth century. It is true that what arouses our admiration when we contemplate the Greek spirit, particularly in such advanced Greeks as Plato and Aristotle, is dependent on the fact that the Greeks did not have such perfect organs of thinking, in the purely physical sense, as had men of the nineteenth century. Depend-

4

ing on one's preference, one might say, "Thank heaven that people in Greek times did not possess thinking organs that were as perfect as those of the people in the nineteenth century!" If on the other hand, one is a pedant like those of the nineteenth century, wishing to cling to this pedantry, then one can say, "Well, the Greeks were just children, they did not have the perfect organs of thought that we have; accordingly, we must look with an indulgent eye upon what we find in the works of Plato and Aristotle. "School teachers often speak in this vein, for in their criticism they feel vastly superior to Plato and Aristotle. You will only fully understand what I have just indicated, however, if you make the acquaintance of people—and there are such!—who have a kind of vision that one may call, in the best sense of the word, a clairvoyant consciousness.

In such people, the presence of clairvoyant consciousness—if there are any in the audience who possess a measure of it, they will please forgive me for telling what is the plain truth—is due to the inadequate development of the organs of intellect. It is quite a common occurrence in our day to meet people who have a measure of clairvoyant consciousness and possess extraordinarily little of what is today called scientific intellect. True as this is, it is equally true that what these clairvoyant people are able to say or write down through their own faculty of perception, may contain thoughts far cleverer than the thoughts of people who show no signs whatever of clairvoyance but function with the best possible organs of intellect. It may easily happen that clairvoyant people who, from the point of view of present-day science are quite stupid—please forgive this expression—produce thoughts cleverer than the thoughts of recognized scientists without being themselves any the cleverer for producing them! This actually occurs. And to what is it due? It comes about because such clairvoyant persons do not need to exercise any organs of thought in order to arrive at the clever thoughts. They create the corresponding images out of the spiritual world, and the images already have within them the thoughts. There they are, ready-made, while other people who are not clairvoyant and can only think have to develop their organs of thought first before they can develop any thoughts. If we were to sketch this, it would be like this. Suppose a clairvoyant person brings something out of the spiritual world in all manner of pictures (see drawing, red). But in it, thoughts are contained, a network of thoughts. The person in question does not think this out, instead, he *sees* it, bringing it along from the spiritual world. He has no occasion to exercise any organ of thought.

Consider another person who is not gifted with clairvoyance, but who can think. Of all that has been drawn in red below, there is nothing at all present in him. He does not bring any such thing out of the spiritual world. Neither does he bring this thought skeleton with him out of the spiritual world (see drawing on left). He exerts his organs of thinking and through them produces this thought skeleton (see drawing on right).

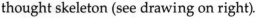

red

In observing human beings today, one can find among everywhere examples of all the stages between these two extremes. For one who has not trained his faculty of observation, it is nevertheless most difficult to distinguish whether a person is actually clever, in the sense that he thinks by means of his organs of reason, or whether he does not think with them at all, but instead by some means brings something into his consciousness, so that only the pictorial, imaginative element is developed in him, but so feebly that he himself is not even aware of it. Thus, there are any number of people today who produce most clever thoughts without having to be clever on that account, while others think very clever thoughts but have no special connection to any spiritual world. To learn to apprehend this distinction is one of the important psychological tasks of our age, and it affords the basis for important insight into human beings at the present time. With this explanation you will no longer find it difficult to understand that empirical supersensible observation shows that the majority of mankind possessed the most perfectly developed organs of thought in the middle of the nineteenth century. At no other time was there so much thinking done with so little cleverness as in the middle of the nineteenth century.

Go back to the twenties of the nineteenth century— only, people do not do this today— or even a little earlier, and read the scientific texts produced then. You will discover that they have an entirely different tone; they do not yet contain the completely abstract thinking of later times which depends on man's physical organs of thought. We need not even mention what came from the pen of people like Herder, Goethe or Schiller; grand conceptions still dwelled in them. It does not matter that people do not believe this today and that commentaries today are written as if this were not the case. For those who write these commentaries and believe that they understand Goethe, Schiller, and Herder simply do not understand them; they do not see what is most important in these men.

It is a fact of great significance that about the middle of the nineteenth century the human organism reached a culmination in respect of its physical form and that since that time it has been regressing; indeed, in regard to a rational comprehension of the world it is regressing rapidly in a certain sense.

This fact is closely connected with the development of materialism in the middle of the nineteenth century. For what is the human organism? The human organism is a faithful copy of man's soul-spiritual nature. It is not surprising that people who are incapable of insight into the soul and spirit of man see in the structure of the human organism an explanation of the whole human being. This is particularly the case when one takes into special consideration the organization of the head, and in the head in turn the organization of the nerves.

In the course of my lectures in Stuttgart,[2] I mentioned an experience that is really suited to throw light on this point. It happened at the beginning of the twentieth century in a gathering of the Giordano Bruno Society of Berlin[3]. First, a man spoke—I would call him a stalwart champion of materialism—who was a most knowledgeable materialist. He knew the structure of the brain as well as anyone can know it today who has studied it conscientiously. He was one of those who see in the analysis of the brain's structure already the full extent of psychology—those who say that one need only know how the brain functions in order to have a grasp on the soul and to be able to describe it. It was interesting; on the blackboard, the man drew the various sections of the brain, the connecting strands, and so on, and thus presented the marvelous picture one obtains when one traces the structure of the human brain. And this speaker firmly believed that by having given this description of the brain he had described psychology. After he had finished speaking, a staunch philosopher, a disciple of Herbart,[4] rose up and said, "The view propounded by this gentleman, that one can obtain knowledge of the soul merely by explaining the structure of the brain, is one I must naturally object to emphatically. But I have no cause to take exception to the drawing the speaker has made. It fits in quite well with my Herbartian point of view, namely, that ideas form associations with one another, and connecting strands of a psychic character run from one idea to another." He added that as a Herbartian, he could quite well make the same drawing, only the various circles and so on would for him not indicate sections of the brain but complexes of ideas. But the drawing itself would remain exactly the same!

A most interesting situation! When it is a matter of getting down to the reality of a subject, these two speakers have diametrically opposed views, but when they make drawings of the same thing, they find themselves obliged to come up with identical drawings, even though one is a wholehearted Herbartian philosopher and the other a staunchly materialistic physiologist.

What is the cause of this? It is in fact this: We have the soul-spirit being of man; we bear it within us. This soul-spirit being is the creator of the entire form of man's organism. It is therefore not surprising that here in the most complete and perfect part of the organism, namely the nervous system of the brain, the replica created by the soul-spirit being resembles the latter in every way. It is indeed true that in the place where man is most of all man, so to speak, namely in the structure of his nerves, he is a faithful replica of the soul-spiritual element.

Thus, a person who, in the first place, must always have something the senses can perceive and is content with the replica, actually perceives in the copy the very same thing that is seen in the soul-spiritual original. Having no desire for soul and spirit and only concentrating, as it were, on the replica, he stops short at the structure of the brain. Since this structure of the brain presented itself in such remarkable perfection to the observer of the mid-nineteenth century, and considering the predisposition of humanity at that time, it was extraordinarily easy to develop theoretical materialism.

What is really going on in the human being? If you consider the human being as such—I shall draw an outline of him here—and turn to the structure of his brain, you find that first of all man is, as we know, a threefold being: the limb being, the rhythmic man, and the being of nerves and senses. When we now look at the latter, we have before us the most perfect part of the human being, in a sense, the most human part. In it, the external world mirrors itself (see drawing, red). I shall indicate this reflection process by the example of the perception through the eyes. I could just as well sketch the perceptions coming through the ear, and so on. The external world, therefore, reflects itself in the human being in such a way that we have here the structure of man and in him the reflection of the outer world.

As long as we consider the human being in this way, we cannot help but interpret him in a materialistic manner, even though we may go beyond the often quite coarse conceptions of materialism. For, on the one hand, we have the structure of the human being; we can trace it in all its most delicate tissue structures. The more closely we approach the head organization, the more we discover a faithful replica of the soul-spiritual

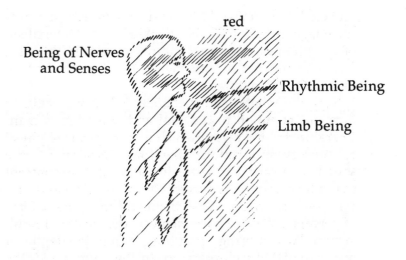

red

Being of Nerves
and Senses

Rhythmic Being

Limb Being

element. Then we can follow up the reflection of the external world in the human being. That, however, is mere picture. We thus have the *reality* of man, on the one hand, traceable in all its finer structural details, and on the other hand we have the *picture* of the world.

Let us keep this well in mind. We have man's reality in the structure of his organs, and we have what is reflected in him. This is really all that offers itself initially to external sensory observation. Thus, for sensory observation, the following conclusion presents itself. When the human being dies, this whole human structure disintegrates in the corpse. In addition, we have the pictures of the outer world. If you shatter the mirror, nothing can mirror itself any longer; hence, the pictures, too, are gone when the human being has passed through death. Since external sense observation cannot ascertain more than what I have just mentioned, is it not natural to have to say that with death the physical structure of the human being disintegrates? Formerly, it reflected the outer world. Human beings bear but a mirror-image in their soul and it passes away. Materialism of the nineteenth century simply presented this as a fact. It could not do otherwise, for it really had no knowledge of anything else.

Now the whole matter changes when we begin to turn our attention to the soul and spirit life of man. There, we enter a region which is inaccessible to physical sensory observation. Take a fact pertaining to the soul that is near at hand, the simple fact that we confront the outer world by observing it. We observe and perceive objects; then we have them within us in the form of percepts. We also have memory, the faculty of recollection. We can bring up in images from the depths of our being what we experience in the outer world. We know how important memory is for the human being.

Let us consider this set of facts some more. Take these two inner experiences: You look through your eyes at the external world, you hear it with your ears, or in some other way you perceive it with your senses. You are then engaged in an immediately present activity of the soul. This then passes over into your conceptual life. What you have experienced today, you can raise up again a few days later out of the depths of your soul in pictures. Something enters into you in some manner and you bring it up again out of your own being. It is not difficult to recognize that what enters into the soul must originate in the external world. I do not wish to consider anything else for the moment except the fact that is clearly obvious, namely, that what we thus remember has to come from the outer world. For if you have seen some red object, you remember the red object afterwards, and what has taken place in you is merely the image of the red object which, in turn, arises again in you. It is therefore something the external world has impressed upon you more deeply than if you occupy yourself only with immediate perceptions in the outer world.

Now picture what happens: You approach some object, you observe it, that is to say, you engage in an immediate and present soul activity in regard to the observed object. Then you go away from it. A few days later, you have reason to call up again from the depths of your being the pictures of the observed object. They are present again, paler, to be sure, but still present in you. What has happened in the interval?

Let me ask you here to keep well in mind what I have just said and compare this singular play of immediate perceptual thoughts and pictures of memory with something that is quite familiar to you, the pictures appearing in dreams. You will easily be able to notice how dreaming is connected with the faculty of memory. As long as the dream images are not too confused, you can easily see how they tie in with the memory images, hence, how a relationship exists between dreams and what passes from living perceptions into memory.

Now consider something else. Human beings must be organically completely healthy if they are to tolerate dreaming properly, so to speak. Dreaming requires that a person has himself fully under control and that at any time a moment can occur when he is certain he has been dreaming. Something is out of order when a person cannot come to the point of perceiving quite clearly: This was a dream! You have met people who dreamed they were beheaded. Suppose they could not distinguish afterwards between such a dream and the actual beheading; suppose they thought they really had been beheaded and yet had to go on living! Just imagine how impossible it would be for such people to sort out the facts without becoming totally confused! They would constantly feel that they had just been beheaded, and if they presumed they had to believe this—one can just about imagine what sort of words would break from their lips!

You can see, therefore, that human beings should be able at any moment to have themselves in hand so well that they can distinguish dreams from the thought life within reality. There are people, however, who cannot do this. They experience all kinds of hallucinations and visions and consider them realities. They cannot distinguish; they do not have themselves well enough in hand. What does this signify? It means that what dwells in dream has an influence on their organization, and that the organization is adapted to the dream picture. Something in their nervous system is not fully developed that should be developed; therefore, the dream is active in them and makes its influence felt.

Thus, if someone is not able to distinguish between his dreams and experienced realities, it means that the power of the dream has an organizing effect on him. If a dream were to possess itself of our whole brain, we would see the whole world as a dream! If you can contemplate such a fact and appreciate its full value, you will gradually learn to apprehend the facts to which ordinary science today does not wish to aspire because it lacks the courage to do so. You will learn to perceive that the very same power that energizes the dream life is present in us as organizing and quickening power, as power of growth. The only reason why the dream does not have the power to tear asunder the structure of our organism is that the latter is too strongly consolidated, that it has so firm a structure as to be able to withstand the effects of the ordinary dream. Thus, the human being can distinguish between the dream experience and that of reality.

When the little child grows up, becoming taller and taller, a force is at work in it. It is the same force as the one contained in the dream; only in the case of the dream we behold it. When we do not behold it, when it is instead active inside the body, then it, the very same power that is in the dream, makes us grow. We need not even go so far as to consider growth. Every day, for example, when you eat and digest and the effects of digestion spread throughout your organism, this happens by means of the force that dwells in dreams. Therefore, when something is out of order in the organism, it is connected with dreaming that is not as it should be. The force we can, from the outside, observe working in dream life is the same as the one that then works inwardly in the human being, even in the forces of digestion.

Thus, we can say that if we only consider the life of man in the right way, we become aware of the working of the dream force in his organism. When I describe this actively working dream force, I actually enter upon the same paths in this description that I must tread when I describe the human etheric body.

Imagine that someone were able to penetrate with his vision everything that brings about growth in the human being from childhood on, everything that causes digestion in man, everything that sustains his whole organism in its state of activity. Imagine that I could take this whole system of forces, extracting it from the human being and placing it before him, then I would have placed the etheric body before the human being. This etheric body, that is, the body that reveals itself only in irregularities in a dream, was far more highly developed prior to the point in time in the nineteenth century to which I have referred. Gradually it became weaker and weaker in its structure. In turn, the structure of the physical body grew correspondingly stronger. The etheric body can conceive in pictures, it can have dreamlike imaginations, but it cannot think. As soon as this etheric body begins to be especially active in a person of our time, he becomes a bit clairvoyant, but then he can think less, because, for thinking, he particularly needs the physical body.

Therefore, it need not surprise us that when people of the nineteenth century had the feeling that they could think particularly well, they were actually driven to materialism. For what aided them in this thinking the most was the physical body. But this physical thinking was connected with the special form of memory that was developed in the nineteenth century. It is a memory that lacks the pictorial element and, wherever possible, moves in abstractions.

Such a phenomenon is interesting. I have frequently referred to the professor of criminal anthropology Moritz Benedikt.[5] Today as well, I would like to mention an interesting experience he himself relates in his memoirs. He had to address a meeting of scientists, and he reports that he prepared himself for this speech for twenty-two nights, not having slept day or night. On the last day before giving the address, a journalist who was supposed to publish the speech came to see him. Benedikt dictated it to him. He says that he had not written down the address at all, having merely impressed it onto his memory. He now dictated it to the journalist in his private chamber; the following day he gave this speech at the meeting of scientists. The journalist printed what he had taken down from dictation, and the printed speech agreed word for word with the speech Benedikt delivered at the meeting.

I must confess, such a thing fills me with admiration, for one always admires what one could never find possible to accomplish oneself. This is indeed a most interesting phenomenon! For twenty-two days, the man worked to incorporate, word for word, what he had prepared into his organization, so that in the end he could not possibly have uttered a single sentence out of the sequence impressed onto his system, so firmly was it imbedded!

Such a thing is possible only when a person is able to imprint the whole speech into his physical organism purely out of the gradually developing wording. It is actually a fact that what one thinks out in this way stamps itself onto one's organization as firmly as the force of nature firmly builds up the bone system of man. Then, the whole speech rests like a skeleton in the physical organism. As a rule, memory is tied to the etheric body, but in this case the latter has imbedded itself completely in the physical organism. The entire physical system then contains something in the way it contains the bones, something that stands there like the skeleton of the speech. Then it is possible to do what Professor Benedikt did. But this is only possible when the nerve structure of the physical organism is developed in such a way that it receives without resistance into its plasticity what is brought into it; gradually, of course, for twenty-two days, even nights, it had to be worked in.

It is not surprising that somebody who relies so much on his body acquires the feeling that this physical body is the only thing working in the human being. Human life had indeed taken such a turn that it worked its way completely into the physical body; people therefore arrived at the belief that the physical body is *everything* in the human organization. I do not think that any other age but ours, which has attached this high value on the physical body, could have come to such a grotesque invention—forgive the expression—as stenography. Obviously, when people did not rely as yet on stenography, they did not attach so great a value to preserving and accurately recording words and the sequence of words such as is the aim in stenography. After all, only the imprint in the physical body can make so fast and firm a record. It is therefore the predilection for imprinting something in the physical body that has brought about the other preference for preserving this imprinted word, but by no means for retaining anything that stands one level higher. For stenography could play no part if we wished to preserve those forms that express themselves in the etheric body. It takes the materialistic tendency to invent something as grotesque as shorthand.

All this, of course, is added only by way of explanation of what I wish to contribute to the problem of understanding the appearance of materialism in the nineteenth century. Humanity had arrived at a certain condition that tended to engrain the soul-spiritual into the physical organism. You must take what I have said as an interpretation, not as a criticism of stenography I do not favor the immediate abolition of stenography. This is never the tendency underlying such characterizations. We must clearly understand that just because one understands something, this does not imply that one wishes to abolish it right away! There are many things in the world that are necessary for life and that yet cannot serve all purposes—I do not want to go further into this subject—and the need for which still has to be comprehended. But we live in an age, and I have to emphasize this again and again, when it is absolutely necessary to penetrate more deeply into the development of nature as well as into that of culture, to be able to ask ourselves: Where does this or that phenomenon come from? For mere carping and criticizing accomplish nothing. We really have to understand all the things that go on in the world.

I would like to sum up what I presented today in the following way. The evolution of mankind shows that in the middle of the nineteenth century a certain culmination was reached in the process of the structural completion of the physical body. Already now, a decadence has set in. Further, this perfection of the physical body is connected with the rise of theoretical materialism. In the next few days, I shall have to say more about these matters from one or another viewpoint. I wished to place before you today what I have just summed up.

LECTURE II
Dornach, April 3, 1921

Before I begin, let me emphasize that this lecture does not form part of the sequence of lectures presented in the context of the courses, [1] but in a certain respect is intended to relate to what I have outlined yesterday evening. There, we dealt with studying that particular form of development within humanity's historical evolution that occurred in the middle and also in the second half of the nineteenth century; the evolutionary impulse of materialism. I said that in these considerations our attention should not be turned so much to materialism in general, which calls for other viewpoints, but rather to theoretical materialism, to materialism as a world view. I drew attention to the fact that this materialism must be confronted with a sufficiently critical mind, but that, on the other hand, materialism has been a necessary phase of evolution in the history of mankind.

We cannot simply speak of rejecting it and say that it is an aberration; materialism needs to be understood. For the one does not exclude the other. Particularly in these reflections it is important to extend the sphere of thoughts relating to truth and error further than is ordinarily the case. It is generally said that in the logical life of thoughts it is possible either to err or to find the truth. What is not mentioned is that under certain circumstances the glance we cast upon the external world may discover errors in outer reality. Difficult though it may be for modern thought to admit to errors in the events of nature—something that spiritual science has to do—it is obvious for people today to admit that there are actual errors in the results that arise in the course of the historical development and manifest themselves, so to speak, in the communal, social sphere. These errors cannot be corrected by mere logic, but demand comprehension based on the conditions that gave rise to them.

In thinking, all we have to do is reject error. We have to extricate ourselves from error and, overcoming it, reach truth. But in the case of errors rooted in the factual realm we must always say that they also have a positive aspect and are of value in a certain sense for the development of mankind. Theoretical materialism of the nineteenth century should therefore not merely be condemned in a narrow, one-sided manner; instead, we should grasp its significance in human evolution.

Theoretical materialism consisted in the fact—and what remained of it still consists in this—that man devotes himself to a conscientious and exact investigation of the external material facts, that in a certain sense he loses himself in this world of facts. Then, proceeding from this investigation of facts, he attains to a view of life that tends to the conclusion that there is no other reality except the world of facts, and that everything pertaining to soul and spirit is, after all, merely a product of the material course of events. Even a conception of life such as this was necessary during a certain epoch of time, and the only danger would be a rigid adherence to it so that it could influence the further development of humanity in an age when other contents have to enter human consciousness.

Let us try today and investigate the actual basis of this evolutionary impulse leading to theoretical materialism. We come to it when, from a certain standpoint, we picture once more the threefold nature of the human organism.[2] I have characterized it on many occasions. I have said: We must distinguish within the whole organization of the human being the part that, in regard to his physical being, may be designated as the organization of the senses and nerves. This is chiefly concentrated in the human head, but in a certain sense it extends over the whole human organism, also penetrating the other parts of it. As a second member we have the rhythmical organization. We encounter it chiefly in the rhythm of breathing and in the circulation of the blood. The third part in a wider sense is the metabolic organization of the human being, including the whole system of the human limbs. The human limb system is a system of movement, and every form of movement is basically an expression of our metabolic processes. One day, when people will investigate more closely what really takes place in the metabolic processes whenever the human being moves, they will discover the intimate connection between the limb system and the metabolic system.

In considering these three systems in the human being, we have, first of all, pointed out the fundamental difference between them. I have already drawn your attention yesterday to the fact that, by means of the same drawing, two men with entirely different world views wanted to clarify matters relating to the human head organization as well as to the processes of human thinking. I pointed out that it so happened that I was once present at a lecture given by an extreme materialist. He wished to describe the life of the soul, but he actually described the human brain, the individual sections of the brain, the connecting fibers, and so on. He arrived at a certain picture, but this picture he drew on the blackboard was, for him, only the expression of what goes on materially and physically in the human brain. At the same time, he saw in it the expression of soul life, particularly the conceptual life. Another man, a philosopher of the school of Herbart, spoke of thoughts, of associations of thoughts, of the effect one thought has upon another, etc., and he said he could make use of the same picture on the blackboard. Here, quite empirically, I should say, we encounter something most interesting. It is this that somebody for whom the observation of the soul life is something quite real, at least in his thoughts — this must always be added in case of Herbartianism — clarifies to himself the activity of the soul life by using the same picture employed by the other lecturer, who depicts the soul life by trying to set forth only the processes in the human brain.

Now, what lies at the foundation of this? The fact is that in its plastic configuration the human brain is indeed an extraordinarily faithful replica of what we know as the life of thought. In the plastic configuration of the human brain, the life of thought really does express itself, we might almost say, in an adequate manner. In order to follow this thought to its conclusion, however, something else is needed. What ordinary psychology and also Herbart's psychology designate as chains of thoughts, as thought associations in the form of judgments, logical conclusions and so on, should not remain a mere idea. At least in our imagination — even if we cannot rise to clairvoyant Imaginations — we should allow it to culminate in a picture; the tapestry of logic, the tapestry presented to us by psychology of the life of thought, the teaching of the soul life, should be allowed to culminate in a picture. If we are in fact able to transform logic and psychology in a picture-like, plastic way into an image, then the human configuration of the brain will emerge. Then we shall have traced a picture, the realization of which is the human brain.

On what is this based? It is based on the fact that the human brain, indeed the whole system of nerves and senses, is a replica of an Imaginative element.[3] We completely grasp the wonderful structure of the human brain only when we learn to investigate Imaginatively. Then, the human brain appears as a realized human Imagination. Imaginative perception teaches us to become familiar with the external brain, the brain we come to know through psychology and anatomy, as a realized Imagination. This is significant.

Another fact is no less important. Let us bear in mind that the human brain is an actual human Imagination. We are indeed born with a brain, if not a fully developed one, at least with a brain containing the tendencies of growth. It tries to develop to the point of being a realized Imaginative world, to be the impression of an Imaginative world. This is, as it were, the ready-made aspect of our brain, namely, that it is the replica of an Imaginative world. Into this impression of the Imaginative world we then build the conceptual experiences attained during the time between birth and death. During this period we have conceptual experiences; we conceive, we transform the sense perceptions into thoughts; we judge, we conclude, and so on. We fit this into our brain. What kind of activity is this?

As long as we live in immediate perception, as long as we remain in the interplay with the external world, as long as we open our eyes to the colors and dwell in this relationship with colors, as long as we open our organs of hearing to sounds and live within them, the external world lives on in us by penetrating our organism through the senses as through channels. With our inner life, we encompass this external world. But the moment we cease to have this immediate experience of the outer world—something I already called your attention to yesterday—the moment we turn our eye away from the world of colors, allow our ear to become inattentive to the resounding of the external world, the moment we turn our senses to something else, this concreteness—our interplay with the external world in perceiving—penetrates into the depths of our soul. It may then be drawn to the surface again in the form of pictures by memory. We may say that during our life between birth and death insofar as our thought life is concerned, our interplay with the external world consists of two parts: the immediate experience of the external world in the form of perceptions and the transformed thoughts. We surrender, as it were, completely to the present; our inner activity loses itself in the present. Then, however, this immediate activity continues. To begin with, it is not accessible to our consciousness. It sinks down into the subconscious but may be drawn to the surface again into memory. In what form, then, does it exist in us?

This is a point that can be explained only by a direct view attainable in Imagination. A person who honestly pursues his way in his scientific striving cannot help but admit to himself that the moment the riddle of memory confronts him he cannot advance another step in his research. For due to the fact that the experiences of the immediate present sink down into the subconscious, they become inaccessible to ordinary consciousness; they cannot be traced further.

But when we work in a corresponding way upon the human soul by means of the soul-spiritual exercises that have frequently been discussed in my lectures, we reach a stage where we no longer lose sight of the continuations of our direct life of perceptions and thoughts into conceptions that make memories possible. I have often explained to you that the first result of an ascent to Imaginative thinking is to have before your soul, as a mighty life-tableau, all your experiences since birth. The stream of experience normally flows along in the unconscious, and the single representations, which emerge in memory, rise up from this unconscious or subconscious stream through a half-dreamy activity. Those who have developed Imaginative perception are offered the opportunity to survey the stream of experiences as in one picture. You could say that the time that has elapsed since birth then takes on the appearance of space. What is normally within the subconscious is then beheld in the form of interconnected pictures. When the experiences that otherwise escape into the subconscious are thus raised to direct vision, we are able to observe this continuation of present, immediate perceptual and thought experiences all the way into conceptions that can be remembered. It is possible to trace what happens in us to any sort of experience we have in our mind, from the point in time when we first lose sight of it until the moment we recall it again. After all, between experiencing something and remembering it again something is taking place continuously in the human organism, something that becomes visible to imaginative perception. It is possible to view it in Imaginations, but it is now revealed in a quite special way.

The thoughts that have lost themselves, as it were, in the subconscious region an activity connected with our life-impulses, our impulses of growth; they stimulate an activity in us that is related to our impulse of death. The significant result revealing itself to Imaginative perception in the way I could only allude to today is the following: Human beings do not connect the memory-activity, leading to the renewal of thinking, of thought and perceptual experiences, with what calls us into physical life and maintains digestion in this life, so that substances that have become useless are replaced by usable ones, and so on. The power of memory that descends into the human being is not related to this ascending life system in man. It is linked to something we also bear within us ever since our birth, something we are born with just as we are born with the forces through which we live and grow. It is connected with what then appears to us, concentrated into one moment, in regard to the whole organism in dying.

Death only appears as a great riddle as long as it is not observed within the continuous stream of life from birth to death. Expressing myself paradoxically, I might say that we die not only when we die. In reality, we die at every moment of our physical life. By developing within our organism the activity leading to memory as recollective thinking—and in ordinary physical life every form of cognition is actually linked up with memory—insofar as this cognition is developed, we die continuously. A subtle form of death, proceeding from our head organization, is forever going on within us. By carrying out this activity that continues on into memory, we constantly begin the act of dying. But the forces of growth existing in the other members of the human organism counteract this process of death; they overcome the death forces. Thus we maintain life. If we only depended on our head organization, on the system of nerves and senses, each moment in life would really become a moment of death for us. As human beings we continuously vanquish death, which streams out, as it were, from our head to the remaining organism. The latter counteracts this form of death. Only when the remaining organization becomes weakened, exhausted through age or some kind of damage, thus preventing the counteraction against the death-bearing forces of the human head, only then does death set in for the whole organism.

Indeed, in our modern thinking, in the thinking of today's civilization, we really work with concepts that lie side by side like erratic blocks, without being able to correctly recognize their interrelationship. Light must enter into this chaos of erratic blocks constituting our world of concepts and thoughts. On the one hand, we have human cognition which is so intimately tied to the faculty of memory. We observe this human cognition and have no idea of its kinship to our conception of death. And because we are completely ignorant of this relationship, what could otherwise be deciphered in life remains so enigmatic. We are unable to connect the experiences of everyday life with the great extraordinary moments of experience. The insufficient spiritual view over what lies around as fragmentary blocks in our conceptual world brings it about that despite the splendid achievements of the nineteenth century life has gradually become so obscure.

Let us now consider the second system, the second member of the human organization, the rhythmical organization. It is also present in the human head organization. The interior of the human head breathes together with the breathing organism. This is an external physiological fact. But the breathing process of the human head lies, as it were, more within; it conceals itself from the system of nerves and senses. It is covered over by what constitutes the chief task of the head organization. Still, the human head has its own concealed rhythmical activity. This activity becomes evident mainly in the human chest organization, in those processes of the human organism that are centered in the organs of breathing and in the heart.

When we observe the outward appearance of this organization, unlike in the case of the head organization, we cannot see in it a kind of plastic image for what exists as its counterpart in the soul, namely, the life of feeling. When we observe the soul experiences, our feelings manifest as something more or less undefined. We have sharp contours in our thoughts. We also have clear concepts of thought associations. In the details pertaining to our life of feeling we have no such sharp outlines. There, everything interpenetrates, moves and lives. You will not find an Herbartian who, in making an outline of the life of emotion, would characterize this in a sketch that might resemble one drawn by an anatomist or a physiologist for the lungs or the heart and circulatory system. Here, you find that such a relationship does not exist between the inner soul element and the outer aspects. This is also the reason why Imaginative cognition does not suffice to bring before the soul this relationship between the soul's life of feeling and the rhythmical system. For this we need what I have characterized in my books as Inspiration, Inspirative perception. This special form of perception through Inspiration attains to the insight that our emotional life has a direct link to the rhythmical system. Just as the system of nerves and senses is linked to the conceptual life, so the rhythmical life is linked to the life of feelings.

But, metaphorically speaking, the rhythmical system is not the wax impression of the emotional life in the same way that the brain's configuration is the wax impression of the conceptual life. Consequently we cannot say that our rhythmical system is an Imaginative replica of our life of feeling. We must say instead that what unfolds and lives in us as the rhythmical system has come about through cosmic Inspiration, independently of any human knowledge. It is inspired into us. The activity carried out in the breathing and in the blood circulation is not merely something that lives within us enclosed by our skin; it is a cosmic event, like lightning and thunder. After all, through our rhythmical system, we are connected with the outer world. The air that is now within me was outside before; it will be outside again the next moment. It is an illusion to believe that we only live enclosed within our skin. We live as a member of the world that surrounds us, and the form of our rhythmical system, which is closely connected to our movements, is inspired into us out of this world.

Summing this up, we can say: As the basis of the human head we have, first of all, the realization of an Imaginative world. Then, in a manner of speaking, below what thus realizes itself as an Imaginative world, we have the realm of the rhythmical system, an Inspired world. Concerning our rhythmical system, we can only say: An Inspirative world is realized within it.

How do matters stand in regard to our metabolic system, our limb-system? Metabolism belongs together with the limb-system, as I have pointed out already. Our metabolic processes stand in a direct relationship with our volitional activity. But this relationship reveals itself neither to Imaginative nor to Inspirative perception. It discloses itself only to Intuitive cognition, to what I have described in my books as "Intuitive knowledge." This explains the difficulty of seeing in the external physical processes of metabolism the realization of a cosmic Intuition. This metabolism, however, is also present in the rhythmical system. The metabolism of the rhythmical system conceals itself behind the life-rhythm, just as the life-rhythm conceals itself behind the activity of nerves and senses in the human head.

In the case of the human head we have a realized Imaginative world; hidden behind it a realized Inspirative world in regard to the rhythm in the head. Still further behind this, there is the metabolism of the head, hence a realized Intuitive element. Thus we can comprehend our head, if we in it the confluence of the realized Imaginative, Inspired, and Intuitive elements. In the human rhythmical system the Imaginative is omitted; there we have only the realization of the Inspired and Intuitive elements. And in the metabolic system Inspiration, too, is omitted; there, we are dealing only with the realization of a cosmic Intuition.

In the threefold human organism, we thus bear within us first the organization of the head, a replica of what we strive for in cognition through Imagination, Inspiration, and Intuition. In trying to understand the human head, we should really have to admit to ourselves that with mere external, objective knowledge gained through the observation of the outer sensory world, which is not even Imagination and does not rise up to the Intuitive element, we should stop short of the human head. For the inner being of the human head begins to disclose itself only to Imaginative knowledge; behind this lies something still deeper that reveals itself to Inspiration. In turn, behind this, lies something that makes itself known to Intuitive knowledge. The rhythmical system is not even accessible to Imagination. It reveals itself only to Inspirative cognition, and what is concealed beneath it is the Intuitive element. Within the human organism, we certainly ought to find metabolism incomprehensible. The true standpoint in regard to the human metabolism can be none other than the following. We can only say that we observe the metabolic processes of the external world; we try to penetrate into them with the aid of the laws of objective perception. Thus we attain knowledge of the external metabolism in nature. The instant this outer metabolism is transformed and metamorphosed into out inner metabolism it becomes something quite different; it turns into something in which dwells the element that discloses itself only to Intuition.

We would therefore have to say: In the world that presents itself to us as the sensory realm, the most incomprehensible of all incomprehensible problems is what the substances, with which we become familiar externally through physics and chemistry, accomplish within the human skin. We would have to admit: we must rise up to the highest spiritual comprehension if we want to know what really takes place within the human organism in regard to the substances we know so well in their external aspects in the world outside.

Thus we see that in the structure of our organism there are, to begin with, three different activities. First of all, something that discloses itself to Intuitive knowledge is active in the structure of the human organism, building it up out of the world's substances. In addition something is active in this organism that reveals itself to Inspirative knowledge; it fits the rhythmical system into the metabolic organism. Finally, something is active in the human organism that reveals itself to Imaginative knowledge; it builds in the nervous system. And when this human organism enters through birth into the external physical world, all that is ready-made, as it were, by virtue of its own nature, then evolves further inasmuch as human beings develop objective knowledge between birth and death.

Concerning this objective knowledge we have seen that it is tied to the activity of memory; it is not connected with constructive but with destructive forces. We have seen that this form of knowledge is a slow dying proceeding from the head. We may therefore say that the human organism was built up through what could be comprehended by means of Intuition, Inspiration, and Imagination. This dwells in this human organism in a manner inaccessible to present-day cognition. On the other hand, what is built into our organism between birth and death by means of our objective insights breaks down and destroys this organism. We actually think and form concepts on the basis of this destruction when we unfold our conceptual life, the life of thoughts.

We really cannot be materialists when we comprehend what this knowledge, so intimately linked with the faculty of memory consists of. For if we wanted to be materialists, we would have to imagine that we are built up by forces of growth; that those forces are active that absorb the substances and transmit them to the various organs in order to bring about, in a wider sense, the digestive processes within our organism. We should have to picture this faculty, inherent in growth, digestion, and the constructive forces in general, continuing and culminating somewhere in the conceptual process, in thinking which arrives at objective knowledge. Yet this is not the case. The human organism is built up through something that is accessible to Intuition, to Inspiration, and to Imagination. Our organism is built up when it has absorbed these forces into itself. But then regression begins, the process of decay, and what brings this decay about is ordinary knowledge between birth and death.

Through the processes of ordinary perception we do not build anything into the constructive forces; rather, by destroying what has been built up, we create, first of all, the foundations for a continuous element of death in ourselves. Into this continuing element of death we place our knowledge. We do not immerse ourselves in material elements when we think; no, we destroy the material element. We hand it over to the forces of death. We think our way into death, into the destruction of life. Thinking, ordinary perception, is not related to growing, budding life. It is related to death, and when we observe human perception, we do not find an analogy for it in the natural formations including the human brain. We discover an analogy only in the corpse that decays after death. For what the decaying body represents, I might say, intensively, in a certain greatness, must continuously take place within us when we perceive objectively in the ordinary sense of the word.

Look upon death if you wish to comprehend the cognitive process. Do not look upon life in a materialistic manner; look upon what represents the negation, the elimination of life. Then you arrive at a comprehension of thinking. To be sure, what we call death then acquires an entirely different meaning; based on life it attains to a different significance.

Even external phenomena enable us to grasp such things. Yesterday, I said to you that the culmination of the materialistic world view lies in the middle or in the last third of the nineteenth century. This culmination viewed death as something that must absolutely be rejected. In a sense people at that time felt noble by viewing death in this way, as ending life. Life alone they wanted to consider and wished to see it as ending with death. Frequently, one looks back somewhat disdainfully upon the "child-like folk-consciousness." Take the word *"verwesen,"* (to decompose) which points to the process of what occurs after death. The prefix *"ver"* always indicates a movement towards what the word expresses. *"Verbruedern"* (to become like brothers, to fraternize) means to move in the direction of becoming brothers; *"versammeln"* (to gather together) indicates moving in the direction of gathering, of meeting. In the vernacular, *"verwesen"* does not mean decomposing, ceasing to be; it means moving in the direction of *Wesen*, of being, of life. Such word formations, connected with a spiritual way of grasping the world during the epoch of instinctive knowledge, have become exceedingly rare. In the nineteenth century people materialized everything; they no longer lived in the spiritual essence permeating the word. Many examples could be cited to show that the culmination of materialism became evident even in speech.

We can therefore understand that after the human being had been developed, as I said yesterday, to a point of culmination by forces that disclose themselves to Inspiration, Intuition, and Imagination, he then attained to the highest culmination in the nineteenth century, followed in turn by a decadence. We can understand that the human being distanced himself, as it were, from the power enabling him to comprehend himself inwardly by developing in the strongest measure the forces that, as conceptual forces, are most akin to death, the forces of abstraction. It is from this point that it is possible, proceeding from today's lecture, to advance to what constitutes the actual, essential impulse within what we may call the materialistic impulse of knowledge in human history.

LECTURE III
Dornach, April 9, 1921

This evening, I do not wish to continue directly with the considerations normally carried on here on Saturdays and Sundays. Instead—in order that the friends of our cause, [1] who have gathered here, can take along as much as possible of what is more or less closely connected with the studies undertaken during this week—we shall venture into still more intimate considerations intended to relate to the questions already touched upon.

Even in reference to fructifying philology by means of anthroposophical spiritual science, I have indicated that an original form of sensibility for language has been lost and that in its place a more abstract orientation towards the things of the surrounding world has come about. I have pointed out that a significant developmental force in human history is represented in the fact that through Aristotle, in the fourth century before Christ, there emerged what subsequently was called logic. For it does indeed signify an orientation towards the world in an abstract sense to find one's way consciously into the logical element, which earlier had been present more unconsciously and instinctively in the constitution of the human soul.

I said that an inner concrete process was still experienced in ancient times that is comparable to what we can study in the processes of puberty. What appears in the child when it learns to speak, is a metamorphosis, a more inwardly developing metamorphosis of the process that unfolds later on in the human being in the process of reaching sexual maturity. And what runs its course inwardly in this process of learning to speak, in ancient times had aftereffects for people's whole life. The human being experienced himself as if through the word something were coming to expression in him that lived also in the things outside, something the things do not express, however, because they have, in a sense, become dumb. As the word resounded, something was felt within that corresponds to processes in the outer world. What was experienced then was much more substantial, much more closely connected to human life than what is inwardly experienced today in comprehending the world through abstract concepts. What human beings then experienced through the word was more organic, I would say, more instinctive, more inclined towards the animalistic soul element than what we can now experience through the conceptual, abstract grasp of things. We were brought closer to the spiritual life through this abstract comprehension. Yet, at the same time, we arrived at abstraction. Thus, at precisely the world-historical moment, when human beings were in a sense elevated to the point of gradually grasping the spirit, their mental experience at the same time suffered a dilution into abstractions—I can express these matters only in a more or less pictorial manner since our language has not yet coined words for it.

Naturally, this process did not develop in the same way in all of humanity. It took place earlier in those folk groups that were the foremost bearers of civilization; others remained behind. I was able to point out that in the eleventh century the population settled in central Europe still occupied a standpoint that must be designated as pre-Aristotelian compared to the Greek development of civilization. In central Europe, people advanced much later beyond the point the Greeks passed with Aristotle. Through Aristotelianism, the Greeks anticipated much of what came about for the central European nations and those counted among them because of their culture only in the first third of the fifteenth century.

Now, two things are connected with this development in regard to the comprehension of language and the abstract element. I have already pointed out one. As human soul life was lifted into abstraction through Aristotelianism—which still was only a symptom for a general comprehension of things within the Greek culture—it became estranged from the direct experience of the word, of language. With this, the portal leading to man's unfolding life in the direction of birth was closed. In their everyday experience, human beings no longer found their way back to the point where they could have realized through the process of acquiring speech how the soul-spiritual element holds sway in them just as it does outside in the world. Due to this, they were also diverted from looking back still further. For the next stages would have shown what one might call overall union of the spirit with physical-corporeal matter. They would have yielded comprehension of preexistence, the insight that the human soul-spiritual element leads an existence in supersensory worlds prior to uniting with the corporeal nature that arises within physical matter. It is true that this insight did not exist in earlier times of humanity's evolution in the definitely conscious form in which we try to acquire it today through spiritual science; instead, it was present in a more instinctive manner. The remnants of it appear to us in the Oriental civilization, which consider looking upon the preexistent human soul a matter of course.

If the human being is then in a position of continuing further, something that is even more difficult to discern than preexistence becomes actual knowledge and perception, namely, repeated earth lives. This view existed in earlier ages of human development, though in an instinctive manner. It survived in a more poetic, imaginative form in the civilizations of the Orient when the former had already fallen into decadence, albeit a most significant, even beautiful decadence.

Thus, when we look back to former epochs of human evolution without the prejudices of modern anthropology, we find a mode of perception that, albeit instinctively, penetrated into things. Inasmuch as human beings still understood the processes of acquiring speech, they also grasped something of the soul activity within outer nature; and inasmuch as they understood the incorporation of the soul-spiritual into the physical corporeal element, they understood something of the spirit vibrating and weaving through the world.

To the extent that historical knowledge of the Greeks reaches back, only the sparse remnants of this ancient spirit perception are contained in the traditions of Greek civilization. If we go back beyond Aristotle and Plato to the Ionic philosophers, to around the turn of the fifth and sixth centuries B.C. in Greek development of thought, we find a philosophy, for example in the work of Anaxagoras, [2] that cannot be comprehended on the basis of today's assumptions. Motivated by a certain healthy insight, the philosophers of the Occident should really admit to themselves that Western philosophy simply lacks the prerequisites to understand Anaxagoras. For what Anaxagoras acknowledges—though already in decadent form—as his nous dates back to those ages I have just spoken of, ages when people still sensed and perceived how the world is infused and woven through by spirit, how, out of spirit, the soul-spiritual being of man descends in order to unite with the physical-corporeal nature. In former times, this was an instinctive, concrete perception. Then it diminished to the knowledge present in the instinctive insight into the process of speech, something that in turn was lost during the Aristotelian age, particularly as far as the most advanced civilizations are concerned.

As I have already explained, when people still had insight into this process of emerging speech, they sensed something in the resounding of the word that was an expression for an objective happening in nature outside. Here, I come to an essential difference: What was conceived as the universal soul by those who can be called "knowledgeable about speech" in the ancient sense, was predominantly thought of as filling space, and human beings experienced themselves as having been formed out of this spirit-soul element filling out space. Yet this was something different from what we discover when we go back further beyond the nous of Anaxagoras. Then we arrive at something leading into the preexistence of human beings; it is something that does not merely deal with the fact that the human soul weaves and exists in the present within the universal spirit and soul. Instead, we find here that this human soul dwells with the universal spirit and soul in time.

We must be familiar with these matters through an inner comprehension, if we wish to gain truly historical insight into a most significant process in the development of civilization in western Asia and Europe. Nowadays, people really have no relevant conception of the state of mind of humanity living in the age when Christendom was established. Certainly, if you consider the general human soul condition of today in its particular configuration, you have to picture the great majority of those people of western Asia and Europe as having been uneducated in comparison to the education of our modern age we are so proud of. Yet, in those times, there were individuals who towered above the great mass of uneducated humanity. I might say, the successors of the ancient initiates stood out because of significant knowledge, knowledge that indeed did not dwell in the soul the same way as does our knowledge, which is permeated everywhere by abstract concepts and has therefore attained to full consciousness. Something instinctive existed even in the highest knowledge of that period. Yet, at the same time, something forceful was inherent in this instinctive knowledge, something that still penetrated into the depths of things.

It is strange that many representatives of present-day traditional confessions have a curious fear of the possibility that somebody might discover that such penetrating knowledge did exist in past times, knowledge that arrived at refined concepts even if these were viewed more through instinctive pictures, as I said, and were expressed in forms of speech, for the comprehension of which there exists little feeling today.

Our anthroposophy is not intended as a renewal of what is called Gnosis, but it is the path that allows us to look into the nature of this Gnosis. In regard to its sources, our anthroposophy has nothing in common with the ancient Indian philosophies. It can nevertheless penetrate into the compelling, magnificent aspects, the outpouring from all things, of the Vedanta, Sankhya, or Yoga philosophies, because it once again attains in a conscious manner to those regions of the world that were then reached instinctively. Likewise, our anthroposophy can penetrate into the essence of the Gnosis. We know that this Gnosis was eradicated by certain sects of the first Christian centuries to the point where very little Gnostic knowledge is still available historically. The Gnosis has actually become known to modern humanity only through the documents of those who tried to disprove it. They included quotes from the recorded texts in their written refutations, whereas the original Gnostic texts themselves were lost. Thus, the Gnosis has really been handed down to posterity only through the documents of its enemies who naturally quoted only what they deemed suitable in conformity with their cleverness.

Just study the quotation skills of our opponents and you will gain an idea of how far one can penetrate into the nature of such a subject. When one has to depend on the documents of the opponents! Insight into the Gnosis has in most cases been dependent on the texts of its opponents—outwardly and historically it depends on them even today. Just imagine, it would certainly be in accordance with the wishes of somebody like Mr. von Gleich, [3] if all anthroposophical texts should be burned up—surely, he would like that best—and that anthroposophy would be handed down to posterity only through his own proclamations! We only have to picture things by means of something that can truly call attention to them.

If, for these reasons, we are unable to look into what already existed in those times, we will go astray with all the treatises, be they ever so well meant and scientific that concern something most important in regard to the comprehension of Christianity. One point, where almost everything remains yet to be done because everything done so far by no means leads to what could be designated by an honest striving for knowledge as true insight, is the Logos concept we encounter at the beginning of the Gospel of John. This Logos concept cannot be comprehended if the soul-spiritual development of human beings belonging to the most advanced civilization of that age is not inwardly understood. This is the case particularly if there is no comprehension of the soul-spiritual development that ran its course in Greek culture and shone across into Asia, casting its shadows into what confronts us in the Gospel of John.

We must not approach this Logos concept merely by means of a dictionary or a superficial philological method. It can be approached only if we inwardly study the soul-spiritual development in question here, approximately from the fourth pre-Christian century until the fourth century A.D. No satisfactory history has yet been written about what then took place inwardly in the most advanced part of humanity and its representatives of wisdom. For this is related to the vanishing of any understanding for the process of learning to speak. The other matter, the comprehension of preexistence, was preserved in traditions until the time of Origen;[4] yet it was lost to inward understanding much earlier than the comprehension of the process of speech, of the resounding of the word in man's inner being.

If we focus on the soul-spiritual condition of the representatives of wisdom in Asia Minor and Europe, we discover that a transition took place. What had existed as a uniform process in perception, namely the resounding of the word and in it the being of the world, became differentiated into an orientation towards abstract concepts, ideas, and a feeling, a dull sensation of what was pushed down more into subconsciousness—the word as such. And what resulted from this? A certain fact came about in regard to the human soul life because of it. The word content and the ideal, conceptual content of consciousness were experienced in an undifferentiated manner by human beings in ancient times. Now, the conceptual content became separated.

Initially, however, it did retain something of what human beings had once possessed in the undifferentiated nature of word, concept, and percept. People spoke of "concepts"; they spoke of "ideas, " but yet it is obvious—for example in Plato's case— that people still experienced the idea spiritually and full of content. As they spoke of the idea, it still contained something of what had earlier been perceived in the undifferentiated word concept. Thus, people already drew closer to the idea that is grasped as a mere concept, but this grasp still retained something of what was comprehended in the ancient resounding of words. As this transition developed, the content of the world grasped spiritually by the human being turned into what was then expressed as the Logos concept. The Logos concept is understood only when it is known that it contains this transition to the idea, but without any remnant of the ancient word concept in grasping this idea. As people spoke of the Logos as the world-creative element, they were not clearly but only dimly aware that this world-creative spirit element has something in its content that was grasped in earlier times through the perception of the word.

We must take into consideration this quite special nuance of the soul's experience of the outer world in the Logos. There existed a very special nuance of soul perception, the Logos perception. Aristotle then worked his way out of it, found his way closer to abstraction and attained from it subjective logic. In Plato, on the other hand, we find the idea as the world-creative principle; in Plato, it is still pervaded by concrete spirituality, because it still contains the remnants of the ancient word concept, being basically the Logos, though in diminished form.

Thus, we can picture that what came with Christ into the man Jesus was to be designated as the world-creative principle out of the views of that age. People had a concept for that, the concept that was indeed retained in the Logos concept. The Logos concept existed. With it, people tried to grasp what had been given to the world in the story of Christ Jesus. the concept, which had developed out of ancient times and had assumed a special form, was utilized to express the starting-point of Christianity; thus, the most sublime wisdom was used to see through this mystery. We must be able to place ourselves completely into that age, not in the sense of an external conception but in inwardly grasping the way people viewed the world at that time.

There is a great break between Plato and Aristotle. On the other hand, the whole style of the Gospel of John is composed in such a way that we see: It came about based on a living comprehension of the world-creative principle and, at the same time, because the one who wrote down the Gospel of John was familiar with the Logos concept that had already been lost. All translation of the Gospel of John is impossible if one cannot penetrate into the origin of the Logos concept. This Logos concept did indeed dwell in all vitality among the wise representatives of the most civilized part of the world between the fourth century B.C. and the fourth century A.D.

When Christianity became a state religion, something from which the later Catholic Church was developed, the era was reached when, in a sense, even the last nuance of the ancient "word, " of the old word concept, was lost from this idea. Fundamentally, Aristotle did nothing but separate subjective logic from the Logos and develop the theory of this subjective logic. Yet, at the time the dominant condition of soul and spirit of mankind paid little heed to what Aristotle had established as subjective logic. On the contrary, Aristotelianism was forgotten, only entering again into the later age by way of the Arabs. It did exist; but aside from being present in this roundabout way through tradition, people still clearly felt that one was dealing on the one hand with subjective logic, on the other with the perception of a world-creative principle in the Logos. In this concept, something was still contained of what one had grasped in the ancient conception of the resounding-of-the-word in man's inner being as the counter-image of the word-become-silent, namely, as the Logos creating nature in this becoming silent.

Then, in the fourth century A.D., this nuance was lost from the Logos concept. It can no longer be discovered; it vanished. It is retained at most in a few secluded thinkers and mystical seekers. It vanished from the general consciousness of even the representative Church Fathers and teachers. What then still appears as a most comprehensive, ideally spiritualized world view in somebody like Scotus Erigena[5] no longer contains the ancient Logos concept, though that term is used. The former Logos concept is utterly filtered into an abstract thought concept. The world-creative principle is now understood not by means of the ancient Logos concept, but only through the sublimated or filtered thought concept. This is what then appeared in the text by Scotus[6] concerning the division of nature, but it is something that basically had already completely disappeared from consciousness: this loss of the Logos concept, this transformation of it into the thought concept.

In regard to European humanity, concerning which I said that it retained for itself a more ancient development into a later age, it was considered necessary to go back even beyond the period during which the Logos concept had been active in its full vitality. But people traced it back in an abstract form, and this return in an abstract form was even dogmatized. At the Eighth Ecumenical Council at Constantinople in A.D. 869, it was set down that the world and the human being are not to be conceived of as being membered into body, soul, and spirit, but merely into body and soul, and that the soul possesses a few spiritual qualities.

The other process of evolution I have just mentioned runs parallel to what had been dogmatically set down there. For a person who studies the development of Occidental civilization from the first Christian centuries, where much was still pervaded by Gnostic elements, up to the fourth and fifth centuries of our Christian era, it is an extraordinarily interesting fact to experience this diminishing of the Logos concept. Later, when the Gospels were translated, nothing, of course, could be brought into these translations of any feeling for the Logos concept as it had held sway within pre-Christian humanity in those eight centuries, in the middle of which lies the Mystery of Golgotha. This peculiarity of the period from which Christendom emerged must be studied also by means of such intimate aspects. Nowadays, people prefer to solve even the most difficult problems by means of the threadbare concepts, concepts that are easily acquired. Historical problems such as I have just mentioned, however allow a solution only if we seek the preparation for the solution in the acquisition of certain nuances of the human soul life, if we are willing to proceed from the honest assumption that in the present cultural age we simply do not possess in our soul life the nuance that leads to the Logos concept as it is meant in the Gospel of John. This is why we should not try to comprehend the Gospel of John with the vocabulary and conceptions of the present. If we attempt to understand the Gospel of John with present-day concepts, superficiality will dictate to us from the very outset. This is something that must be discerned with an alert eye of soul and this must be done in regard to history in these areas, for things are in a bad way at the present in regard to this history.

Only recently, I have had to call to mind an extraordinarily important fact in reference to this subject. A letter written by one of the most recognized theologians was brought to my attention—it was not addressed to me.[7] This esteemed theologian of the present expressed himself on anthroposophists, Irvingites, and similar rabble. He confused everything. In his exposition, one point in particular stands out strangely. He says of himself that he has no sense for the sort of view that points to the supersensible such as anthroposophy tries to do; he has to limit himself to what is given in human experience.

This is a theologian whose vocation it is to speak on and on about the supersensible. He has become famous for having written fat historical volumes about the life of the supersensible in human evolution. He is an authority for countless people of stature at present. Such a modern theologian admits that he has no sense for the supersensible but, instead, wishes to stick to "human experience!" Yet he talks about the supersensible and does not say, I wish to remain within human sensory experience; therefore, I negate all theology. Oh no, in our age, he becomes a famous theologian! My dear friends, it is so important for us to be alert to everything that is in a certain sense a determining factor today among our young people, yet at the same time proves itself to be an inner impossibility.

It is necessary to grasp with inner energy how one is to proceed to sincere and honest insight. Perhaps it can be discerned particularly in problems such as the Logos problem, and a person who sees what anthroposophy as to set forth about such a problem should realize from this that anthroposophy is certainly not taking the easy way out. It tries to do research earnestly and honestly and it is only because of this that it comes into conflict with a number of contemporary trends. For today people actually have either hatred or fear of such thoroughness, which must, however, be striven for and is needed in all areas of scientific life. I ask you: does the opposition, which so readily dispenses shallow judgments concerning anthroposophy, even know what anthroposophy occupies itself with? Does it know that this anthroposophy struggles with problems such as the Logos problem, which, after all, is only one detail, albeit an important one? It really would be the duty of those who are leaders in the sciences to at least have a look at what they judge from the outside. But this is the problem, that external life can be made comfortable—and this applies to many people—if one shuns the inconvenience of searching in an earnest manner. To be sure, for all this love of convenience, one is not aware of the strong forces of decline in our present civilization. The attitude of "after us the deluge" powerfully dominates the currently prevalent scientific world.

This is what I wished to illustrate today by means of one important problem of philological and historical research. After all, it is my hope that if particularly the esteemed students will realize more and more how the conscientious attempt is made to focus especially on those problems current research ignores, the young people above all others will come to the realization that such paths have to be pursued. I harbor the hope and I also know: If we work sufficiently in the direction of developing enthusiasm and confessing to the truth, what is needed to achieve again forces of regeneration in human civilization will be attained after all. Perhaps certain forces of darkness can suppress for a while what is being striven for here. In the long run, they will be unable to do so if the reality corresponds to the will, if, in fact, something light-filled is contained in what anthroposophy wills. Indeed, truth has means that only truth can discover and that are undiscoverable for the powers of darkness. Let us unite, old and young, young and old, in order to attain a clear view for discovering such paths to truth!

A study I began before our course started will become fully comprehensible only if we go back even further in considering the development of humanity in recent history. Basically, we have only given a few indications concerning the developments in the nineteenth century. It will be our purpose today to follow the spiritual development of mankind further back in time, giving special attention to an extraordinarily important and incisive event in the evolution of Western civilization. It is the turning-point that came about in the fourth century. There emerged at that time a figure still vivid in the memory of Western civilization, namely, Aurelius Augustinus.[1] We find in him a personality who had to fight with the great intensity, on the one hand, against what had come down from ancient times, something attempting during those first Christian centuries to establish Christianity on the basis of a certain ancient wisdom. On the other hand, he had to struggle against another element, the one that eventually was victorious in Western civilization. It rejected the more ancient form and limited itself to comprehending Christianity in a more external, material way, not to penetrate Christianity with ideas of ancient wisdom, but simply to narrate its events factually according to the course it had taken since its establishment, comprehending it intellectually as well as that was possible at that time.

These conflicts between the two directions—I would like to say, between the direction of a wisdom-filled

Christianity and a Christianity seemingly tending toward a more or less materialistic view—these conflicts had to be undergone particularly by the souls of the fourth and the early fifth century in the most intense way. And in Augustine, humanity remembers a personality who took part in such conflicts.

In our time, however, we have to understand clearly that the historic documents call forth almost completely false ideas of what existed prior to the fourth century A.D. As clear as the picture may be since the fifth century, as unclear are all the ordinary ideas concerning the preceding centuries. Yet, if we focus on what people in general could know about this period prior to the fourth century A.D., we are referred to two areas. One area is that of knowledge, cultivated in the schools; the other is the area of ritual, of veneration, of the religious element. Something belonging to very ancient times of human civilization still extends into these two areas. Though cloaked in a certain Christian coloring, this ancient element was still more or less present during the first Christian centuries in both the stream of wisdom and that of ritual.

If we look into the sphere of wisdom, we find preserved there a teaching from earlier times. In a certain sense, however, it had already begun to be replaced by what we today call the heliocentric world system—I have spoken of this in earlier lectures here. Nevertheless, it still remained from former astronomical teachings, and might be designated as a form of astronomy, but now not from the standpoint of physical cosmological observation. In very ancient times, people arrived at this astronomy—let us call it etheric in contrast to our physical astronomy—in the following way: People of old were still fully aware of the fact that human beings by nature belong not only to the earth but also to the cosmic surroundings of the earth, the planetary system. Ancient wisdom had quite concrete views concerning this etheric astronomy. It taught that if we turn our attention to what makes up the organization of the upper part of the human being—and here I make use of expressions that are familiar to us today—insofar as we view the etheric body of man, the human being stands in interaction with Saturn, Jupiter, and Mars. People thus considered certain reciprocal effects between the upper part of the human etheric body and Saturn, Jupiter, and Mars. Furthermore, people found that the part of the human being that is of a more astral nature has a sort of interrelationship with Venus, Mercury, and the Moon. The forces that then lead man into his earthly existence and that bring it about that a physical body is fitted into this etheric body, these are the forces of the earth. Those forces, on the other hand, that cause the human being to have a certain perspective leading beyond his earthly life, are the forces of the sun.

Thus it was said in those ancient times that the human being comes out of unknown spiritual worlds he passes through in prenatal life but that it is not as if he merely entered into terrestrial life. Rather, he enters from extraplanetary worlds into planetary life. The planetary life receives him as I have described it, relating him to the sun, moon, earth, Mercury, Venus, Mars, Jupiter, and Saturn. The orbit of Saturn was considered to be the approximate sphere the human being enters with his etheric body out of extraplanetary into planetary life. Everything that is etheric in the human being was definitely related to this planetary life. Only insofar as the etheric body then expresses itself in the physical body, only to that extent was the physical body related to the Earth. Insofar as the human being in turn raises himself with his ego beyond the etheric and astral body, the ancients related this to the sun.

Thus, one had a form of etheric astronomy. It was certainly still possible for this etheric astronomy not merely to look upon the physical destinies of the human being in the way physical astronomy does. Instead, since people viewed the etheric body, which in turn stands in a more intimate relationship to the spiritual aspect of the human being, in an interplay with the same forces of the planetary system, the following possibility existed. Since the forces of destiny can express themselves out of the planetary system by way of the etheric body, it was possible to speak of the human constitution and to include in the latter the forces of destiny.

In this teaching of antiquity, this etheric astronomy, which was continued even after people already had developed the heliocentric system as a kind of esoteric-physical science, a last wisdom teaching had emerged from ancient instinctive wisdom investigations and had been retained as a tradition. People spoke of the influences of heaven in no other way but by saying, Indeed, these influences of heaven exist; they bear not only the affairs of nature but also the forces of human destiny. Thus, there certainly existed a connection between what we might call a teaching of nature, namely cosmology, and what passed over later into all that people now consider as astrology, something that in ancient times, had a much more exact character and was based on direct observation.

It was thought that when the human being has entered the planetary sphere on his way to a new birth and has been received by it insofar as his etheric body is concerned, he subsequently enters the earth. He is received by the earth. Yet, even here, people did not merely think of the solid earth. Rather, they thought of the earth with its elements. Apart from the fact that the human being is received by the planetary sphere — whereby he would be a super-earthly being, whereby he would be what he is only as a soul — it was said that like a child he is received by the elements of the earth, by fire or warmth, by air, water, and the solid earth. All of these elements were considered the actual earth. Consequently, it was thought, the human being's etheric body is so tinged by these external elements, so saturated, that now the temperaments originate in it. Thus, the temperaments were pictured as closely tied to the etheric body, hence to the life organization of the human being. Therefore, in what is actually physical in man — or, at least, in what manifests through the physical body — this ancient teaching also saw something spiritual.

The most human aspect of this teaching, I would say, was something that can still be clearly discerned in the medical science period. The remedies and the teaching of medicine were certainly a product of this view of the relationship of the etheric body to the planetary system as well as of the way the etheric human being penetrate, as it were, into the higher spheres, into air, water, warmth, and earth, so that the physical impressions of the etheric soul temperaments found their way into his organization: black gall, white gall, and the other fluids, phlegm, blood, and so on. According to this commonly held view the nature of the human constitution can be known from the body fluids. It was not customary in medicine in those days to study the individual organs, of which drawings could be made. The intermingling of the permeation with fluids was studied, and a particular organ was viewed as a result of a special penetration of fluids. People then thought that in a healthy person the fluids intermingled in a specific manner; an abnormal intermingling of fluids was seen in a sick person. Thus we may say that the medical insight resulting from this teaching was definitely founded on the observation of the fluid human organism. What we call knowledge of the human organism today is based on the solid, earthly organism of man. In regard to the view of the human being, the course taken has led from an earlier insight into the fluid man to a more modern insight into the solid human being with sharply contoured organs.

The direction taken by medicine runs parallel to the transition from the ancient etheric astronomy to modern physical astronomy. The medical teaching of Hippocrates[2] still corresponds essentially to etheric astronomy, and, actually, the accomplishments of this medical conception concerned with the intermingling of fluids in man remained well into the fourth century A.D. in an exact manner, not only in tradition as it was later. Just as this ancient astronomy was subsequently obscured after the fourth century and physical astronomy took the place of the old etheric astronomy in the fifteenth century, so, too, pathology and the whole view of medicine was then based on the teachings of the solid element, of what is bounded and expressed by sharp contours in the human organism. This is in essence one side of humanity's evolution in the inorganic age.

Now we can also turn our attention to what has remained of those ancient times in cultic practices and religious ceremonies. The religious ceremonies were mainly made available to the masses; what I have just been describing was predominantly considered to be a treasure of wisdom belonging to centers of learning. Those cultic practices that found their way from Asia into Europe and that, insofar as they are religious endeavors, correspond to the view I have just explained, are known as Mithras worship.[3] It is a worship we find even as late as the first Christian centuries extending from East to West; we can follow its path through the countries of the Danube as far as the regions of the Rhine and on into France. This Mithras worship, familiar to you as far as its outer forms are concerned, may be briefly characterized by saying that along with the earthly and cosmic context the conqueror of the Mithras-Bull was depicted imaginatively and pictorially in the human being, riding on the bull and vanquishing the bull-forces.

Nowadays, we are easily inclined to think that such images—all cultic pictures, religious symbolizations which, if we may say so, have emerged organically out of the ancient wisdom teachings—are simply the abstract, symbolic product of those teachings. But it would be absolutely false if we were to believe that the ancient sages sat down and said, Now we must figure out a symbol. For ourselves we have the teaching of wisdom; for the ignorant masses we have to think up symbols that can then be employed in their ceremonial rites, and so on. Such assumptions would be totally wrong. An assumption approximately like that is entertained by modern Freemasons; they have similar thoughts about the nature of their own symbolism. But this was certainly not the view of the ancient teachers of wisdom.

I should now like to describe the view of these sages of old by referring in particular to the connections of the Mithra worship to the world view I have just outlined above. A fundamentally important question could still be raised by those who had retained a vivid view of how the human being is received into the planetary world with his etheric body, of how man is subsequently received into the sphere of earthly elements into warmth or fire, air, water, and earth, of how through the effects of these elements on the human etheric being black gall, white gall, phlegm, and blood are formed. They asked themselves a question that can occur now to a person who truly possesses Imaginative perception. In those times, the answer to this question was based on instinctive Imaginative perception, but we can repeat it today in full consciousness. If we develop an Imaginative conception of this entrance of the human being from the spiritual world through the planetary sphere into the terrestrial sphere of fire, air, water, and earth, we arrive at the realization that if something enters from the spheres beyond into the planetary sphere, hence into the earth's sphere, and is received there, this will not become a true human being. If we develop a picture of what is actually evolving there, if we have an Imaginative view of what can be beheld in purely Imaginative perception outside the planetary sphere, then enters into and is received by the planetary sphere and is subsequently taken hold of by the influences emanating from the earth sphere, we see that this does not become a human being. We do not arrive at a view of man; instead we attain to a conception that can be most clearly represented if we picture not a human being but a bull, an ox.

The ancient teachers of wisdom knew that no human beings would exist on earth if there were nothing besides this extraplanetary being that descends into the planetary sphere of evolution. They saw that at first glance one does arrive at the conception of the gradual approach of an entity out of extraplanetary spheres into the planetary and hence the earth sphere. But if one then proceeds from the content of these conceptions and tries to form a vivid Imaginative view, it does not turn into a human being; it becomes a mere bull. And if one comprehends nothing more in the human being but this, one merely comprehends what is bull-like in human beings. The ancient teachers of wisdom formed this conception. Now they said to themselves, In that case, human beings must struggle against this bull-like nature with something still higher. They must overcome the view given by this wisdom. As human beings, they are more than beings that merely come from the extra-planetary sphere, enter into the planetary sphere, and from there are taken hold of by the terrestrial elements. They have something within them that is more than this.

It is possible to say that these teachers of wisdom came as far as this concept. This was the reason they then developed the image of the bull and placed Mithras on top of it, the human being who struggles to overcome the bull, and who says of himself, I just be of far loftier origin than the being that was pictured according to the ancient teaching of wisdom.

Now these sages realized that their ancient teaching of wisdom contained an indication of what is important here. For this teaching did look upon the planetary sphere, upon Saturn, Jupiter, Mars, Mercury, Venus, moon, and so on. It also said that as the human being approaches the earth, he is constantly lifted up by the sun so as not to be submerged completely in the terrestrial elements, so as not to remain merely what proceeds from the etheric body and the mixture of black and white gall, phlegm, and blood when it is received by the planetary sphere and when the astral body is received

61

by the other planetary sphere through Mercury, Venus, moon. What lifts man upward dwells in the sun. Therefore, these sages said, Let us call man's attention to the sun forces dwelling in him; then he will turn into Mithras who is victorious over the bull!

This then was the cultic image. It was not meant to be merely a thought-out symbol but was actually to represent the fact, the cosmological fact. The religious ceremony was more than a mere outer sign; it was something that was extracted, as it were, out of the essence of the cosmos itself.

This cultic form was something that had existed since very ancient times and had been brought across from Asia to Europe. It was, in a sense, Christianity viewed from one side, viewed from the external, astronomical side, for Mithras was the sun force in man. Mithras was the human being who rebelled against the merely planetary and terrestrial aspects.

Now, a certain endeavor arose, traces of which can be observed everywhere when we look back at the first Christian centuries. The tendency arose to connect the historical fact, the Mystery of Golgotha, with the Mithras worship. Great were the numbers of people at that time, especially among the Roman Legions, who brought with them into the lands on the Danube and far into central Europe, indeed even into western Europe, what they had experienced in Asia and the Orient in general. In what they brought across as the Mithras worship there lived feelings that, without reflecting the Mystery of Golgotha, definitely contained Christian views and Christian sentiments. The worship of Mithras was considered as a concrete worship relating to the sun forces in man. The only thing this Mithras worship did not perceive was the fact that in the Mystery of Golgotha this sun force itself had descended as a spiritual entity and hand united itself with the human being Jesus of Nazareth.

Now there existed schools of wisdom in the East up until the fourth century A.D. that by and by received reports and became aware of the Mystery of Golgotha, of Christ. The further east we go in our investigations, the clearer this becomes. These schools then attempted to spread a certain teaching throughout the world, and for a time there was a tendency to let flow into the Mithras cult what agrees with the following supersensory perception: The true Mithras is the Christ; Mithras is his predecessor. The Christ force must be poured into those forces in man that vanquish the bull. To turn the Mithras worship into a worship of Christ was something that was intensely alive in the first Christian centuries up until the fourth century. One might say that the stream intending to Christianize this Mithras worship followed after the spreading of the latter. A synthesis between Christendom and the Mithras worship was striven for. An ancient, significant image of man's being—Mithras riding on and vanquishing the bull— was to be brought into relationship with the Christ Being. One might say that a quite glorious endeavor existed in this direction, and in a certain respect it was a powerful one.

Anyone who follows the spread of Eastern Christianity and the spread of Arianism[4] can see a Mithras element in it, even though in already quite weakened form. Any translation of the Ulfilas-Bible[5] into modern languages remains imperfect if one is unaware that Mithras elements still play into the terminology of Ulfilas (or Wulfila). But who pays heed nowadays to these deeper relationships in the linguistic element? As late as in the fourth century, there were philosophers in Greece who worked on bringing the ancient etheric

63

astronomy into harmony with Christianity. From this effort then arose the true Gnosis, which was thoroughly eradicated by later Christianity, so that only a few fragments of the literary samples of this Gnosis have remained.

What do people really know today about the Gnosis, of which they say in their ignorance that our anthroposophy is a warmed-over version? Even if this were true, such people would not be able to know about it, for they are familiar only with those parts of the Gnosis that are found in the critical, Occidental-Christian texts dealing with the Gnosis. They know the quotes from Gnostic texts left behind by the opponents of the Gnosis. There is hardly anything left of the Gnosis except what could be described by the following comparison. Imagine that Herr von Gleich would be successful in rooting out the whole of anthroposophical literature and nothing would remain except his quotations. Then, later on, somebody would attempt to reconstruct anthroposophy based on these quotes; then, it would be about the same procedure in the West as that which was applied to the Gnosis. Therefore, if people say that modern anthroposophy imitates the Gnosis, they would not know it even if it were the case, because they are unfamiliar with the Gnosis, knowing of it only through its opponents.

So, particularly in Athens, a school of wisdom existed well into the fourth century, and indeed even longer, that endeavored to bring the ancient etheric astronomy into harmony with Christianity. The last remnants of this view—man's entering from higher worlds through the planetary sphere into the earth sphere—still illuminate the writings of Origen; they even shine through the texts of the Greek Church Fathers. Everywhere one can see it shimmer through. It shines through particularly in the writings of the genuine Dionysius the Areopagite.[6] This Dionysius left behind a teaching that was a pure synthesis of the etheric astronomy and the element dwelling in Christianity. He taught that the forces localized, as it were, astronomically and cosmically in the sun entered into the earth sphere in Christ through the man Jesus of Nazareth and that thereby a certain previously nonexistent relationship came into being between the earth and all the higher hierarchies, the hierarchies of the Angels, of Wisdom, the hierarchies of the Thrones and the Seraphim, and so on. It was a penetration of this teaching of the hierarchies with etheric astronomy that could be found in the original Dionysius the Areopagite.

Then, in the sixth century, the attempt was made to obliterate the traces even of the more ancient teachings by Dionysius the Areopagite. They were altered in such a way that they now represented merely an abstract teaching of the spirit. In the form in which the teaching of Dionysius the Areopagite has come down to us, it is a spiritual teaching that no longer has much to do with etheric astronomy. This is the reason he is then called the "Pseudo-Dionysius." In this manner, the decline of the teaching of wisdom was brought about. On the one ʰnd, the teachings of Dionysius were distorted; on the ⹁ ɪer hand, the truly alive teaching in Athens that had tried to unite etheric astronomy with Christianity was eradicated. Finally, in regard to the cultic aspect, the Mithras worship was exterminated.

In addition, there were contributions by individuals such as Constantine.[7] His actions were intensified later by the fact that Emperor Justinian[8] ordered the School of Philosophers in Athens closed. Thus, the last remaining people who had occupied themselves with bringing the old etheric astronomy into harmony with Christianity had to emigrate; they found a place in Persia where they could at least live out their lives. Based on the same program, according to which he had closed the Athenian Academy of Philosophers, Justinian also had Origen declared a heretic. For the same reason, he abolished Roman consulship, though it led only a shadowy existence, people sought in it a kind of power of resistance against the Roman concept of the state, which was reduced to pure jurisprudence. The ancient human element people still associated with the office of consul disappeared in the political imperialism of Rome.

Thus, in the fourth century, we see the diminishing of the cultic worship that could have brought Christianity closer to man. We observe the diminishing of the ancient wisdom teaching of an etheric astronomy that tried to unite with the insight into the significance of the Mystery of Golgotha. And in the West, we see an element take its place that already carried within itself the seeds of the later materialism, which could not become a theory until the fifteenth century when the fifth post-Atlantean epoch began, but which was prepared in the main through taking the spiritual heritage from the Orient and imbuing it with materialistic substance.

We must definitely turn our minds to this course of European civilization. Otherwise, the foundations of European civilization will never become quite clear to us. It will also never become really clear to us how it was possible that, again and again, when people moved to the Orient, they could bring back with them powerful spiritual stimuli from there. Above all else, throughout the first part of the Middle Ages, there was lively commercial traffic from the Orient up the Danube River, following exactly those routes taken by the ancient

Mithras worship, which, naturally, had already died away at the beginning of the Middle Ages. The merchants who traveled to the Orient and back again, always found in the East what had preceded Christianity but definitely tended already towards Christianity. We observe, moreover, that when the Crusaders journeyed to the Orient, they received stimuli from the remnants they could still discern there, and they brought treasures of ancient wisdom back to Europe.

I mentioned that the ancient medical knowledge of fluids was connected with this old body of wisdom. Again and again, people who traveled to the Orient, even the Crusaders and those who journeyed with the Crusades, upon their return always brought back with them remnants of this old medicine to Europe. These remnants of an ancient medicine were then transmitted in the form of tradition all over Europe. Certain individuals who at the same time were ahead of their age in their own spiritual evolution then went through remarkable developments, such as the personality we know under the name Basilius Valentinus.[9]

What kind of personality was he? He was somebody who had taken up the tradition of the old medicine of fluids from the people with whom he had spent his youth, at times without understanding it from this or that indication. Until a short time ago—today it is already less often the case—there still existed in the old peasant's sayings remnants of this medical tradition that had been brought over from the Orient by the many travelers. These remnants were in a sense preserved by the peasantry; those who grew up among peasants heard of them; as a rule they were those who then became priests. In particular those who became monks came from the peasantry. There, they had heard this or that of what was in fact distorted treasure of ancient wisdom that had become decadent. These people did undergo an independent educational development. Up until the fifteenth and sixteenth centuries, the educational development an individual went through by means of Christian theology was something much more liberal than it was later on. Based on their own spirituality, these priests and monks gradually brought a certain amount of order into these matters. They pondered what they had heard; out of their own genius, the connected the various matters. Thus originated the writings that have been preserved as the writings of Basilius Valentinus.

Indeed, these conditions also gave rise to a school of thought from which Paracelsus[10] even Jacob Boehme[11] learned. Even these individuals still took up the treasure of ancient medical wisdom that lived, I might say, in the folk group soul. One can notice this primarily in Jacob Boehme, but also in Paracelsus and others, even if one considers their writings only in a superficial way. If you look closely at, for example, Jacob Boehme's text "De Signatura Rerum," you will find in the manner of his presentation that what I have said is very obvious. It is a form of old folk wisdom that basically contained distorted ancient wisdom. Such old folk wisdom was by no means as abstract as our present-day science; instead, there still existed a sensitivity for the objective element in words. One felt something *in* the words. Just as one tries to *know* through concepts today, one *felt* in the words. One knew that the human being had drawn the words out of the objective essence of the universe itself.

This can become evident in Jacob Boehme's efforts to feel what really lies concealed in the syllable, "sul," or again in the syllable, "phur" of "sulphur". See how Jacob Boehme struggles in "De Signatura Rerum," to draw something out of a word, to draw out an inner word-extract, to draw something out of the word "sulphur" in order to come to an entity. The feeling is definitely present there that when one experiences the extract of words, one arrives at something real. In former times, it was felt, something had settled into the words the human soul absorbed when it moved from spheres beyond through the planetary sphere into earthly existence. But what the soul placed into the words due to its closeness to the intermingling of fluids when the child learned to speak was still something objective. There was still something in speech that was like instruction by the gods, not merely like human instruction. In Jacob Boehme we see this noble striving that can be expressed somewhat as if he had felt, I would like to consider speech as something in which living gods work behind the phenomena into the human organization in order to form speech and, along with speech, a certain treasure of wisdom.

Thus we see that the ancient body of wisdom does indeed continue on into later ages, though already taken up by modern thinking, which, it is true, is yet barely evident in such original and outstanding minds like Jacob Boehme and Paracelsus. Into what has thus been brought forth the purely intellectualistic, theoretical element is now imprinted, the element that is based on man's physical thinking and takes hold only of the physical realm. We see how, on the one hand, purely physical astronomy arises, and how, on the other hand, physiology and anatomy come about, which are directed exclusively upon the clearly defined organs of man—in short, the whole medical adumbration.

Thus, the human being gradually find himself surrounded by a world that he comprehends only in a physical sense and in which he himself as a cosmic being certainly has no place. Concerning himself, he grasps only what he has become by virtue of the earth; for it is thanks to the earth that he has become this solidly bounded, physical, organic being. He can no longer reconcile what is revealed to him of the universe through physical astronomy with what dwells in his form and points to something else. He turns his attention away from the manner in which the human form indicates something else. He finally loses all awareness of the fact that his striving for erect posture and the special manner and means by which he attains to speech out of his organism cannot originate from the Mithras-Bull, but only from Mithras. He no longer wishes to occupy himself with all this, for he is sailing full force into materialism. He has to sail into materialism, for religious consciousness itself, after all, has absorbed only the external, material phenomenon of Christianity. It has then dogmatized this external, material phenomenon without attempting to perceive through some wisdom how the Mystery of Golgotha took place, but instead trying to determine through stipulations what truth is.

Thus we observe the transition from the ancient Oriental position of thinking based on cosmic insight to the specifically Roman-European form of observation. How were matters "determined" in the Orient, and how could something be "determined" about the Mystery of Golgotha based on Oriental instinctive perception? If we take the insight coming out of the cosmos, looking up at the stars, that insight, though it was an instinctive, elemental insight, should lead to, or was at least supposed to lead to, the meaning of the Mystery of Golgotha. This was the path taken in the Orient. Beginning with the fifth century, there was no longer any sensitivity for this path. By replacing the Asiatic manner of determination more and more with the Egyptian form, earlier Church Councils had already pointed out that the nature of the Mystery of Golgotha should not be determined in this manner, but that the majority of the Fathers gathered at the Councils should decide. The juristic principle was put in the place of the Oriental principle of insight; dogmatism was brought into the juristic element. People no longer had the feeling that truth must be determined out of universal conscience. They began to feel that it was possible to ascertain, based on resolutions of the Councils, whether the divine and the human nature in Christ Jesus was two natures or one, and other such things. We see the Egyp-to-Roman juristic element pervading the innermost configuration of Occidental civilization, an element that even today is deeply rooted in human beings who are not inclined to permit truth to determine their relation-ship to it. Instead, they wish to make decisions based on emotional factors; therefore, they have no other measure for determining things except majority rule in some form.

We shall say more about this tomorrow.

LECTURE V
Dornach, April 16, 1921

Yesterday I referred to the significant turning point in the development of Occidental civilization in the fourth century A.D. I pointed out that, on the one hand, this was the time when Greek wisdom disappeared from European culture, wisdom through which people had tried to bring to expression the depths of Christianity in a wisdom-imbued way. The time of the outer expression of this disappearance falls somewhat later, namely, when Emperor Justinian declared the writings of Origen heretical, abolished Roman consulship, and closed the Greek Academy of Philosophy at Athens. The guardians of Greek wisdom thus had to flee to the Orient, withdrawing, as it were, from European civilization. The wisdom teaching that had extended from the East as far west as Greece and had assumed its special form there, is one aspect of the picture.

On the other hand, the Mithras worship was supposed to indicate in a significant external ritual how, with their soul-spiritual nature, human beings were to raise themselves above all that could be comprehended through the interplay of beings of the planetary sphere with terrestrial forces, how the human being could sense his full humanity. This was the object of the Mithras cult. This Mithras worship, which was intended to reveal to man his own being, likewise disappeared after it had spread through the regions along the Danube and on into central and western Europe. These two streams, one a cultic stream, the other a stream of wisdom, were

73

replaced in Europe by factual narrations of the events of Palestine. Thus, one has to say that neither a cultic worship, which would have recognized in Christ Jesus the victor over all the human being, was meant to bring under his control in the course of world evolution, nor a wisdom that would have tried to grasp the actual mysteries of Christendom in a wise manner were able to enter Europe. Instead, the superficial narration of the events of Palestine became popular. The concepts that should have been found in these happenings in Palestine were instead steeped in the flood of juristic thinking, which replaced the investigation of cosmic secrets with the determination of dogmas by means of majority resolutions in Church Councils, and so forth.

This very fact indicates that a change of great and far-reaching significance had taken place in the fourth century A.D. in the development of Western civilization, and consequently in the evolution of the whole of mankind. Proceeding from the Orient, all the influences that had laid hold of eastern European civilization were in a sense pushed back again towards the Orient. Only the increasing tendency towards abstract thinking in the Roman world maintained itself in the Occident alongside the comprehension of the external, sensory world of facts.

How alive the conceptions of the Greek gods had been among the Greeks, and how conceptually abstract the ideas were the Romans entertained of their gods! Actually, in the later period, what the Greeks possessed of ideas concerning the supersensible world was already lifeless, although quite alive as such within itself. Yet, it was a lifeless element in comparison to the living conceptions of the supersensible worlds present during the ancient Persian and Indian civilizations, which represented a living within these higher worlds. In those times, albeit with a purely instinctive human perception, people lived in communion with the supersensible worlds just as mankind in the present communes with the sensory world. For human beings in the ancient Orient, the spiritual world was readily accessible. For them, the beings of the spiritual world were present just as other human beings, our fellowmen, live side by side with us. Out of this living, supersensible world, the Greeks built up their system of concepts. In the ages before Aristotle, up to the fourth century B.C., Greek ideas were not abstract ideas gained through external sensory observation and then lifted up into abstraction. These Greek ideas still originated from the living, supersensible world; they were born of a primeval power of vision. These living Greek ideas still imbued a person with soul sustenance and warmth; insofar as he could share in them, they bestowed on him the necessary enthusiasm for his form of social order. Certainly, we must never forget that a large part of the Greek people was denied a share in this life of thought; this was the extensive world of the slaves. But the bearers of Greek culture certainly participated in a realm of ideas that was basically a downpouring of supersensible, spiritual powers into the world of the earthly sphere.

In comparison with this, the Roman world—separated from Greece only by the sea—definitely had a quite abstract appearance. The Romans described their gods in the same prosaic, unimaginative ways as, shall we say, our modern scientists speak of the laws of nature. Although this is an indication of the significant change I have to point out here, we confront this change in a special way of we turn our attention to a factor in the life of soul that found only partial realization in world history and did not develop to its full potential.

Consider for a moment the destiny of the ancient Greek people. It is fraught with a certain tragedy. After its period of great glory, Greek culture pined away and, in essence, vanished from the stage of world history, for what replaced it in that territory cannot be said to have been a true successor. The Greek nation went into decline in a severe, world-historical illness, and from its ancient ideas it produced what, I would say, represents the dawn of all later culture. It brought forth Stoicism and Epicureanism, [1] systems or views of life in which the more abstract mode of thought, characterizing the later Western civilization, already found an early expression. But we can see in Stoicism and Epicureanism, even in the later Greek mysticism, that they express a decline of ancient Greece.

Why was it that this culture of Greece was destined to decline and ultimately to pass away from the stream of world evolution?[2] One could say that this decline and death of the ancient Greek people indicates a significant mystery in world history. With faculties of vision handed down to them as an echo of the ancient Oriental world view, the ancient Greeks still beheld the soul-spiritual human being in his full light. After all, in the earlier periods of Greek culture, every individual knew himself to be a being of soul and spirit that had descended through conception and birth from the spiritual worlds, that has its home in a supersensible sphere and is destined for supersensible spheres. Yet, at the same time, even in its prime, Greece sensed its decline in world history—I have often referred to this. It sensed that human beings cannot fully attain to humanity on earth by merely looking up into supersensible worlds. It felt itself surrounded and pervaded by the earth's forces. Hence the ancient saying: "Better it is to be a beggar in the sense world than a king in the realm of shades."[3] The Greeks of earlier periods had still beheld all the shining glory of the supersensible world; at the same time, by attaining full humanity in ancient Greece, they sensed that they could not maintain this radiance of the spiritual worlds. They felt they were losing it and that their soul nature was becoming ensnared in the things of the earth. Fear of death arose in them because they realized that life between birth and death can estrange the soul from its spiritual home. Greek culture must definitely be described in accordance with this feeling.

Men like Nietzsche basically had true insight into these matters.[4] Nietzsche had the right feeling when he designated the period of Greek development preceding the Socratic and Platonic age as the tragic epoch of Greek culture. For already in thinkers such as Thales, [5] and particularly Anaxagoras[6] and Heraclitus,[7] we observe the twilight of a magnificent world view which modern history does not mention at all. We note the fear of becoming estranged from the supersensible world, of becoming tied to what alone remains from the passage through life between birth and death, namely, of becoming linked to the world of Hades, the world of shades, which basically becomes man's lot. Nevertheless, the Greeks preserved one thing; they saved what appeared at its height in the Platonic idea. There emerged amid the onset of progressive decline this world of Platonic ideas, the last glorious remnant of the ancient Orient, though it, too, was then fated to perish in Aristotelianism.

Yet these Greek ideas did appear, and Greek thinking constantly sensed how the human ego is really something that is becoming lost in human life. This was a fundamental experience of the Greeks. Take the description I gave concerning ego evolution in my book *Riddles of Philosophy*,[8] where I described that the ego was then connected with thinking, with external perception. But since the whole ego experience is bound up with thinking, the human being experienced his *I* not so much within his own corporeality. Rather, he felt it linked to all that lives in the world outside, to the blossoming of the flowers, to lightning and thunder in the sky, to the billowing clouds, to the rising mist and the falling rain. The Greeks experienced the ego connected to all this. They sensed with the forces of the ego, as it were, but without the housing of this ego. Instead, they felt, When I look out upon the world of flowers, *there* my ego is attached, *there* it blossoms in the flowers.

It is justifiable to say that this Greek culture could not have continued. What would it have become if it had continued? It was not inherently possible for it to continue on a straight line. What would it have become? Human beings would gradually have come to consider themselves earth beings that are subhuman. The actual soul-spirit being in us would have been experienced as something that really dwells in the clouds, the flowers, the mountains, in rain, and sunshine, a being that occasionally comes to visit us. If the development of Greek culture had continued in the same direction, human beings increasingly would have felt that at night, when they had fallen asleep, they could experience the approach of their own ego in all its radiance and that it paid them a special visit then. But upon waking in the morning and becoming involved in the world of the lower senses, they also would have felt that insofar as they are a being of the earth they are but the outer housing of the ego. A certain estrangement from the ego would have been the consequence of an unbroken development of what can be noticed or sensed as the fundamental keynote or actual basic temperament of Greek nature.

It was necessary that this ego, which was escaping, as it were, into nature and the cosmos, should be firmly anchored in the inner constitution of the human being, an organic being moving about on the earth. A powerful impulse was required for this to happen. It was, after all, the peculiar characteristic of the Oriental world view that while it clearly drew attention to the ego— precisely because of its teaching of repeated earth lives—it also had the inherent tendency to alienate this ego from the human being, to deprive us of the ego. This is how it came about that the Occident, unable to rise to the heights attained by Greece, lacked the inner strength to assimilate the wisdom of Greece in its full strength and allowed it instead to flow back, so to speak, towards the Orient. The West also lacked the strength to take possession of the Mithras cult and allowed it to flow back to the Orient. By dint of the robust, sturdy forces of human earthly nature, the West was capable only of listening to purely factual narrations of the events of Palestine and then of having them affirmed by dogmas laid down in the Councils. At the outset, the Europeans were confronted with a materialistic view of the human personality.

This became most evident in the transition in the fourth century. All knowledge that would have been capable of producing a deeper comprehension of Christianity gradually withdrew back into Asia, all insight that could have brought about a cult in which the Christ Triumphant would have appeared rather than He who is overwhelmed by the burdens of the Cross, whose triumph can only faintly be surmised behind the shadow of the Crucifix. For the Occident, this ebbing away of the wisdom and the ancient ceremonial worship was initially a matter of securing the ego. From the robust force dwelling in the barbaric peoples of the north, the impulse emerged that was intended to supply the power to attach the ego to the earthly human organism.

While this was happening in the regions around the Danube, somewhat south of there, and in southern and western Europe, Arabism was transplanted from the Orient in forms differing from those of the earlier Oriental wisdom. Arabism then made its way as far as Spain, and southwestern Europe became inundated by a fantastic intellectual culture. This was a culture that in the external field of art could not achieve anything more than the arabesque, since it was incapable of permeating the organic realm with soul and spirit. Thus, in regard to the cultic ceremonies, Europe was filled, on the one hand with the narration of purely factual events; on the other hand, it was engrossed in a body of abstract, fantastic wisdom that, entering Europe by way of Spain, turned in filtered form into the culture of pure intellect.

Within this region, where the stories about the events of Palestine referring solely to the external aspects prevailed, where only the fantastic intellectual wisdom from Arabism existed, there a few individuals emerged—after all, a few isolated individuals appear now and again within the totality of mankind—who had an idea of how matters really stood. In their souls a feeling dawned that there is a lofty Christian mystery, the full significance of which is so great that the highest wisdom cannot penetrate it; the most ardent feeling is not strong enough to develop a fitting ceremonial worship for it. Indeed, they felt that something emanated from the Cross on Golgotha that would have to be comprehended by the highest wisdom and the most daring feeling. Such ideas arose in a few individuals. Something like the following profound Imagination arose in them. In the bread of the Last Supper, a synthesis of sorts was contained, a concentration of the force of the outer cosmos that comes down to the earth together with all the streams of forces from the cosmos, penetrating this earth, conjuring forth from it the vegetation. Then, what has thus been entrusted to the earth from out of the cosmos, in turn springs forth from the earth and is synthetically concentrated in the bread and sustains the human body.

Still another element pierced through all the clouds of obscurity that covered the ancient traditions. Something else was passed on to these European sages, something that, it is true, had had its origin in the Orient but penetrated through the cloud cover and was understood by some individuals. This other mystery, which was linked with the mystery of the bread, was the mystery of the holy vessel in which Joseph of Arimathea had caught the blood flowing down from Christ Jesus. This was the other aspect of the cosmic mystery. Just as the bread was regarded a concentrated extract of the cosmos, so the blood was regarded as the extract of the nature and being of man. In bread and blood—of which wine is merely the outer symbol—this extract expressed itself for these European sages. They had truly stepped forth as if out of the hidden places of the mysteries and towered far above the masses of the European population who could only hear the facts of Palestine, and who, if they advanced to scholarliness, found their way only slowly into the abstract fantasy of Arabism. In these wise men, who distinguished themselves by something that was like the overripe fruit of Oriental wisdom and at the same time the ripest fruit of European perception and feeling, there developed what they called the Mystery of the Grail. But, so they told themselves, the Mystery of the Grail is not to be found on earth.

People have grown accustomed to developing the kind of intelligence that found its highest form in Arabism. They are in the habit of not looking for the meaning of external facts, but are satisfied with being told of these outer facts from the aspect of sensory reality. One must penetrate to an understanding of the Mystery of the Bread, which is said to have been broken by Christ Jesus in the same chalice in which Joseph of Arimathea caught His blood. As legend tells it, this chalice was then removed to Europe, but was preserved by angels in a region high above the surface of the earth until the arrival of Titurel[9] who created for this Grail, this sacred chalice, a temple on Mont Salvat. Through the clouds of abstraction and narrations of mere facts, those who had become European mystery sages in the manner described above wished to behold in a sacred, spiritual temple the Mystery of the Grail, the mystery of the cosmos that had disappeared along with etheric astronomy and the Mystery of the Blood that had vanished along with the ancient view of medicine. For just as the ancient medicine had fallen victim to abstract thinking, the old etheric astronomy, too, had passed over into abstract thought.

At a certain period in time, this whole trend of abstract thinking had reached its prime and had been brought to Spain by the Arabs. It was precisely in Spain where the Mystery of the Grail could not be found outwardly anywhere among people. Only abstract intellectual wisdom prevailed. Among the Christians, there was only narration of bare, external facts; among the Arabs, the Moors, there existed a fantastic development of the intellect. Only in the heights, above this earth,

hovered the Holy Grail. This spiritual temple, this Holy
Grail, this temple that encompassed the mysteries of
bread and wine, could be entered only by those who
had been endowed by divine powers with the necessary
faculties. It is not by chance that the temple of the Grail
was supposed to be found in Spain, where one literally
had to move miles away from what earthly actuality
presented, where one had to break through brambles in
order to penetrate to the spiritual temple that enshrined
the Holy Grail.

It was out of such prerequisite feelings that the conception of the Holy Grail developed. The invisible
Church, the supersensible Church, which is nevertheless to be found on earth—this was what concealed itself
in the Mystery of the Grail. It was an immediate presence that cannot be discovered, however, by those who
turn their mind indifferently to the world. In ancient
times, the priests of the mysteries went out into the
world, looked around among human beings, and based
on seeing their auras, concluded, Here is one we must
receive into the mysteries; there is another one we must
accept into the mysteries. People did not need to ask;
they were chosen. Inner initiative on the part of the
individual was not required; one was chosen and bid-
den to enter the sacred mystery centers. This age was
over already around the eleventh, twelfth, and ninth
and tenth centuries.

The impulse urging a person to ask, What are the
secrets of existence? had to be grounded in the human
being through the Christ force, which had moved into
European civilization. No one could approach the Grail
who passed through the outer world with a drowsy,
apathetic mind. It was said that he alone could penetrate into the miracles, that is, the mysteries of the Holy

Grail, who in his soul felt the inclination to ask about the secrets of existence, both the cosmic secrets and those of man's inner being. Fundamentally speaking, it has remained so ever since. After the first half of the Middle Ages, however, when human beings had been earnestly directed to pose questions, had been told that they *should* indeed ask questions, a great reaction set in beginning with the first third of the fourteenth century. By that time, those who asked about the Mysteries of the Holy Grail had become fewer and fewer in number, and inertia was creeping into the souls of men. They turned their attention wholly to the outer forms of human life on earth, to all that may be seen, counted, weighed, measured, and calculated in the cosmos.

Nevertheless, the sacred challenge had already entered European civilization in the early Middle Ages, the sacred challenge remained: To enquire into the mysteries of the cosmos as well as into the inner mysteries of man, namely, the mysteries of the blood. After all, it was in a great variety of phases that humanity has passed through what materialism with all its forces by necessity had to bring into European civilization. Momentous, stirring words were uttered, though in many instances they have died away. We have to consider how great the possibility was for momentous words to be spoken within European civilization. What was destined for a certain age, namely, the factual narration of the events of Palestine, the permeation of these outer facts with Arabism, which was accomplished by scholasticism[10] in the Middle Ages, was indeed of great significance for that particular age. But just as it developed out of an age of greater wisdom and ceremonial practices, both of which had only been pushed back to the East, it also did not understand how to listen to the supersensible mys-

84

teries of Christianity, the mysteries of the Holy Grail. All the truly compelling voices that resounded in the early Middle Ages—and there were more than a few of them—were silenced by Rome's Catholicism, which was becoming more and more engulfed in dogmatism, in the same way as the Gnosis—as I pointed out again yesterday—was eradicated root and branch.

We must not form a negative judgment of the period between the fourth and the twelfth and thirteenth centuries merely on the basis of the fact that of the numerous voices raised, as it were, in holy, overripe sweetness throughout European civilization—which, for the rest was barbaric—only the somewhat awkward voice of one man has remained who could not write, that of Wolfram von Eschenbach.[11] For all that, he was still great; he was spared by the dogmatism that had gripped Europe and had basically eradicated the powerful voices that had called amid strife and bitterness for the quest of the Holy Grail. Those who raised this call for the Holy Grail meant to let it resound in the spirit of freedom dawning in the dull souls. They did not wish to deprive the human being of his freedom; they did not mean to push anything on him; he was to be the questioning one. Out of the depths of his own soul he was to ask about the miracles of the Grail.

This spiritual life that later became extinct was truly greater than the spiritual life opposing it, although the latter, too, was not without a certain greatness. When what has been described by the servants of the Holy Grail as a spiritual path was then superseded by the earthly path of the journey to the physical Jerusalem over in the East, namely, when the crusade to the Grail was replaced by the crusades to the terrestrial Jerusalem, when Gottfried of Bouillon[12] set out to establish an external kingdom in Jerusalem in opposition to Rome, letting his cry, "Away from Rome!" ring out, his voice was really less persuasive than that of Peter of Amiens.[13] His voice sounded like a mighty suggestion to translate into something materialistic what the servants of the Holy Grail had intended as something spiritual.

This, too, was one of the paths that was taken because of materialism. It led to the physical Jerusalem, not to the spiritual Jerusalem, which was said to enshrine in Titurel's temple what had remained of the Mystery of Golgotha as the Holy Grail. Legend held that Titurel had brought this Holy Grail down to the earth's sphere from the clouds, where it had hovered, held by angels during the age of Arabism and the factual narration of the events of Palestine. The age of materialism, however, did not begin to ask about the Holy Grail. Lonely, isolated individuals, people who did not have a share in wisdom but dwelled in a kind of stupor, like Parsifal, were the ones who set out to seek the Holy Grail. But they also did not really understand how to ask the proper, appropriate question. Thus, the path of materialism, which began in the first third of the fourteenth century, was preceded by that other path of materialism already expressed in the turn to the East, the eastward journey to the physical Jerusalem. This tragedy was experienced by modern humanity; human beings had to and still have to undergo this tragedy in order to comprehend themselves inwardly and to turn properly into people asking questions. Modern mankind had to and still has to experience the tragedy that the light that once had approached from the East had not been recognized as spiritual light. The spiritual light had been rejected, and instead people set out to find a physical country, the physical materiality of the Orient. In the Middle

Ages, humanity began to seek the physical East after the spiritual East had been rejected at the close of antiquity.

Such, then, was the situation in Europe, and our age today is still a part of it. For if we understand the true, inner call resounding in human hearts, we still are and should be seekers for the Holy Grail. The strivings of humanity that emerged beginning with the crusades still await their metamorphosis into spiritual endeavors. We have yet to arrive at such a comprehension of the cosmic worlds so that we will be able to seek for the origin of Christ in these cosmic worlds. As long as these cosmic worlds are investigated only with the methods of external, physical astronomy, they naturally cannot be conceived of as the home of Christ. From what the modern astronomer teaches as the secret of the heavens, which he describes only by means of geometry, mathematics, and mechanics and observes only with the telescope, the Christ could not have descended to earth in order to incarnate in the human being Jesus of Nazareth. Neither can this incarnation be understood on the basis of knowledge about the physical nature of the human being, knowledge that is obtained by moving from people in actual life to the clinic, where the corpse is dissected for the purposes of research so that views concerning the living human being are arrived at based on the corpse.

People in antiquity possessed an astronomy inbued with life and medical knowledge filled with life. Once again, our quest must be for a living astronomy, a living medicine. Just as a living astronomy will reveal to us a heaven, a cosmos, that is truly pervaded by a spirituality and from where the Christ could descend, so an enlivened medicine will present to us the being of man in a way that enables us to penetrate with insight and understanding to the Mystery of the Blood, to the organic inner sphere where the forces of the etheric body, the astral body, and the ego transform themselves into the physical blood When a true medical knowledge has grasped the Mystery of the Blood and a spiritualized astronomy has understood the cosmic spheres, we shall comprehend how it was possible for the Christ to descend from these cosmic spheres to the earth, how He could find on earth the human body that could receive Him with its blood. It is the Mystery of the Grail that in all earnestness must be sought in this manner, namely, by setting out on the path to the spiritual Jerusalem with all that we are as human beings, with head and heart. This, indeed, is the task of modern humanity.

It is strange how the essence of what ought to come to pass weaves objectively through the sphere of existence. If it is not perceived in the correct way, it is experienced outwardly, it is superficially materialized. Just as formerly the Christians flocked to Jerusalem, so now large numbers of Jewish people travel to Jerusalem,[14] thus expressing yet another phase of materialism that indicates how something that ought to be understood spiritually by all of modern humanity is interpreted only materialistically. The time must come when the Mystery of the Grail will once again be comprehended in the right way. You know that I have mentioned it in my *An Outline of Occult Science*.[15] It is, in a manner of speaking, woven into the text that refers to all we must seek to discover along this path of spiritual science. Thus, I indicated what we have to acquire as a kind of picture and Imagination for what must be sought in earnest striving of the spirit and with profound human feeling as the path to the Grail.

Tomorrow, we will discuss this further.

LECTURE VI
Dornach, April 17, 1921

During the last few days, I have tried to show how Western civilization originated and that a significant and mighty turning point can be noted in mankind's overall evolution in the fourth Christian century. It was also necessary to point out how Greece gradually developed in the direction of this twilight, so to speak; how, based on quite different impulses, the civilization of central and western European culture came about, and how a comprehension of Christianity developed under these influences. To begin with, let us try and refer to the facts under consideration once more from a certain different viewpoint.

Christianity originated in the western Orient from the Mystery of Golgotha. Insofar as its specific nature was concerned, Oriental culture certainly was already in decline. The ancient, primordial wisdom existed in its last phases in what developed in Asia Minor and Greece as Gnosticism. The Gnosis, after all, was a form of wisdom that combined, in the most manifold ways, what presented itself to the human being as phenomena of the cosmos and nature. This not withstanding, in comparison to the directly perceived, instinctive insight into the spiritual world that was the foundation of Oriental development, Gnosticism already had a more, shall we say, intellectual, rational character. The spiritual life that permeated all human perception in the ancient Orient was no longer present. It was actually from the last vestiges of the ancient wisdom that people sought to fit together the philosophical and humanistic view that was then employed as a body of wisdom for understanding the Mystery of Golgotha. The substance inherent in the Mystery of Golgotha was clothed in the wisdom retained from the Orient in Greece.

Now let us consider this wisdom from the point of view of spiritual science. If we view human beings as they devoted themselves once upon a time to this wisdom, we find that the main thing in the ancient Orient was that people saw the world with what was active in their astral body, with what they could experience in their soul through their astral body—even though their sentient soul and rational or intellectual soul had already developed. It was the astral body that worked into these soul members and enabled people to actually turn their glance away from the earthly phenomena and to still perceive quite clearly what enters in the spiritual, supersensible sphere from the cosmos. As yet, human beings did not have a view of the world based on the ego. Their self expressed itself only dimly. For the human being the ego was as yet not an actual question. Human beings dwelled in the astral element, and in it they still lived in a certain harmony with the world phenomena surrounding them. In a sense, the really puzzling world for them was the one they beheld with their eyes, the one that ran its course around them. For them, the comprehensible world was the supersensible world of the gods, the world in which the spiritual beings had their existence. Human beings looked across to these spiritual beings, to their actions, their destinies. It was indeed the essential characteristic of the view of the ancient Orient that people's attention was directed towards these spiritual worlds. People wished to comprehend the sensory world on the basis of these spiritual worlds.

Today, finding ourselves within our civilization, we take the opposite view. To us, the physical-sensory world is given. Proceeding from it, in one way or another, we try to comprehend the spiritual world—if we attempt that at all, if we do not reject doing so, if we do not remain stuck in pure materialism. The material world is seen as given by us. The ancient Orientals saw the spiritual world as given. On the premise of the physical world, we try to discover something with which to comprehend the wondrousness of the phenomena, the purpose of the structure of the organisms, and so on; based on this physical, sensory world, we try to prove to ourselves the existence of the supersensory world. The ancient Orientals tried to comprehend the physical, sensory environment on the basis of the superphysical, supersensory world given to them. Out of it, they wished to receive light—indeed, they did receive it, and without it, the physical, sensory world was to them only darkness and trepidation. Thus, they also experienced what they sensed to be their innermost being as still completely illuminated by the astral body, as having emerged from the spiritual worlds. People then did not say, I have grown out of earthly life. Rather, they said, I have grown and descended out of divine-spiritual worlds; and the best I bear within me is the recollection of these divine spiritual worlds. Even Plato, the philosopher, speaks of the fact that the human being has insights, memories, of his prenatal life, the life he led prior to descending into the physical material world. The human being certainly viewed his ego as a ray emerging from the light of the supersensible world. For him, the material world, not the supersensory world, was puzzling.

This world view then had its offshoots in Greece. The Greeks already experienced themselves within the body, but in it they discovered nothing that could have explained this body to them. They still possessed the traditions of the ancient Orient. They viewed themselves in a certain sense as a being that had descended from the spiritual worlds but that in some ways had already lost the awareness of these spiritual worlds. It was actually the final phase of the Oriental life of wisdom that appeared in Greece, and it was on the basis of this world view that the Mystery of Golgotha was to be understood. After all, this Mystery presented the human being with the profound, tremendous problem of life, with the question how the supersensible, cosmic being from other worlds, the Christ, could have found His way into a human corporeality. The permeation of Jesus by the Christ was the great problem. We see it light up everywhere in the Gnostic endeavors. People had no such insight of their own concerning a link between the supersensible aspect of their own nature and the sensory-physical element of their being, and because they had no perception of the connection between the soul-spiritual and the corporeal-physical in reference to themselves, the Mystery of Golgotha became an unsolvable problem for the thinking influenced by the Greek world view. It was, however, a problem with which Greek culture struggled and to which it devoted its finest resources of wisdom. History records much too little of the spiritual struggles that took place then.

I have called attention to the fact that the body of Gnostic literature was eradicated. If it were still available, we would be able to discern this tragic struggle for a comprehension of the living union of the supersensible Christ with the sense-perceptible Jesus; we would observe the development of this extraordinarily profound problem. This struggle was extinguished, however, an end was put to it by the prosaic, abstract attitude originating from Romanism which is only capable of carrying inner devotion into its abstractions by means of whipping up emotions. The Gnosis was covered up and dogmatism and Church Council decisions were put in its place. The profound views of the Orient that contained no juristic element were saturated with a form assumed by Christianity in the more Western world, the Western world of that age, the Roman world.

Christianity emerged from this Romanism imbued, as it were, with the legal element; everywhere, legal concepts moved in as the Roman political concepts spread out over Christianity. Christianity assumed the form of the Roman body politic, and from what was once the world capital, Rome, we see the emergence of the Christian capital city of Rome. We see how this Christian Rome adopts from ancient Rome the special views on how human beings must be governed, how one's rule must be extended over men. We observe how a kind of ecclesiastical imperialism gains ground because Christianity is poured into the Roman form of government. What had been molded in spiritual forms of conception was transformed into a juristic and human polity. For the first time, Christianity and external political science were forged together and Christianity spread out in that form. Such mighty forces and impulses dwell in Christianity that they could, of course, be effective and survive despite the fact that they were poured into the mold of the Roman political system. And as the Roman political system took hold of the Western world, side by side with it, the humble narrations, the factual reports concerning what had taken place in Palestine, continued on.

In this Western world, however, people had been pre-

pared in a quite special way for Christianity. This preparation consisted in the fact that the human being was
aware of himself based on his physical nature; he sensed
his ego by means of his physical being. Here, the difference became evident between the way Christianity had
passed, as it were, through the Greek world, which then
declined, and the form of Christianity that then turned
into the actually political Christianity, the governmen-
tal, Roman Christianity. Then, more from the northern
regions, another form of Christianity emerged that was
poured into the northern people, called Barbarians by
the Greeks and Romans. It streamed into those northern people who due to their nature and in concentrating
their own being, so to speak, sensed their ego. Out of
the totality of man in the physical-sensory realm, out of
the human physical and sensory ego incarnation, they
arrived at self-comprehension. Now they also tried to
grasp what reached them as a simple story about the
events in Palestine. Thus, in this Barbarian world, the
humble tale of the events in Palestine encountered the
ego-feeling, I would like to say, the blood-ego-feeling,
particularly in the central and northern European
realm. These two aspects came together. On the premise
of this ego comprehension of man, people tried to grasp
the simple report of the events in Palestine. They did not
wish to comprehend its deeper content. They did not
try to permeate it with wisdom. They only tried to draw
it into the physical-sensory, human sphere.

In the Heliand, [1] we can observe how these tales concerning the events in Palestine appear drawn completely down to the human level, into the world of
European people, the ego-world. We see how everything is brought down to the human level; unlike the
way it was in Greece, people later had no ability to pene-

94

trate the Mystery of Golgotha with wisdom. The urge developed to picture even the activity of Christ Jesus as humble human activity without looking up into the supersensible, and increasingly to imbue these tales with the merely human element. Furthermore, into this were fitted the Church Council resolutions spreading out dogmatically from the Roman-Christian Empire. Like two worlds that were alien to one another, these two merged—the Christianity that in a sense had Europeanized the report from Palestine and the Christianity representing the Greek spirit in juristic, Romanized, abstract form. This is what then lived on through the centuries.

Only a few individuals could place themselves into this stream in the manner I described yesterday, when I spoke of the sages who developed the conception of the Grail. They pointed out that the impulse of Christianity had indeed once been couched in Oriental wisdom, but that the bearer of this Oriental view, the sacred vessel of the Grail, could be brought to Europe only by means of divine spirits who hovered above the earth, holding on to it. Only then, so they said, a hidden castle was built for it, the Castle of the Grail on Mont Salvat. To this was added that a human being could only approach the miracles of the Holy Grail through inaccessible regions. Then these sages did not say that the surrounding impassable region a person has to penetrate in order to reach the miracles of the Grail is sixty miles wide. They put it in a much more esoteric way when they described this path to the Holy Grail. They said, Oh, these people of Europe cannot reach the Holy Grail, for the path they must take in order to arrive at the Holy Grail takes as long as the path from birth to death. Only when human beings arrive at the portal of death, having tread the path, impassable for Europeans, the path that extends from birth to death, only then will they arrive at the Castle of the Grail on Mont Salvat.

This was basically the esoteric secret that was conveyed to the pupil. Because the time had not yet come when human beings would be able to discern with a clear consciousness how the spiritual world might once more be discovered, the pupils were told that they could enter into the sacred Castle of the Grail only by way of occasional glimpses of light. In particular, they were given strict injunctions that they had to *ask*, that the time had come in human development when the human being who does not ask—who does not develop his inner being and does not seek the impulse of truth on his own but remains passive—cannot arrive at an experience of his own self. For man must discover his ego by means of his physical organization. This *I*, which discovers itself through the physical organization, must in turn raise itself up by its own power in order to behold itself where, even in the early Greek culture, this self was still beheld, in supersensible worlds. The *I* must first lift itself up in order to recognize itself as something supersensible.

In the ancient Orient, people saw what occurred in the astral body; the consequences of former earth lives were beheld in it. This is why one spoke of karma. In Greece, this conception was already obscured. The cosmic events were observed only with dim astral vision. This is why people spoke vaguely of destiny, of fate. This view of destiny is only a diminished, weaker form of the fully concrete conception held by the ancient Orient concerning man's passage through repeated earth lives, the consequences of which make themselves known to experience within the astral body, though only instinctively. Thus, the ancient Orientals could speak of karma developing in the recurring incarnations on earth, the consequences of which were simply present in astral experience.

Now the development moved westward to the ego experience. This experience of the ego was initially tied to the physical body. It was egotistically self-enclosed. The first ego experience dwelled in dullness, even when it contained a strong impulse towards the supersensible worlds. Parsifal, who undertook his pilgrimage to the Holy Grail, is described as a dim-witted man. It must be clearly understood that when the Mithras worship spread across the West from the Orient, it was rejected by the West; it was not comprehended. For he who sat on the bull, who was to become the victor over the base forces, experienced himself, after all, as emerging from these lower forces. If Western man beheld Mithras riding on the bull, he did not comprehend this being, for this being could not be the one the ego felt and experienced out of its own physical organization. An understanding for this riding Mithras faded away and disappeared.

It can be said that all this had to come to pass, for the ego had to experience its impulse in the physical organization. It had to connect itself firmly with the physical organization, but it must not allow itself to become set in this firm experience within the physical organization.

It was a profound reaction to the Orient's treasures of wisdom, when the West increasingly aimed for what developed out of the purely physical element. This reaction was a necessity. Any number of views did come together in Europe to make this reaction a very strong one. But it was not proper for it to extend into this spiritual striving for more than a few centuries. A new spirituality has indeed emerged since then in the first third of the fifteenth century, but it was an abstract spirituality, a sublimated, filtered spirituality.

Human beings took hold of physical astronomy and physical medicine, and, to begin with, they had to have this stimulus based on the ego impulse sensing itself in the physical element. But it must not continue to become firmly set in European civilization if this European culture wishes to avoid its decline. Truly, more than enough forces of decline are present, vestiges which should only be vestiges and which should be recognized as such.

Just remember how the most up-to-date theology—I have often emphasized this—has lost the faculty for comprehending Christ; increasingly it has arrived at the point of turning Christ Jesus completely into an earth being, a human being. It has put the "humble man from Nazareth"[2] in the place of Christ Jesus. Proceeding from Romanism, out of a materialistically oriented principle of authority, the living spirituality, by means of which the human being can really become familiar with the Mystery of Golgotha, was lost more and more. And observe how in modern times a science is developing that tries to comprehend everything external but that does not wish to penetrate to the human being. As a result of this science, see how impulses arise in society that try only to bring about a human, physical order but that do not want to penetrate the human, physical structures with any divine-spiritual, supersensory, spiritual principle.

During all this it is as if in human souls, in a few human souls, there remained an individual glimpse of light. When a ray of the astral element still dwelling within them combined with the ego, these individuals received such glimpses of light. It is part of the most impressive phenomena of modern Europe when we observe how, out of the East, there resounds a mighty admonition in the religious philosophy of Soloviev, [3] a religious philosophy steeped, so to speak, in Eastern sultriness. But something resounds from there to the effect that a supersensible, spiritual element must permeate the earthly social order. In a sense, we see how Soloviev dreams of a kind of Christ-state. He is capable of that because within him are the last vestiges of a subjective astral experience illuminating the ego.

Compare these dreams of a Christ-permeated state with what has been established in the East accompanied by the negation of all spiritual elements, something that harbors only forces of decline—what an overwhelming, colossal contrast! The world should pay attention to such a colossal contrast. If people had already today sufficient objectivity to observe these things, they would be able to see, on the one hand, the one who raises the demand of the Christ-permeated state, the Christ-permeated social structure, Soloviev. They would view him as somebody still stimulated by the Oriental element and casting, so to speak, a final spark into this Europe growing torpid, in order to revive it again from this viewpoint. On the other hand, Czar Nicholas or his predecessors could well be placed together with Czar Lenin; the fact that they give vent to different ideas in the historical development of mankind does not constitute a fundamental difference between them. What matters are the forces living in them and shaping the world, and the same forces dwell in Lenin that dwell in the Russian Czar; there really is no fundamental difference. It is naturally difficult to find one's way within this melee of forces that extend into European civilization from earlier times. Initially, it is indeed a melee of forces and a firm direction must be sought. Such a firm direction can be found in no other way than by lifting the ego up to a spiritual comprehension of the world. Through a spiritual comprehension of the world, the Christian impulse must be reborn. What has been striven for in regard to the external world since the first third of the fifteenth century must be striven for in reference to the totality of the human being; the whole human being has to be understood based on the knowledge of the world.

The comprehension of the world must be viewed in harmony with the understanding of humanity. We must understand the earth evolution in phases, in metamorphoses. We have to look at earlier embodiments of our earth, but we must not consider a primordial nebula devoid of human beings. We have to look at Saturn, sun, and moon as already permeated with the activity of human beings; we must observe how the present structure of the human being originated from the earlier metamorphoses of the planet earth and how the human form in an early phase was likewise active there. We must recognize the human being in the world, and out of this knowledge of man in the world an understanding of the Mystery of Golgotha can well up once again. Human beings must learn to understand why an impassable region surrounds the Castle of the Grail, why the path between birth and death is difficult terrain. When they understand why it is difficult, when they grasp that the ego experiences itself based on the physical organization, when they sense how impossible a merely physical astronomy, a merely physical medicine are, then they themselves will clear the paths. Then people will bring something into this hitherto difficult terrain between birth and death that comes into being through their own soul efforts.

Out of the substance of the soul and spirit, human

beings have to fashion the tools with which to break the ground on the field, the soul-field, leading to the Castle of the Grail, to the Mystery of Bread and Blood, to the fulfillment of the words, "Do this in remembrance of me" [Luke 22:19]. For this remembrance has been forgotten; people are no longer aware of what dwells in the words, "Do this in remembrance of me." For this is truly done in remembrance of the mighty moment of Golgotha if the symbol of the bread, that is what develops out of the earth through the synthesis of cosmic forces is understood. It is done rightly if we understand once again how to comprehend the world through a spiritualized cosmology and astronomy, and if we learn to comprehend the human being based on what his extract is, namely, the element where the spiritual directly intervenes in him—if we grasp the Mystery of the Blood. Through work on the inner being of human souls the path must be discovered that leads to the Holy Grail. This is a task of cognition, this is a social task. It is also a task that, to the greatest extent possible, is hated in the present

For due to being placed within the ego education of Western civilization, human beings develop above all a longing to remain passive inwardly in the soul, not to allow earthly existence to give to them what could bring progress to their souls. The active taking hold of the soul forces, the inward experiencing, and this does not necessarily mean occult development but merely the experience of soul nature in general; yet this is something European humanity does not like. Instead, it wishes to continue what was natural for the epoch directly preceding it, namely, the ego development, which does, however, lead to the most blatant egotism, to the blindest raging of instincts, when it is extended beyond its own age. This ego feeling, extending beyond the time properly assigned to it, first of all has penetrated the sentiments of national chauvinism. It appears in national chauvinism; from these feelings arise the spirits who wish to keep the path to the Holy Grail in an impassable condition. But it is our obligation to do everything that can be done in order to call human souls to activity in the area of knowledge as well as in the social sphere. Yet, all those forces filled with hatred against such activity of the soul emerge in opposition to such a call. After all, haven't people been conditioned long enough so that they concluded, We must consider heretical all our own soul efforts to free ourselves from guilt; we must properly cultivate the awareness of sin and guilt, for we must not progress by means of our own efforts, but must be redeemed in passivity through Christ?

We fail to understand Christ if we do not recognize Him as the cosmic power that completely unites with us when through questions and inner activity we work our way through to Him. Everywhere today, from the denominations, from theology and those who were always connected to theology, from the military and science—from all this we see arise those powers today that try to obstruct the path of inner activity.

For a long time, I have had to call attention to the fact that this is the case, and I have had to say again and again: the arising opposing powers will become more and more vehement. Indeed, to this day this has certainly come true. It is definitely not possible to say that the opposition has already reached its greatest strength. Not by a long shot has it attained its culmination. This opposition has a strong, organizing power in concentrating together all the elements that, while they are in reality destined to decline, can obstruct in their very decline for the time being everything working with the forces of upward striving progress. The forces fostering the activity of souls are weak today in comparison to the opposing elements. Those forces that, based on the comprehension of the spiritual world, try to turn the progressive forces into forces of their own soul are weak. The world has taken on an ahrimanic character. For it was inevitable that the ego, having comprehended itself in the physical element, is taken hold of by ahrimanic forces if it remains in the physical element and does not lift itself up at the right time to a spiritual understanding of itself as a spiritual being. Indeed, we see this process of usurpation by the ahrimanic powers; we observe it in the fact that, little as the sleepy souls would be willing to admit this, an actual tendency towards evil is making itself felt everywhere today.

An inclination towards evil is clearly noticeable, for example, in the manner opponents fight against anthroposophical spiritual science and everything related to it. From the most questionable sources come the means with which individuals battle today against spiritual science, even individuals who enjoy a prestigious standing in the world in scientific or theological circles. The truth is not what people are concerned with. It is only a matter of what slander suits these individuals best and what they like better. It is truly a matter of humanity being strongly possessed by the forces of evil, by a love for evil. Those who are unable today to reckon with this tendency for evil, with this ever increasing love for evil in the battle against anthroposophy, will not be able to develop a feeling, an awareness of the kind of opposing forces and powers that will yet arise in the future. For years, reference has been made to this ever increasing development. If nothing more can be attained than a clear feeling of it, then this clear feeling, which is, after all, also a force, must at least be maintained. We have to look into the world and be aware of the way it surrounds us. With a sober mind we must realize what is really facing us in the filthy slander that is now emerging from among our opponents and that is the more impressive the more tarnished its source.

It is really necessary to become acquainted with this particular tendency, with this love of evil, that will become more and more prevalent. It is truly necessary not to wallow groggily in excuses that the opponents are convinced of what they say. Do you really believe that in individuals such as the one who has emerged as the newest opponent against anthroposophical spiritual science even the possibility for an inner force of conviction is present? Not even the possibility of conviction is present in him. He acts out of quite different deeper motives. It is indeed a clever move to seek particularly in this direction, to seek for the manner of viewing things that is based on fooling the opponent. Who is the better commander? He who can best fool the enemy! But when this principle is transferred to the means of battling against truth, then such a battle is a battle of the lie, of the personified lie against truth. We must realize that this battle of the personified lie against truth is capable of anything, that it will definitely attempt to take away from us what we have tried and are still trying to attain in the way of outward supports in order to find bearers of truth in this civilization. It is not exaggerated to say that there exists the most profound and thoroughgoing wish to deprive us of the Waldorf School and this building.[4] And if we pay no attention to this; if we do not even develop in us a feeling concerning the ways and means of this opposition, then we remain sleeping souls. Then we do not take hold with inner alertness of what is trying to pour forth out of anthroposophical spiritual science.

Basically, we should not be surprised now that the opponents could turn out the way they did for that could have been known long ago. The overwhelming impression for us today certainly is that there are two few individuals who can be active representatives of our spiritual movement. It is generally still easier to be effective among human beings by means of force, control, and injustice than by means of freedom. The truth that is to be proclaimed through anthroposophical spiritual science is permitted to count only on human freedom. It must find people who ask questions. One certainly cannot say, Why doesn't this truth possess in itself the strength to compel human souls by virtue of divine-spiritual power? It does not wish to do that; it cannot do that. The reason is that it will always consider inner freedom, the freedom of the human being in general, to be something absolutely inviolable. If the human being is to come to anthroposophy out of his own judgment, he must become one who asks questions; out of the innermost freedom of judgment he must convince himself. The word of spiritual truth will be spoken to him; convincing himself of it is something he must do on his own. If he wishes to cooperate and be active in society, he must do so out of the innermost impulse of his heart. Those who belong in the truest sense of the word to anthroposophical spiritual science must become people who ask questions.

What do we encounter on the side of the opposition? Do not believe that only those who band together who are in some way one-sided in any one creed. No, in a

Catholic church in Stuttgart, a sermon tells its listeners, Go to the lecture by Herr von Gleich.[5] There you can invigorate your Catholic souls and can vanquish the opponents of your Catholic souls! And these Catholic souls go there; the Catholic, General von Gleich, gives a lecture and concludes with a song by Martin Luther! A fine union of one side and the other—the opponents organize as one! It certainly matters not if they agree in any way in their faith, their convictions.

For us, what matters is the strength to stand firmly on the ground of what we recognize as right. Yes, nothing will be left undone to undermine this ground; of this you can be sure. I had to bring this up one more time, particularly in connection with the considerations concerning the course taken by European civilization; for it is necessary that at least the intention develops to place oneself firmly on the ground we must recognize as the right one. It is also necessary that among ourselves we do not give ourselves up to the popular illusions concerning the various oppositions. Their aim is to undermine the ground we stand on. It is up to us to work as much as is humanly possible, and then, if the ground under us should become undermined and we do slide down into the chasm, our efforts will nevertheless have been such that they will find their spiritual path through the world. For what appears now are the last convulsions of a dying world. But even if it is in its last throes of death, this world can still strike out like a raving maniac, and one can lose one's life due to this frantic lashing out. This is why we must at least recognize what kind of impulses give rise to this mad lashing out. Nothing can be achieved by what is timid; we must appeal to what is bold. Let us try to measure up to such an appeal!

I had to include this so that you would sense that we face an important, significant, and decisive moment, and that we have to consider how we are to find the strength to persevere.

Dornach, April 22, 1921

A future study of history will record these days as belonging among the most significant ones of European history, for today central Europe's renunciation of a will of its own became known.[1] It remains to be seen in what direction matters will develop further in the next few days, but whatever takes place, it is, after all, an action that much more so than many that have preceded it in our catastrophic age, is connected with human decisions of will that originated in the full sense of the word from the forces of decline in European civilization. Such a day can remind us of the periods from which emerged everything within European civilization, the origin of which I described in the past few weeks. It has its point of departure, as it were, in what is described so superficially by history but what so profoundly influenced the civilization of mankind after the fourth Christian century.

We have characterized these events from several perspectives. We have outlined how after the fourth century the element that could be termed the absolutely legalistic spirit invaded the ecclesiastical and secular civilization of the Occident and then became more and more intensified. We then indicated the sources from which these matters originated. Indeed, already earlier we have called attention to the fact that in the middle of the nineteenth century modern humanity underwent a crisis that, although given little notice, can even be described from an anatomical, physiological standpoint, as we saw here a few weeks ago.[2] All that then took its course in the second half of the nineteenth century, particularly in the last third, culminating in the unfortunate first two decades of the twentieth century, stands under the influence of what occurred in the middle of the nineteenth century.

This day in particular gives us cause to introduce these considerations we intend to pursue in the next few days with the contemplation of a certain personality. This is something we have done already on several occasions, but it might be especially important from the viewpoint I wish to assume today. One could say that this is an individual who, partly as a spectator and partly as one undergoing the events of history as a tragic personality, experienced what was present in the form of forces of decline within European civilization in the last third of the nineteenth century. I am referring to Friedrich Nietzsche.[3]

We are not assuming our standpoint today in order to biographically consider the personality of Nietzsche in any way. We only do so in order to demonstrate a number of aspects of the last third of the nineteenth century through the person of Nietzsche. After all, his activities fall completely within this period of the nineteenth century. He is the personality who participated, I would like to say, with the greatest sensitivity in all the cultural streams pervading Europe during that period. He is the one who sensed the forces of decline inherent in these trends in the most terrifying manner and who, in the end, broke down under this tragedy, under these horrors.

Naturally, one can approach the picture we have in mind from any number of directions. We shall focus on a few of them today. Friedrich Nietzsche grew up in a parsonage in central Germany. This implies that he was surrounded all through his childhood by what can be designated as the modern confinements of culture, the narrowness of civilization. He had around him all that expresses itself in a philistine, sentimental manner and yet simultaneously exhibited smugness, conceit, and trivial contentment. I say complacent, conceited, for this culture believed it had a grasp on the untold number of secrets of the universe in threadbare, superficial sentiments. I say content with trivialities because these sentiments are indeed the most commonplace. They penetrate philistine sentimentality from the very simplest human level and, at the same time, are valued by this philistine sentimentality as if they were the pronouncements God uttered in the human mind.

Nietzsche was a product of this narrowness of culture, and as a young man he absorbed everything someone can acquire who passes through the present-day higher forms of education as a, let me say, unworldly youth. Already during his early teens, Nietzsche was attracted with all his heart to everything that streams out of Greek tragedies such as those by Sophocles or Aeschylus.[4] He imbued himself with all that strives out of Greek humanism towards a certain spiritual-physical world experience. And with all of his human nature, with his thinking, feeling, and willing, Nietzsche wanted to stand within this experience of world totality of which man can feel himself to be a part, an individual member.

Time and again, the soul of young Friedrich Nietzsche must have confronted the mighty contrast existing between what the majority of modern humanity in its philistine sentimentality and narrow, trivial self-contentment calls reality and the striving for loftiness

111

inherent in the tragic poets and philosophers of early Greek antiquity. Certainly, his soul swung back and forth between this philistine reality and the striving for sublimity in the Greek spirit that surpasses all trivial human striving. And when he subsequently entered the sphere of modern erudition, the lack of spirit and art, the mere intellectual activity of this modern scholarship was particularly irritating to him. His beloved Greeks, through whom he had most intensely experienced the striving for loftiness, had for him been remolded by modern science into philological, formal trivialities. He had to find his way out of the latter. Hence he acquired his thorough antipathy against that spirit he considered the source of modern intellectualism. He was seized with profound antipathy against Socrates[5] and all Socratic aspirations.

Certainly, there are the impressive, positive sides of Socrates; there is all that one can learn in a thorough manner through Socrates. Yet, on the one hand, we have Socrates as he once existed within the world of Greece and, on the other hand, there is Socrates, the ghostly specter haunting the descriptions of modern high school teachers and university philosophers. With whom could young Nietzsche become acquainted when he initially observed his surroundings? Only with the ghostly specter Socrates! This is how he acquired his dislike against this Socrates, out of what has arisen through this Socratism within European civilization. Thus, he saw in Socrates the slayer of human wholeness that in the art and philosophy of the pre-Socratic age had streamed through European civilization. In the end, it seemed to him that what overlooks the world from the foundation of existence is a reality turned philistine and desolate. He felt that any lofty, noble striving

112

to ascend to the spiritual spheres of life must struggle to overcome such a reality.

Nietzsche was unable to discover such noble tendencies in anything that could have emerged from the prevailing striving for knowledge; he could find it only in what originated from efforts of artistic character. For him, what had developed as tragic art out of ancient Greece illuminated the philistine atmosphere into which Socratism had finally turned. He saw Greek tragedy reborn, as it were, in what Richard Wagner was endeavoring to create as tragedy out of the spirit of music towards the end of the 1870's and beginning of the 1880's.[6] In the musical drama to be created he saw something that by ignoring Socratism was connected directly with the first Greek age of total humanism. Thus, he recognized two streams of art, on one hand, the Dionysian, orgiastic one that, arising from unfathomable depths, attempts to draw the whole human being into the world, and, on the other hand, the one that eventually was so perverted in Europe that it lost all its luster and decayed into the absolute spiritual sclerosis of modern scholarship, namely, the Apollonian stream. Nietzsche strove for a new Dionysian art. This pervades his first work, *The Birth of Tragedy out of the Spirit of Music* (*Die Geburt der Tragoedie aus dem Geist der Musik*). Right away, he had to experience how the typical philistine railed at what expressed itself in this book out of a knowledge borne aloft by wings of imagination. Immediately, the leading philistine of modern civilization, Wilamowitz[7], mobilized. (Subsequently he became the luminary of the University of Berlin and clothed the Greek creators of tragedy in modern, trivial garments that won the undying admiration of all those who penetrate as deeply into the Greek word as they are distant from the Greek spirit.) Right away the collision occurred between the stream that, borne by the spirit, tried to penetrate the artistic element based on knowledge and the other that does not feel comfortable within this richly imaginative spirit of knowledge, this knowledge borne by the spirit, and that therefore escapes into philistine pedantry.

Everything his soul could experience through this contrast was then poured out by Nietzsche in the beginning of the 1870's in his four so-called *Thoughts Out of Season*[8] (*Unzeitgemaesse Betrachtungen*). The first of these contemplations was dedicated to the educated philistine proper of the modern age. These *Thoughts Out of Season* have to be considered in the right light. They were certainly not intended as attacks against individual persons. In the first contemplation, for example, the otherwise quite worthy and upright David Strauss[9] was not meant to be attached personally. He was to be considered as the typical representative of modern philistinism in education which is so infinitely content with the trivialities developing out of this modern life. We actually experience this again and again, because, basically, matters have not improved since those days, they have only intensified.

This is approximately the same experience as the one we have when we attempt to contribute something to the comprehension of the world out of the depths of spiritual science. Then people come and say that although what is being said concerning an etheric and astral body and spiritual development may all be true, it cannot be proven. One can only prove that two times two is four. Above all else, one has to consider how this unprovable spiritual science relates to the certain truth that two times two is four. You can hear today in all possible variations—although perhaps put not quite so bluntly—that the objection that two times two is four must be raised against every utterance concerning soul and spirit land. As if anybody would doubt that two times two is four!

Friedrich Nietzsche wished to strike out against the philistinism of modern education when he described its prototype, David Friedrich Strauss, the author of *Old and New Faith* (*Alter und neuer Glaube*), this arch-philistine book. He also tried to demonstrate how desolate things stood with modern spirituality. We need only recall some important facts to show just how desolate they are. We need only remember that in the first half of the nineteenth century there still existed fiery spirits, for example, the historian Rotteck, [10] who lectured on history in a one-sidedly liberal form but with a certain fiery spirituality. We only have to recall that in Rotteck's *History* (*Geischichte*) something of the totality of man holds sway, albeit a somewhat withered one, something of the human being who at least brings into the whole experience of mankind's development as much spirituality as there is rationality in it. We need only compare this with the people who said later, It will lead nowhere to try and develop a national constitution or social conditions out of human reason. Instead, we ought to study ancient times, concentrate on history. We should study the way everything developed and accordingly arrange matters in the present.

This is the attitude that, in the end, bore its dull fruits in the teachings of political economy represented, for instance, in somebody like Lujo Brentano,[11] the attitude that only wished to observe history, and actually held that anything productive could only have been brought into humanity's evolution in ancient times. It held that nowadays one would really have to empty out the human being and then, like a sack, stuff him full with what can still be gained from history so that modern man, aside form his skin—and at most a little of what lies under the skin—would, underneath this tiny area, be stuffed full with what former ages have produced, and would in turn be able to utter ancient Greek insights, old Germanic knowledge, and so on. One did not think nor wished to believe that the modern human soul could be imbued with any productivity. History became the catchword of the day. Nietzsche in the 1870's was disgusted by this and wrote his book *The Use and Abuse of History in Life* (*Vom Nutzen und Nachteil der Historie fuer das Leben*) in which he indicated how modern man is being suffocated by history. And he demanded that productivity be attained once again.

The artistic spirit still lived in Nietzsche. After he had turned to Wagner, "a philosopher, as it were, "[12] he again dealt with another philosopher, namely Schopenhauer.[13] In Schopenhauer's ideas he saw something of the reality of the otherwise dull and dusty spirit of philosophy. Nietzsche regarded Schopenhauer as an educator of modern humanity, not only as someone who had been but as someone who ought to become such a teacher. And he wrote his book *Schopenhauer as Educator* (*Schopenhauer als Erzieher*). He followed this with *Richard Wagner in Bayreuth*, pointing out in an almost orgiastic manner how a revival of modern civilization through art would have to come about.

Strange indeed are the depths from which *Richard Wagner in Bayreuth* originated. Friedrich Nietzsche himself had painstakingly edited out everything he had written in addition to what was then published under the title, *Richard Wagner in Bayreuth*. One could almost

116

say that for each page of this book, printed in 1876, there exists a second page that contains something completely different. While Bayreuth and its activities are enthusiastically celebrated in this book, in addition to each page Nietzsche wrote another, as it were, different page filled with deeply tragic sentiments concerning the forces of decline in modern civilization. Indeed, even he could not believe in what he was writing; he could not believe that the power to truly transform the forces of decline into those of ascent lay in Bayreuth. This tragedy prevails especially in those pages, deleted at that time, that remained in manuscript form and were made public only after Friedrich Nietzsche had fallen ill. It was at that time that the great change came over him, actually already in 1876. This period of Nietzsche's life ended tragically in the agony over the forces of decline inherent in modern culture.

Already in 1876 the disgust concerning the decline was stronger in his mind than the joy over the positive forces he had initially noted in Bayreuth. Above all, his soul was inundated by the observation of all that has pervaded modern civilization of untrue elements, of the present-day lack of truthfulness. And I would like to say this concentrated itself in his mind into a picture of what affects this modern civilization on the human level. He was actually no longer able to discover in this modern culture any redeeming spirituality that could surmount the philistine view of reality. Thus, he entered his second period in which he opposed the distorted self-concept of human beings in modern times with what he called the "all-too-human" (*Allzumenschliche*), with the true concept of the human being, of which people these days do not want to know anything.

One would like to say, Just look at those individuals who have celebrated modern history in this manner,

117

such as Savigny[14], Lujo Brentano, Ranke[15] and the other historians and ask what they are actually doing? What is woven into the tapestry of the active spirit of the times? Something is being produced that is supposed to be true. Why is it presented as truth? Because those individuals who speak of such a truth are in reality themselves spiritually impotent. They deny the spirit because they themselves do not possess it and cannot discover it. They dictate to the world: You must be thus and thus—for they lack the light they are supposed to shed over the world. The all-too-human, the whole all-too-narrow attitude is what is built up to the human element and presented as absolute truth to mankind. From 1876 on, this dwelled as a feeling in Nietzsche while he wrote his two volumes *Human, All Too Human* (*Menschliches, Allzumenschliches*); then *Dawn* (*Morgenroete*, and finally, *Joyful Science* (*Froehliche Wissenschaft*), by means of which Nietzsche plunged as if intoxicated into nature so as to escape from what had actually surrounded him.

Nevertheless, a tragic feeling was present in him. Northern Germany, northern Europe in general and central Europe had had an effect on him; he absorbed all that and from Schopenhauer and Richard Wagner in particular he found his way to Voltairism; the text *Menschliches, Allzumenschliches* was dedicated to Voltaire.[16] He attempted to revive Socratism by trying to breathe new life into it, but he did this by seeking the all-too-human truth, human narrowness, behind the lie of modern civilization. He tried to reach the spirit out of this human narrowness. He did not find it behind the accomplishments of men of more recent times. He believed he could find it through a kind of intoxicated plunge into nature. He endeavored to experience this intoxicated plunge into nature in his life by traveling south repeatedly during his vacations in order to forget, in the warm sun and under the blue sky, what men have produced in the modern age. This drunken plunge into nature underlies his *Morgenroete* and the *Froehliche Wissenschaft* as the basic feeling. He did not find joy through it; his sense of tragedy remained. It is especially pronounced when we see him express his sentiment in poetry and hear:[17]

Die Krähen schrei'n
und ziehen schwirren Flugs zur Stadt:
bald wird es schnei'n, —
wohl dem, der jetzt noch—Heimat hat!

(The ravens shriek
and fly with flutt'ring wings to town;
soon it will snow, —
how fortunate is he
who now still has—a home!

Nietzsche, too, had no home. "Fly, bird! Rasp your song in sounds of wasteland birds." He had no home because this is the impression he had of himself, as if ravens were shrieking round him when he fled again and again from Germany to Italy. Soon, however, it became evident that he could not remain in this mood. There are verses by Nietzsche in which he remonstrates against anybody who takes this mood expressed in the lines, "The ravens shriek and fly with flutt'ring wings to town," too seriously. He did not wish to be considered only as a tragic person; he also wanted to laugh about everything that had occurred in modern culture.

119

As I said, just read the few lines that follow after the above poem in the most recent Nietzsche edition. So in the last third of the nineteenth century we have, in a sense, in Nietzsche a spirit predestined to abandon everything people in the modern age have produced, to flee everything the arts and the sciences have accomplished, in order to find something original, to discover new gods and smash the old

We might say that this individual was too deeply wounded by his age for these wounds to heal, much less for them to give rise to a productive new impulse. Thus, from these wounds sprang forth creations and ideas devoid of content. The *Superman* appeared, pervaded by sensuous, bleeding lyricism. In the last third of the nineteenth century, it was no longer possible for Nietzsche to penetrate to the true human being on the basis of natural science, which had extinguished man, or on the basis of sociology or the social structures of the last century, an age that possessed machines but no longer the human being, except as he stands in front of the machine. Nietzsche did, however, experience the urge to escape through negation, to flee what was no longer known and felt to be human. Instead of a comprehension of the human being out of the whole cosmos, instead of an "occult science, " there emerged the abstract, lyrical, sultry and overheated, pathological and convulsive *Superman*, appearing in visions before his soul in *Thus Spoke Zarathustra* (*Also sprach Zarathustra;*[18] visions that in part touch the deepest aspects of human nature but that basically always sound disharmonious in some way, expressing intentional disharmony.

Then, there is the other negation, or rather idea devoid of content. This life between birth and death cannot be understood if it is not at the same time seen as extending beyond the one earth life. Those who truly possess a feeling for grasping the one life between birth and death, who take hold of it with such a profound feeling and lyricism as did Friedrich Nietzsche, those sense in the end: This life cannot be comprehended as a single one, it must be viewed in its development through many lives. But as little as Nietzsche could bestow a content on the human being and therefore proceeded in a convulsive manner to his negation, the *Superman*, as little could he give substance to the idea of repeated earth lives. He hollowed these lives out; they turned into the desolate, eternal return of the same. Just think for a moment what can arise in our mind concerning repeated earth lives, which are linked to each other in karma through a mighty progression of destiny. Just picture how one life pours content into the following one; then imagine these earth lives as shadowy, empty husks, emptied of all content, and there you have the eternal return of the same, the caricature of the repeated earth lives.

Impossible to penetrate to the image of the Mystery of Golgotha by means of what the modern confessions represent—this is how what could have disclosed itself to him through Christianity appeared to Nietzsche! It was impossible to penetrate the religious conceptions that had come about since the fourth century and to arrive at an idea of what had occurred in Palestine at the beginning of the Christian era. Yet, Nietzsche was filled with a profound desire for truth. The all-too-human had come before his soul in a saddening form. He did not wish to participate in the lie of modern civilization; he was not fooled by an image of the Mystery of Golgotha such as the one presented with absolute mendacity to the world by the opponents of Christianity, by the likes of Adolf Harnack.[19] Even in the lie, present as actual reality, Nietzsche still tried to discern the truth. This was the reason for his distortion of the Mystery of Golgotha in his *Antichrist*.[20] In the *Antichrist*, he depicted the image one has to present on the basis of the modern religious conceptions if, instead of lying, one wishes to speak the truth based on this form of thinking and yet, at the same time, is unable to penetrate what modern knowledge offers and to come to what in truth is present in the Mystery of Golgotha.

This is approximately Nietzsche's state of mind in the years 1886 and 1887. He had abandoned everything offered by modern cultural insights. He had passed on to the negation of man in the *Superman*, because he could not attain to the idea of man in modern knowledge, which has eradicated the human being from its field. From his feeling concerning the one earth life he had received an inkling of repeated earth lives, but modern thinking could not give him any content for them. Thus, he emptied out what he sensed; he no longer had any content; only the formal continuation of the eternally same, of the eternal repetition, stood before his soul. And in his mind, he beheld the travesty of the Mystery of Golgotha, as he described it in his *Antichrist*, for if he wished to cling to the truth, he could find no way leading from what modern theology offers to a conception of the Mystery of Golgotha

He had been able to study quite a bit concerning the Christian nature of modern theology in the writings of Overbeck,[21] the theologian from Basle. The fact that this modern theology is not Christian is in the main proven in Overbeck's texts dealing with modern theology. All the unchristian elements pervading modern Chris-

tianity had lived deeply in Nietzsche's soul. The hope-
less lack of vision in this modern knowledge had
deprived him of a true overview of what is produced in
the human being in one life for the next one. Thus arose
in him the empty idea of the return of sameness. The
Christian impulse had been taken from him by what
calls itself the Christian spirit in the modern age, and
he saw the untruthfulness of his age, and he could not
even believe any longer in the truthfulness of art in
which he had tried to believe at the beginning of his
ascending career. He was already filled with this tragic
mood when utterances burst forth from his soul, such
as "And the poets lie too much..."[22] Out of their innermost human nature, poets and artists of the modern
culture have indeed lied too much and lie too much to
this day. For what the forces of the future need most and
what modern civilization possesses least of all is the
spirit of truth.

Nietzsche strove for this spirit of truth; which alone
can present to the human being the true idea of himself.
Through the development in repeated earth lives, it
alone can bestow on this one earth life a meaning other
than that of the senseless return of the same. Through a
sense for truth, he thirsted for the true conception of
the One Who tread the earth in Palestine. He found
only a travesty of it in modern theology and present-day
Christian demeanor. All this broke him. Therefore, the
personality of Friedrich Nietzsche expresses the break-
down of the spirit striving for truth amid the falsehood
that has arisen since the point of crisis in modern times,
namely, since the middle of the nineteenth century. The
rise of this untruthfulness is so powerful that people do
not even have an idea of how deeply they are enmeshed
in its nets. They do not even give a thought any more to

how truthfulness should replace falsehood at every moment.

In no other way, however, than by realizing that our soul has to be imbued with this fundamental feeling that truth instead of falsehood must prevail, only through this profound feeling can anthroposophical spiritual science live. Modern civilization has been educated in the spirit of untruth, and it is against this spirit of falsehood—this can really be cited as an example—that anthroposophic spiritual science has to fight the most. And today, matters have reached the point, as I mentioned already at the conclusion of my last lecture,[23] where even in regard to our anthroposophically oriented spiritual science we find ourselves in a deep, intense crisis. What we need to do very much is to work, to be intensely active out of enthusiasm for truth. For the malaise our culture suffers from is exemplified in what is happening hourly and daily, the malaise that will cause its downfall if humanity does not take heart.

In the last issue of a weekly magazine,[24] which usually expresses widely prevailing public opinion, we read of agitation against Simons' political policies. It goes without saying that neither anthroposophic spiritual science nor the threefold social order have anything to do with Simons' politics. Anthroposophic spiritual science, however, is thrown together today with Simons' politics by a far-reaching spirit of falsehood. People know what is achieved by such means, and much will be achieved. Something of the whole rotten mendacity comes to expression when one reads a sentence that with quotation marks, appears in this magazine and is supposed to characterize Simons: "He is the favorite disciple of the theosophist Steiner, who has prophesied a great future for him. He stands firmly on the gospel of the threefold social order, but in the spirit of his home town of Wuppertal he is also a devout Christian."

Well, there are as many lies here as there are words! I did not say there were as many lies as there were sentences, I said on purpose, There are as many words as there are brazen lies—with the exception of the last sentence—but the first sentences are lies word for word.

By adding this last sentence to the preceding ones, absolute paralysis is added to mendacity. Just imagine the creature that would come into being if somebody would become my favorite pupil, if I would predict a great future for him, if he would firmly cling to the "gospel of the threefold social order" and, on top of that, if he would be a pious Christian in the sense of the good citizens of Wuppertal! Imagine such a person! This, however, is present-day civilization. As insignificant as it may appear, it is a clear symptom of modern civilization. For those who frequently attack such things, attack with the same lies and the same paralysis. And the others are not even aware of the strange figures that are "conjured up before their stupid eyes"[25]—forgive me but I am merely quoting something that is said by the gnomes in one of my mystery plays. They do not notice at all what is conjured up before their, let us say, "intelligent" eyes—intelligence in the sense of modern civilization. People actually swallow anything today, because the feeling for truth and veracity is lacking, and the enthusiasm is missing from the assertion of truth and truthfulness in the midst of an untruthful, lying culture.

Things cannot progress as long as these matters are not taken seriously. A different picture must be placed before the soul today. These days, it becomes quite clear that Europe is intent on digging the grave of its own civilization, that it wishes to call on something outside of Europe so that, above the closed grave of the old civilization as well as above the already closed grave of Goetheanism, something completely different can arise. We shall see whether anything can still come out of that culture for which the politicians are now digging the grave. We shall see whether something can emerge from it that will truly receive the forces of progress; that will discover the human being, find the only true impulse of the idea of eternity in repeated earth lives, and discover the true Mystery of Golgotha and Christianity as the right impulse in the face of all that appears in this area as untruth and falsehood.

LECTURE VIII
Dornach, April 23, 1921

Today, I shall have to turn to a seemingly more remote topic that will fit in, however, with yesterday's and tomorrow's subjects. I have frequently mentioned that when the evolution of humanity is surveyed, people proceed too much from the premise that the general condition of human soul life has basically remained the same ever since any human development can be traced historically or in prehistory. However, this assumption simply does not correspond to the facts. It is difficult, of course, to ascertain what the successive metamorphoses of human soul evolution were like if one is merely in a position to study the facts recorded in historical documents. If, on the other hand, one is able to look back further than these facts allow, then even the historical traditions present themselves in a different light. It then becomes evident that the human soul condition was not always what it is today or what it was in the ages still discernible by external means.

Above all, people believe the following: Human beings utilize something like geometry, like arithmetic, which, as we know, is mainly the theory of counting. Furthermore, they master the art of weighing, of determining weights of given objects. People then consider what measuring and measures represent and contemplate the way one counts and weighs things today. Then people think: Surely, in the age when, according to modern, prevalent opinion, human beings were still completely childlike, they were incapable of measuring, counting, and calculating anything. But ever since human beings were capable of that, these matters have been carried out approximately in the same way we execute them nowadays.

This is not the case at all, and even though it will lead us into a more remote subject, as I said, we must acquire a more exact idea of measures, numbers, and weights before we go into the historical considerations about mankind. Even according to external historical tradition the views concerning numbers prevailing in the Pythagorean School differed somewhat from those of today. As all of you realize, the Pythagoreans connected certain ideas with the numbers one, two, three, four, and so no. They linked quite definite conceptions with an even and an odd number. In short, they spoke about numbers in a certain qualitative sense, not merely in a quantitative one.

When the underlying reason for this is considered from the standpoint of spiritual science, we arrive at the realization that the Pythagorean School, which as yet was still a kind of esoteric school, represented basically only the last vestige of a much more ancient wisdom of numbers, going back to primordial times of which only the traditions have been preserved. And what is handed down to us concerning a science of numbers by Pythagoras is in fact already a decline from a much older teaching of numbers. When these matters are pursued further with the methods of spiritual science, we arrive by way of measure, number, and weight at concepts essentially different from those we possess today. As I said, even though it might create difficulties for some of you, we must make it somewhat clear to ourselves how these concepts of measuring, counting, and weighing are constituted today.

Measuring—how do we measure? We can only have *one* measure and it must assumed in some manner. We cannot claim that this measure on which we base everything, such as the metric measure today, is somehow determined absolutely. It is determined as a certain segment of the northern quadrant of the earth's meridian that passes through Paris, and this segment, the ten millionth part, is not even exactly contained in that original prototype meter located in Paris. It is assumed, however, and we say that we proceed from a certain measure. With it, we then measure other lengths or surface areas by forming a square measure out of the unit of length. Yet, the figures arrived at concerning the object being measured refer to something completely arbitrary that was at one time assumed. It is important to make it clear to ourselves that we actually take an arbitrary measure as the basis, hence, that we always arrive only at a relation of some object to this arbitrarily assumed measure when we measure an object.

It is somewhat different in the case of numbers. In the abstract manner of our life today, we count, 1, 2, 3; we do this when counting apples or people, horses or chairs. To the object that is to be determined by the number it matters not what we designate as 1. We apply our peculiar way of counting to all things we count off, which, as a unit, represent an integrated totality.

Please note that in measuring we proceed from an arbitrary measure and we then relate everything to this arbitrary unit of measure. This unit of measure is something, so to speak; it exists. It is even conceivable, as it were, almost like a thing, an object. The unit of numbers cannot be pictured in this way. The unit of number is a completely abstract concept applicable to anything. No matter whether we count years or people or stars, we are led into total abstraction, into something that cannot stand for any particular reality since it could stand for all realities. When we take the arithmetic unit as the basis, the minute objective element still retained in measuring is lost to us.

When weighing something, we do not see the whole extent of what we take as the basis of weighing. There, the whole matter escapes us even more than in the case of numbers. When we count chairs, for example, and we say, "one," "two," "three," we are at least finished when we come to the third chair that stands before us as a unit. In the case of a scale, on the other hand, we place a weight on one side of the scales—a weight in itself is nothing if it is not subject to earth's gravity, as we say— and the object we weigh is equal to the weight of the weights. Here, however, we are no longer by ourselves; basically, the whole earth is involved. Our point of reference here lies somehow completely beyond the realm we oversee. We enter into a complete abstraction when we say that something weighs five kilograms. Just think what you actually picture when you say that something weighs five kilograms. You place a five kilogram weight on a scale, but this weight by itself is really nothing! We are not dealing with a property of the thing itself. When I say, "one chair," this *one* is at least integrated in the chair. The five kilograms, on the other hand, must relate themselves to the earth. You merely deal with something that relates to something else the whole extent of which you do not see at all, namely, the whole body of the earth. And when weighing the other object on the scale, which is to weigh five kilograms, again, you have something that escapes you completely, belonging again to a totality that is even less than an abstraction.

Let us proceed from numbers. In former times, and here we actually go back as far as the second post-Atlantean epoch, all thinking concerning numbers was dealt with in a significantly different manner from the way we treat it today in the outside world. People then really had concepts of 1, 2, and 3. For us, 2 is nothing but the presence of two units of 1; 3 is the presence of three, 4 that of four units of 1. Thus we continue counting by always adding 1 more. hence repeating the same act of thinking. We can repeat it indefinitely.

This was not the case in the second post-Atlantean epoch. Back then, people sensed the same difference between, let's say, *two* and *three* that we today feel only between different objects. In the number 3, one sensed a significantly different element from that in the number 2. Not only was it the addition of one unit; rather, one sensed something integrated in the 3, something where three things relate to one another. The 2 had an open element, something where two things lie indifferently side by side. People recalled this indifference in lying side by side when they said "two." They did not sense this in the number 3, but only something that belongs together, where each thing relates to all the others. Concerning 2, a person could imagine that one thing escapes to the left, the other to the right. The 3 could not be pictured that way; instead, it was felt that if one unit would disappear, the remaining two would no longer be what they had been, for then, they would exist indifferently beside each other. The 3 combined the 2 in a totality, so to speak; it made them a whole. The form of arithmetic we have today, our elementary counting, this repetition of the same act, did not exist at all in those former times. Only now, through spiritual science, we are once again directed in a certain sense to the qualitative element of numbers.

I can illustrate this with an example long since familiar to you so that you will realize that it is necessary to add not only 1 to 1, and so on, but to delve into the reality of existence with the numbers. In order to give you at least a very elementary idea of this matter, let me outline the following. In my book, *Theosophy*,[1] the individual members of the human being are described:

1. Physical Body
2. Ether Body
3. Astral Body
4. Sentient Soul
5. Intellectual or Mind Soul
6. Consciousness Soul
7. Spirit Self
8. Life Spirit
9. Spirit Man

To list the members of the human being side by side like this, however, signifies counting them off abstractly one after the other; it means that we do not delve into reality. Because these nine do not exist, we cannot count them like that at all: "1. physical body, 2. ether body, 3. astral body, 4. sentient soul. "You cannot count like that when you wish to comprehend the human organization and observe human beings today in their reality. In fact, it must be put like this: The physical body is delimited as an integrated whole, so is the etheric body. Pass on to the third member, on the other hand, it is not something self-enclosed. In the case of the actual human being, we cannot just add the sentient soul to the astral body. Instead, these two, the astral body and the sentient soul, must definitely be combined and thereby, passing from *one* to *two* to *three* in reality, we can, as it were, count off realistically, not merely finding in the 3 the simple addition of 1.

What develops in us as the "astral body" and the "sentient soul," which interact with each other, is simply a third element, abstractly speaking, but by passing in reality to this third element, a third unit can no longer merely be added to the first two. Instead, we must realize that this third element is in itself different from the first two.

Then, the fourth member is counted off, which is actually the fifth, and again, in the modern human being, we must basically add together the sixth and seventh. Thus, we arrive at the way they are actually listed in my *Theosophy*: 3, 4, 5, 6, 7. We have seven actual components, which, when they are abstractly counted off, are nine:

1	1.	Physical Body
2	2.	Ether Body
3	(3.)	Astral Body
	(4.)	Sentient Soul
4	5.	Intellectual Soul
5	(6.)	Consciousness Soul
	(7.)	Spirit Self
6	8.	Life Spirit
7	9.	Spirit Man

Based on reality, we learn to say: By proceeding according to their inherent rules, one thing is not indifferent to the others. Just because this is the third member (see above, 3), it is something different. Certainly, due to our customary abstract thinking about numbers, we have to illustrate this a little, for this older way of thinking about numbers is foreign to ordinary consciousness. In ancient times, on the other hand, in the first and second period of the post-Atlantean epoch, it would not have occurred to anybody to imagine an indifferent addition in progressing from one number to the next. Instead, people experienced something when they passed from, say, 2 to 3, just as we experience something here when we pass from 2 to 3 (see above list). Today you can barely sense it in this example, but not yet in the number itself. In those former times people could sense it in the numbers themselves. They spoke of numbers in reference to their mutual relationships. Anything that existed in twos, for example, was felt to have a quality of openness towards the world, of not being closed off. Something existing in threes, as an actual *three*, was something closed off. You might now say that depending on what is counted a distinction has to be made. When you count, one man, one woman, one child, man and woman are equal to a duality, hence not closed off to the world; the child closes this duality off, forms a totality. When you count apples, on the other hand, we can indeed not say that three apples are more closed off than two. It was true that external matters were merely sensed in this way, but the number itself was experienced quite differently.

You might recall that certain aboriginal tribes still use their ten fingers to count, comparing to them the amount of objects present in their surroundings. So we could say that if we have three apples here, this is equal to three fingers.

For 1, 2, 3, however, these primitive people would not have said—naturally in the words of their own language—"thumb," "index finger," and "middle finger." Although the objects they counted off in the outside world remained undefined, what represented those objects inwardly was very clearly defined, for the three fingers differ from one another. Well, mankind has now advanced so splendidly in the fifth period of the post-

Atlantean epoch—basically, it was already like this in the fourth period—that we no longer need to count by means of our fingers. Instead, we say, "one, two, three." The genius of language is not taken into consideration anymore. For if you would listen to what is contained in the words, purely based on feeling you would say: "*Eins, entzwei*" ("one, in two—cut in two.")* It is still retained in the language, and when you say: "*Drei*" ("three"), and you are sensitive to the sounds, you have something closed off. Three: when pictured correctly, three things can only be imagined as lying in a circle, connected to each other; two: into two (*entzwei*); three: self-enclosed, the genius of language still retains that.

Well, as I said, we have "advanced so far" that we can abstractly add one unit to another. Then we feel that this is 2, that is 1; in case of 3, one more has been added, and so on. Yet, why is it that we can count in the first place? In reality, we don't accomplish it any differently from primitive peoples. Only they did it with their five physical fingers. We, too, count with the fingers, but with those of our etheric body, and we no longer know it. It takes place in our subconscious, and we leave that out of

---

*Translator's note: In the original German, Rudolf Steiner's example is quite clear. This is the reason the German words were retained and the English translation given in parenthesis.

consideration. We actually count by means of the etheric body; in reality, a number is still nothing but a comparison with what is contained within us. The whole of arithmetic is in us; we brought it to birth within us through our astral body. It actually emerges from our astral body, our ten fingers being merely replicas of the astral and etheric. These two are only utilized by the external finger, whereas, when we do sums, we express in the etheric body what brings about the inspiration of numbers in the astral body; then we count by means of the etheric body, with which we think in the first place.

Therefore, we can say that, outwardly, counting is something quite abstract for us today; inwardly, the reason we count is connected with the fact that *we* are counted in the first place, for we are counted out of universal being and are structured according to numbers. It is most interesting to trace the various methods of counting among the different folk groups in the world—according to the number 10, the decimal system, or the number 12—and how this relates to their different etheric and astral constitutions. Numbers are inborn into us, woven into us out of the cosmic totality. Outwardly, numbers are gradually becoming a matter of indifference to us; within us, this is not the case. Within ourselves, each number has its own definite quality. Just try and imagine that you could eliminate numbers from the universe and then see what things formed in numbers would look like if one thing were merely added to the other. Imagine the appearance of your hand, if the thumb were here, and the next finger would be added as the same unit and then the next, and so on. You would have five thumbs on your hand and five on the other! This would then correspond to abstract counting.

The spirits of the universe do not count like that. They create forms according to numbers, and they do it in the manner formerly connected with numbers during the first and even the second period of the post-Atlantean epoch. The development of abstract numbers out of the quite concrete concept of the element and quality of numbers is something that only evolved in the course of humanity's evolution. We have to realize that it has profound significance that the tradition handed down to us from the ancient mysteries relates that the gods fashioned man according to numbers. The saying that the world abounds in numbers implies that everything is fashioned according to numbers and that the human being, too, is formed on the basis of numbers. Hence, the modern way of counting did not exist in those ancient times; on the other hand, an imaginative thinking in the qualities of numbers did exist.

As I said, this leads us back to an age of long ago, namely, the first and second post-Atlantean periods, the ancient Indian and Persian eras, in which our present form of counting was not at all possible. In those times people connected something entirely different from two times one with the number 2. And likewise they associated something other than two plus one with three. As you can see, the human soul constitution has indeed changed considerably in the course of time.

Turning now to the somewhat later period of time, the third period of the post-Atlantean epoch, we find that the measure was something quite different. Today, we measure on the basis of an assumed and arbitrary unit of measurement. Even in the third post-Atlantean period, for example, people did not really refer to such an arbitrary unit of measure. In measuring, they had in mind something quite pictorial. What they focused on may perhaps become clear to you from the following. Here, for instance, we see one column, there is another one (see sketch below); we look at these two columns. If we experience things abstractly, we say that the second column is twice as high as the first one; we measure it by the first one.

That, however, is a very abstract conception. Picturing it concretely, we can interpret it in approximately the following manner: When we evoke a feeling for the column on the left, we experience it to be weak in comparison to the one on the right. We feel that it must grow, and when it grows and grows and reaches this point up here (pointing to the taller column), it has become something special. It has put so much energy into this growth that it now possesses a strength such that its two parts are both equally strong. You can sense something qualitative there. You can go further and say: I have a structure here; I measure it against the other one and thus arrive at the symmetry; the concept of the measure expands for me, entering into the picture.

In this way, we gradually come to the idea that measure actually has to do with something that is still sensed dimly when we speak of moderation* in which case we are not thinking of measuring something. For example, when a person consumes only a certain quantity of some food, we might designate that as being moderate (*maessig*) without having measured the amount. We classify something else as immoderate (*unmaessig*). We are not measuring anything here, we make no comparison, measuring the stomach with what enters it, and so on. We don't measure the piece of meat and then eat it; we do not measure it against the size of the person. Instead, we refer to a quality when we speak of a moderate or immoderate intake of food. We arrive at something that is not so very different from what we term a measure today but it does show us that we refer to something abstract today when we speak of *measure*, namely, "the unit of measure contained in a certain quantity," whereas formerly people defined it as something that was qualitatively connected with objects.

Above all, people sensed the measured symmetry of each member of man in relation to the totality of the human being without thinking at that point of a unit. One thing has remained from this, namely, that it seems abhorrent to us if, as artists, we are supposed to measure anything; for, if an artist actually has to take measurements so that the nose, for example, does not turn out to be too long or too short, this is not considered artistic. But we consider the work artistic when we see that the thing has the proper size for an organism.

*Translator's note: In German, this example is immediately clear. *Mass* means "measure;" *maessig* and *massvoll* mean "moderate."

Therefore, we do not deal with an abstract process here but with something related to the pictorial element.

Finally, consider the unit of measure that still plays a certain role today, namely the so-called golden mean or golden section. It is not connected with measurements but only with a qualitative element. The smaller element is to the medium-sized one as the medium-sized one is to the whole. The smaller element may be any size, but it must always be to the medium-sized one as the medium-sized one is to the whole. We do not have a measurement in mind but something that reveals a certain interrelationship when we look at it. Yet, we speak of the harmonious measure that comes to expression in the golden mean. We cannot base the golden mean on any kind of unit of measure in the abstract sense as we do otherwise. Therefore, as we examine the various periods of humanity's evolution in regard to measuring, we find that in the fourth post-Atlantean period, the Greco-Roman age, this vivid awareness of measure and symmetry gradually transformed itself into abstract measuring. This was actually not the case until the fourth post-Atlantean period. In the third period people experienced the relationships of measure, the proportions, much more the way we only experience the golden mean. Likewise, as we go back into ancient times, our abstract counting can be traced back to an experience of the inner quality of numbers.

In the case of weight, human beings are already far removed from what existed in the first post-Atlantean period as an experience of weight. You need only recall a well-known phenomenon that most of you have experienced in observing an athlete who lifts a heavy weight with the inscription, "200 kilograms"; he tries and tries to lift it, sweating all the while, and you almost perspire with him. Then, when he's let you sweat long enough, he suddenly lifts it up and carries it off. The whole thing really has no absolute weight; that has only been feigned. You feel the weight because of the abstract inscription "200 kilograms." The experience of weight is something we are deprived of nowadays. Therefore, it is one of the most profound experiences when, in regard to natural phenomena, the experience of absolute weight appears in clairvoyant consciousness, as is indeed the case.

It is really true that in the first post-Atlantean epoch, designated as the ancient Indian epoch, a human being still experienced something of weight relationships within himself. I have pointed out many times that our brain actually floats in the cerebral fluid and therefore—according to the well known law whereby a floating body seemingly becomes lighter by the amount of the weight of water it displaces—loses a considerable amount of its weight. Otherwise, the brain would crush the blood vessels lying underneath. The brain floats in the cerebral fluid, but people in their abstract awareness no longer notice this today; neither are they aware of any other relationships within themselves. We no longer experience weight, pay it no attention. There is a major difference between experiencing one's weight at age twelve, and when one is, say five times that age. Most people have forgotten, however, how heavy they appeared to themselves at age twelve, and therefore they cannot very well make the comparison. But let's assume that according to the scales you have the same weight at two ages. Yet this does not matter; what matters is the experience of the weight. This experience of weight that for people today is present only in regard to the earth, was something absolute during the first post-Atlantean epoch.

Today, we experience only a remnant of that in art but there in a very pronounced manner. I need only call your attention to the following. Let us assume that I draw two figures. According to my view, this is really something unclear and unresolved, something that should not be. Two objects like that side by side induce me to draw a third one. But I can shape the third object only in such a way that it appears larger, in a sense, holding the other two together. Then I have the feeling that the three are floating in air and can mutually support each other.

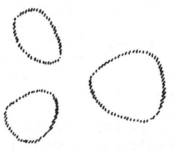

When a painter nowadays draws three angels who are, after all, not viewed in connection with gravity, and he is concerned with composition, he distributes them in space in such a manner that they support each other, that one is borne by the other. Artistically, it would be the worst thing simply to draw three angels side by side on a canvas; such a painter would have no true artistic feeling. One must have a feeling for the weight of each one, how one thing carries the other. In artistic feelings, a slight touch has remained of what was mainly experienced inwardly by people in the post-Atlantean age as producing weight, as giving him weight.

The experience of weight, number, and measure developed during the first three post-Atlantean periods according to the way human beings experienced themselves within the cosmos. And based on what had shaped them from out of the cosmos, the other matters were judged, namely, what they produced. When people observed what their astral body pushed into the etheric body, they had to tell themselves that the astral body counts, counts in a differentiating way thus forming the etheric body. Numbers are found between astral and etheric body and they are something alive and active within us.

Something else is located between etheric body and physical body. Through the inner relationships something is formed out of the etheric body that we can then behold. Basically, even our organism is structured according to the golden mean: the forehead is to a certain other part of the head as that in turn is to the whole length of the head, and so on. All this is imprinted by the etheric body into our physical body out of the cosmos and its relationships. Contained within us, measure and symmetry represent the transition from the etheric to the physical body. Finally, in the transition from the ego to the astral body lives what can be inwardly experienced as weight. I have often pointed out that the ego was actually born in the course of human evolution. The people of the ancient Indian period did not yet experience such an ego. They did, however, experience within themselves something causing weight, the condition of possessing form; hence, they sensed this heaviness, this downward pull, as well as their buoyancy, their ascent. They sensed within themselves what is overcome when the child changes from a being that crawls on all fours to one that walks. The people in ancient India did not experience their ego, but they did sense that they were fettered by the Ahrimanic forces to the earth, that they were weighted down by them, and that, on the other hand, they were borne upwards, lifted up by the Luciferic forces. All this, they experienced as their position of equilibrium. If we were to study the ancient terms for the ego we would find that the above experience was contained in the formulation of the words themselves. Just as the words were fitted together in the verbs according to their inner configuration, so the ancient words for the ego contained the balance between floating and falling.

I — Astral Body — Etheric Body — Physical Body
Weight   Number   Measure

Weight, which isn't abstract anymore, for we confront something completely unknown; number, something quite abstract, for it is totally unrelated to what is being counted; measure, which has become increasingly abstract for us—these abstract conceptions of ours are actually projected from our inner being to the outside. Something that has very real significance within the human being since he is fashioned according to measure, number, and weight is transferred by him to the indifferent external things. In this process of abstraction the human being dehumanizes himself. It is therefore possible to say that mankind's evolution tends in the direction of losing the inner experiences of weight, number, and measure, retaining only a slight touch of them in the artistic realm. We no longer experience them in such a manner that we sense ourselves as having been formed out of the cosmos according to weight, number, and measure.

The geometry we have when we compare congruent and similar figures, when we say that an ellipse is generated by a point so moving that its distance from a fixed point divided by its distance from a fixed line is a positive constant, is something abstract. There, we basically measure the distances and find that their sum is always equal to the large axis of the ellipse. Even if it was not pictured in any way, the ellipse was nevertheless experienced by people in the third post-Atlantean period in this peculiar relationship of two different quantities. In the relationship of one to the other they already sensed the elliptic element, just as they sensed the circle during the same age. And in the same way the nature of numbers was experienced. Humanity evolved in this way from concrete experience to something abstract, developing geometry out of the ancient experience of measure, arithmetic out of the former experience of numbers, and having completely lost the ancient experience of weight and thus having utterly dehumanized themselves, human beings developed only external observation out of it.

All this slowly prepared the way tor the increasing abstractness of inner human experience, a development that culminated in the nineteenth century. Thus, the human being became lost to his own conception. He can no longer comprehend himself; he no longer has any idea that *he* produces geometry because he has been formed according to measure out of the cosmos, that he counts through his very nature. He is surprised when the so-called savages use their fingers in order to compare external objects with them. He has forgotten that he has been fashioned according to numbers out of the cosmos. He does not know that in this regard he, too, always remains a "savage," that his etheric body had imprinted the numbers into his astral body in accordance with the inner qualities of the numbers themselves so that he could later experience the numbers also outside himself. In the course of humanity's evolution, geometry, arithmetic, and the science of weight and weighing have all moved into the abstract domain and have contributed to the fact that the human being could henceforth only devote himself to a science and a form of scientific research that observes these matters externally.

What do we do when we are involved in scientific research today? We measure, count, and weigh. Nowadays, you can indeed read of strange definitions of existence. We already have thinkers who state that existence, being, is that which is measurable. Yet, they naturally refer only to measuring with an arbitrary unit of measure. It is odd that existence is traced back to something actually based on arbitrariness. Therefore, the human being dwells in something that has been completely detached, excluded from him and in regard to which he has utterly lost the connection with himself. Due to such influences, the human being has lost himself in modern knowledge; something I have emphasized from a number of viewpoints, particularly during this lecture course.

As I have often said, the human being has been lost in our perception of ourselves as merely the last step in the evolution of the animals. In society we have lost sight of the human being, for though we have invented extremely sophisticated machines, we are unable to integrate the significance of the people operating these machines into our social processes We must learn to penetrate mankind's evolution; above all we must observe in this way how the process of man's intellectualization has come about. Just think how different people's frame of mind was in the first post-Atlantean period when they continuously experienced a changing equilibrium in placing one leg in front of the other. They always felt themselves become heavy, sensed a falling and floating. Picture how different it was when human beings felt that numbers permeate their own form, that they are built up according to measures. Think of how different that was from superficial measuring, counting, and weighing, leaving out the human being altogether. As I already indicated, at most it is possible for a person with a more sensitive awareness for language to gain some insight into the nature of numbers by means of what is in fact contained in the numerals, the words naming the numbers; or, from an artistic viewpoint, it is possible to sense that this, for example, in the sketch below is feasible:

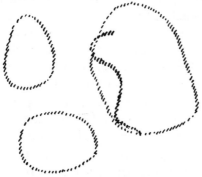

but that this is impossible in this connection:

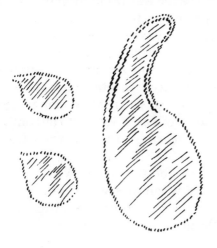

Such a person then has just a touch of the feeling for the inner condition of weight, the inner balance. If, by means of a line, I can follow some relationship in the other object, I have them balancing each other. However, if I sketch a protrusion over here, on the object on the right of second sketch, where there cannot be one, then I have no feeling for this balance. See how mankind has struggled to produce the external proportions out of its inner being, so to say, the outer appearance in contrast to the inward experience. Take a look at the painting by Raphael—it is actually true of all of Raphael's paintings but especially obvious in this one—depicting the "Marriage of Mary and Joseph,"[2] and see how the figures are positioned and painted in such a way that they support each other and that the viewer thus loses the feeling that anything exerts a downward pull. In particular, however, when ancient painters drew some flying creature, study how that was motivated, how you can clearly discern from this figure that it is not pulled down by weight but, rather, supports itself somehow by means of the relationship to other elements in the painting.

So, here we have the transition from the experience of the inner weighting to the external determination of weight: thus, here we have the course of mankind in the post-Atlantean epoch from inward experience to intellectualism, this struggling ascent to the intellect where everything experienced in our concepts is divorced from the human being; where we no longer experience the tearing in the word *entzweien*, ("to fall out with each other"; literally: "tearing in two") when we say *Zwei* ("two").

All this comes about slowly. When this term is employed further, when we say, *zweifeln*, "to doubt," we sense the derivation from *entzweien*. After all, one who doubts something implies: Perhaps this is correct, perhaps it is not. It is open in both directions, the feeling of *entzweien* is inherent in the conceptual act. It is also already contained in the word for the number 2, *zwei*.

Three—there you cannot experience this in the same manner when you apply it to something. Apply it to a judgment, where you have the major premise, the minor premise and the conclusion: a triad, a matter enclosed within itself. Take the syllogism about the most famous logical personality, the one about Gaius Julius Caesar:

All men are mortal;
Gaius is a man;
therefore Gaius is mortal

It all belongs together, the major and minor premise and the conclusion. However, if you take merely the first two, the matter remains open.

Hereby, I only wished to indicate to you what mankind's path to abstraction was like and how, in fact, by losing himself, man brought the intellect into his evolution.

We shall continue with this tomorrow. Today's subject was intended only as an episode, but you will see how it will fit in with further considerations.

LECTURE IX
Dornach, April 24, 1921

In the course of the last week we reflected on a number of considerations suited to throw light on the spiritual condition of the present and the immediate future. Recently, we have referred in particular to the decisive turning point of humanity's development in Europe in the fourth century. Earlier, at least in the south of Europe, people understood the Mystery of Golgotha to some extent on the basis of Oriental wisdom. They still grasped with a certain comprehension something that is viewed today with such antipathy by some circles, namely, the Gnosis. The Gnosis was indeed the final remnant of Oriental primeval wisdom, that primeval wisdom which, though proceeding from instinctive forces of human cognition, did penetrate deeply into the nature of the world's configuration. With the aid of the conceptions and feelings acquired through Gnostic knowledge, people were able to have insight into what had taken place in the Mystery of Golgotha. But the Christian stream that increasingly flowed into the Roman political system and took on its form was actively involved in destroying this Gnostic world outlook. Except for a few quite insignificant remainders from which little can be gained, this Christian stream eradicated everything that once existed as Gnosis. And, as we have seen, nothing was left behind of ancient Oriental wisdom in the consciousness of mankind in Europe except for the simple narrations, clothed in material events, about what took place in Palestine at the time of the Mystery of Golgotha.

To begin with, these narrations were clothed in the form that originated in ancient paganism, as you can see in the *Heliand*. They were adopted by European civilization. But there was less and less of a feeling that these stories should be penetrated with a certain cognitive force. People increasingly lost the feeling that a profound world riddle and secret should be sought for in the Mystery of Golgotha. For concerning the one who had been united with Jesus as Christ dogmas determined by council decisions had been established. The demand had been raised that people believe in these established dogmas; thus, gradually all living knowledge that had still existed up until the time of the fourth Christian century passed over into the solidly structured system of doctrines of the Roman State Church.

Then, if we have an overview of this whole system of the Occidental Christian church stream, we see that the nature of the Mystery of Golgotha was enveloped in certain firm, rigid, and more and more incomprehensible doctrines, and that any living spiritual knowledge was in fact eradicated.

We are faced with a strange factor in European evolution. One might say that the fertile, living Oriental wisdom flowed into the doctrines adopted by the Roman Church and became rigid. In dogma, it continued on through the ensuing centuries. This dogma existed. One must remember that there were some people who to some extent knew what to make of these dogmas, but it had become impossible for the general consciousness of humanity to receive anything but a dead form. Certainly, we encounter a number of splendid minds. We need only to recall some of those who came from the Irish centers of knowledge; we need only recall Scotus Erigena who lived at the court of Charles the Bald.[1] In individuals like him, we have people who received the doctrines and still sensed the spirit in them, or discovered it more or less. Then we have scholasticism, often mentioned here in a certain connection, which attempted in a more abstract form to penetrate the doctrines with its thinking. We face the fact that an extensive system of religious content was present in rigidified doctrines and was handed down from generation to generation; it survived as a system of dogmas. On the one hand, there were the theological dogmas, on the other, the narrations concerning the events of Palestine clothed in materialistic pictures.

Now, if we wish to comprehend our modern age, we must not forget what these Roman-Catholic dogmas couched in Roman political concepts are fundamentally all about. Among them are doctrines of great significance, splendid doctrines. There is, above all, the doctrine of the Trinity, which, in other terminology of later times, points to the Father, the Son, and the Spirit. An ancient and profound primordial wisdom was frozen into this doctrine, something great and mighty that human perception once possessed instinctively. Yet, only the brilliant, inspired insight of a few could fathom what is contained in such a doctrine.

Running through the various council resolutions, there was what finally rigidified into the dogma of the two persons of Christ and Jesus in one man. There were dogmas concerning the birth, the nature of Christ Jesus, the death, the Resurrection, and the Ascension. Finally, there were dogmas establishing the various festivals; and all this was basically the skeleton, the silhouette of a wondrous, ancient wisdom. Now this shadowy image, this skeleton, continued on through the centuries. One particular reason why it was able to go on was that it assumed a certain form of ancient cults. The content of what was thus expressed in dogmas, in the most sublime dogmas, such as the dogma of the transubstantiation of the bread and wine into the body and blood of Christ, could spread because it was clothed in the form of an ancient, sacred cult, namely, the Sacrifice of the Mass. The ancient cult was just altered a bit but as such continued on. The various metamorphoses of the Christian festivals lived on through the whole ecclesiastical year. Those aspects lived on that you know as the sacraments. They were intended to lift the human being out of the ordinary material life through the agency of the Church, so to speak, into a higher, spiritual sphere. Because of all this and because of its link with the impulse of Christianity, this content lived on throughout the centuries of historical development in Europe. Side by side with this, as I have said, existed the humble narration of the events in Palestine, but garbed in materialistic formulas.

Because of its significant content and because people basically had nothing else with which to establish a relationship to the supersensible worlds, all these doctrines together were something that affected minds striving for such higher knowledge. Due to the ritual and the simple narration of the Gospel, however, these doctrines could also unfold that form of activity that gained influence over the broad masses of Europe's population.

In addition to this, another separate and different cult system spread, one that counted less on Christianity as such but frequently accepted it. It was basically not organically connected with Christianity but proceeded more from older cults. This other system culminated in the dogma of present day Freemasonry, which, indeed, had and still has only a superficial relationship to Christianity. As you know, the element that clothed itself in the form of Roman-Catholic dogmatism and the element that in Masonic tradition is linked to other cults and symbolism fight each other tooth and nail to this day.

This development can be traced more or less if only we focus our soul on the historical facts with some sense. But what presents itself can be fully comprehended only when we look to that turning point of European evolution in the fourth Christian century that, in a sense, sank all the ancient spiritual wisdom and its aftereffects into a sort of abyss. Due to that, people in Europe knew little of Oriental primeval wisdom throughout the ensuing centuries.

As I pointed out yesterday, the inner faculties that enabled human beings in ancient times to experience weight, number, and measure in their own being had gradually disappeared. Measure, numbers, and weight then turned into abstractions. With these abstractions, people then established in the fifth post-Atlantean epoch what has today become our natural scientific world view, something that could not include human beings in its sphere and stopped short of them, unable in any way to comprehend them. By means of the abstractions of weight, number, and measure, it did, however, grasp the external natural phenomena with a certain excellence and arrived at a kind of culmination point in the nineteenth century.

People today do not yet have enough distance from these matters; they do not yet realize that a quite special point in time was actually reached in European development in the middle of the nineteenth century. Intellectual striving, pure rational effort, attained to its fullest and greatest unfolding at that time. It was the trend that resulted from those same sources from which the modern natural scientific views have been flowing since the first third of the fifteenth century. Yet, at the same time, this was the trend that ultimately could no longer make anything of the cult that had spread; indeed, this trend basically had been unable for a long time to do anything with the ritual and dogmatic formulas established by the Church councils. Merely a few vestiges had survived, a few remnants; for example, the vestige of the Council of 869,[2] where it had been resolved that the human being consists not of body, soul, and spirit, but merely of body and soul, with the latter possessing a few spiritual qualities. This vestige remained and lived on in the modern philosophical views that believed themselves to be objective but actually only reiterated what had originated in this Catholic dogmatism.

The modern mood of European civilization, which tended increasingly to a purely intellectual, rational view of the universe, formed out of all these directions. Having been prepared for centuries, this mood reached its culmination in the middle of the nineteenth century. How can we understand this culmination if we observe the human being from a soul-spiritual standpoint? We have to focus on human nature, as it was in ancient times and as it has gradually changed. We have done this already from a number of different viewpoints and shall do so again today from yet a certain other standpoint.

Let us place the human being schematically before us. Take, first of all, man's physical body (red). As I said, I am making a schematic drawing.

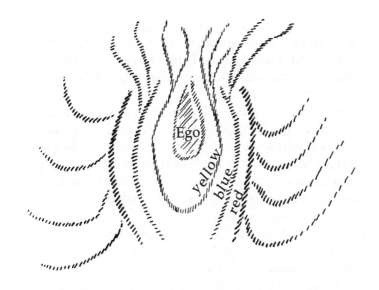

This is man's etheric body (blue); that is the human astral body (yellow); here we have man's ego. Let us first consider the human being as he was in ancient times, those ancient times when instinctive clairvoyance still existed, which then faded, withered, and gradually disappeared. The ego is basically a product of the earth and we need to give it less consideration. But we must be clear about the fact that the whole world actually dwells in man's physical, etheric, and astral bodies. We can say, in this physical body lives the element that represents the whole world. The corporeality is born out of it and continues to reconstruct itself through the intake of nourishment. In the etheric body, the whole world lives as well; in the most diverse ways, influences enter constantly into it and send their effects into the human being in a superphysical manner, effects that express themselves in the forces of growth, for example in the circulation of the blood, in the breath, and so on. They are by no means identical with the forces that are present in the intake of food and in digestion. In addition, there are all the influences living in our astral body that receive impressions from the world through the senses, and so forth. It is like this to this day and was like this in the days when the human being still lived with his ancient instinctive clairvoyance, but in that age, he was more intimately connected with his physical body, his etheric, and astral bodies than he is today. When he woke up in the morning, he submerged with his ego and astral body into his physical and etheric bodies. A close connection developed between his ego and astral body and his etheric body and physical corporeality. And he not only dwelled in his physical body, he also lived in the forces that worked within the latter.

Let me give you a vivid description of this. Imagine that a person possessing ancient clairvoyance ate a plum. It seems almost grotesque to a human being of today when something like this is described, but it is profoundly true. Assume that such an ancient clairvoyant ate a plum; this plum contains etheric forces. If a person eats a plum today, he is not aware of what goes on within this plum. The ancient clairvoyant ate a plum; it was then in his stomach, was digested, and he experienced how the etheric forces in the plum passed over into his body. He cosmically participated in this experience. When he inwardly made comparisons between the various things he ingested into his stomach, he saw that all the relationships in the outside world continued inside the human being, and he perceived them inwardly. From waking in the morning to going to sleep at night, such a person was filled with the vivid inner perception of the life lived outside by the plums, by the apples, and by much else that he ate. Inwardly, through the breathing process, he was aware of the essential, spiritual being of the air. Through the warmth that coursed through his circulation process, he was familiar with the warmth forces of the cosmos in his surroundings. He did not stop short at merely sensing the light in his eyes. He felt how the light rays streamed in through the nerves of his eyes; how, in his own etheric body, they encountered the physical limbs and dwelled within them.

Such a person experienced himself quite concretely within the cosmic element. While it was a dim consciousness, it was present. During the day, it was muted by what a person perceived outwardly even in those days. But even in the early times of Greek civilization, it was true that human beings still retained an aftereffect of what is possessed today only by creatures other than man. I have already mentioned several times that it is most interesting to look with spiritual sight upon a meadow where cows are lying down and digesting. This whole activity of digestion is a cosmic experience for the cows. It is even more so the case with snakes; they lie down and digest and do indeed experience cosmic events. Out of their organism, something blossoms and sprouts that is "world" to their perception. Something arises out of their inner being that is much more beautiful than anything we are ever able to see with our eyes from outside. Something like this was present as an underlying mood in human beings who still possessed ancient, instinctive clairvoyance. While it was muted throughout most of the day by external perceptions, when these people fell asleep, they carried with them what they had thus experienced and received into their astral body and ego. Then, when their ego was alone with its astral body, these experiences arose powerfully in the form of true dreams. Then, in the form of true dreams, these people experienced after the fact what they had only dimly experienced during the day.

You see, I am referring you to the inner soul-bodily manner of experiencing on the part of human beings of ancient times; because they were able to experience in this way, they had cosmic experiences. It was in this that they found their cosmic, supersensible perception. Then, when people in the Orient drank the Soma drink,[3] they knew the nature of the Spirit of the Heights. This Soma drink permeated, surged, and wove through their inner being, enlivening their blood. When these people subsequently fell asleep and the ego and astral body, which had been active in the blood, took along the forms that had come into being through the digestion of the Soma drink, then their being widened out in the widths of space and, in their nocturnal experience, they felt the spiritual beings of the cosmos.

Such an experience was still present in those among whom the ancient Zarathustra found willing listeners in the ancient Persian epoch. If one is unaware of these things, one does not understand what finally came down to us from the Oriental scriptures that have survived. This living cosmic perception gradually became extinguished. Already in the historical Egyptian age, little of it can be found, only its aftereffects are still present. And except for final vestiges that have always been retained among primitive human beings, it then disappeared in the fourth Christian century. From then on, the intellect, the rational element, increasingly struggled to come to the fore in the human being, the element that is completely tied to the mere physical body in its isolation from the world.

If you have a pictorial imagination and enter into your body, you cannot help but experience something cosmic. If you have retained something of the inner quality of numbers and enter into your body with it, you cannot help but experience the number element of the cosmos. The same is true for the ratios of weight. However, if you enter into the human organism with the power of the ego, which is active as a purely rational, intellectual element, then you immerse yourself only in the isolated human body, in what the human body is by virtue of its own nature, without its relationship to the cosmos. You enter into the earthly human body in its total isolation. Thus, if I would try to sketch this from the point of view of the intellect, I would have to do it like this:

The etheric body, the astral body, and the ego (see above, blue, yellow, and shape in the middle) are present there too. But the ego no longer experiences anything of the cosmic element here within the human being. It only has a dim experience of its own existence, of its own immersion in the isolated human organism. Therefore, when this purely intellectual ego goes into its surroundings in sleep, it takes nothing along. The fact that it takes along nothing is the reason that at most reminiscences, dream images of an unrealistic kind, can arise in the human being, and that this ego can in no way be permeated by anything from the cosmos. Basically, from the moment of falling asleep until awakening, the human being experiences nothing of significance, because his whole manner of experiencing is calculated for the isolated human organism, which in turn affects the ego with those forces that have nothing to do with the cosmos. This is why the ego is dulled from the moment of falling asleep until waking up.

Indeed, it must be so, for though instinctively clairvoyant ancient human beings possessed cosmic vision and dwelled in instinctive Imaginations, Inspirations, and Intuitions, they possessed no independent rational thinking. If this independent rational thinking, this actual intellectual thinking, is to develop, it has to make use of the instrument of the isolated human body. It has to be dull during sleep and therefore brings nothing along when it awakens. The ancient human being, on the other hand, having carried his experiences in the body out into the cosmos, brought with him what he had experienced in the encounter of the cosmic aftereffects with the actual spiritual-cosmic occurrences out there. Again, he brought back aftereffects of what he had experienced there and thus enjoyed a lively relationship with the cosmos. What is attained by the human being through intellectual thinking is acquired in the period from waking up until falling asleep and dims down after sleep begins. Human beings now have to depend on the time when they are awake.

We come across the strange phenomenon that in ancient times the human being was bound more to his body than he is today, but that he experienced in this body the spiritual aspect of the cosmos. Modern man has lost this experience in the body. The human being today is more spiritual but he has the most rarefied spirit; he lives in the intellect and can dwell in the spirit only from the time he awakens until he falls asleep. When he enters the spiritual world with his completely rarefied intellectual spirit, his consciousness is dimmed.

Why have we developed materialism? And why did ancient humanity not have materialism? The ancients did not have it because they dwelled within the matter of the body; modern men have materialism because they dwell only in the spirit, because they are completely free of a cosmic connection to their body. Materialism actually comes about because the human being became spiritual, but spiritual in a rarefied manner. People were most spiritual during the mid-nineteenth century. But they lied to themselves in an ahrimanic way inasmuch as they did not recognize that it was the rarefied spirit in which they dwelled. Into the most spiritual element possible for the human being, he only absorbed the concept of materiality. The human being had turned into a completely spiritual vessel, but into this vessel he only let flow the thoughts of material existence. It is the secret of materialism that human beings turned to matter because of their spirituality. This is modern man's negation of his own spirituality. The culmination point of this spiritual condition was in the middle of the nineteenth century, but human beings did not grasp this condition of spirituality.

As I said, this developed slowly through the centuries. The ancient instinctive spirituality had slowly died down in the fourth Christian century; beginning in the first third of the fifteenth century, the new spirituality dawned; the time between is in a sense an episode of purely human experience. Now, however, after this point in time in the first third of the fifteenth century and after that century as a whole this dependence of man on his isolated physical body made itself felt. Now he no longer developed any relationship to what was frozen into dogmatic council doctrines and what, although rigidified, still possessed a grandiose content. Now, too, human beings basically could no longer find any relationship to the humble narrations of Palestine. For a while yet, they forced themselves to connect some meaning with them. However, meaning can be connected with them only when they are penetrated by knowledge. In particular, modern human beings no longer could connect any meaning with the cults, the ritual itself. The Sacrifice of the Mass, a religious act of the greatest cosmic significance, turned into an external, symbolic act because it was no longer understood. The sacrament of the Transubstantiation, which had survived through the Middle Ages and which has profound cosmic significance, became part of purely intellectual disputes. Certainly it goes without saying that when people began to question with their isolated intellect how the Christ could be contained in the sacraments of the altar, they could not comprehend it, for these matters are not suited for comprehension by the intellect. But now human beings began to try to understand them by means of the intellect.

This then led to the emergence of debates of great importance in world history known as the "Eucharist-Dispute, "[4] and linked to names like Hus[5] and others. The most progressive individuals in Europe, those most advanced in the rational comprehension of the world, then arrived at the various forms of Protestantism. It is the intellect's reaction against something that had emerged from a much broader, much more intense power of cognition than is the intellect itself. The powers that had developed in the modern soul as intellectual faculties and what dwelled in the rigid dogmas yet containing something great and mighty, these two confronted each other as two alien views! Protestant confessions of the greatest variety arose as compromises between the intellect and the ancient traditions. The sixteenth, seventeenth, eighteenth and nineteenth centuries passed, and in the middle of the nineteenth century the human being reached the culmination of his intellectual development. He became a spiritual being through and through.

With this spirituality, he could comprehend what exists in the outer, sensory world, but he did not comprehend himself as spirit. People hardly had an inkling any longer of the meaning of a sentence such as the one by Leibnitz that states, "Nothing dwells in the intellect that did not dwell earlier in the senses, except for the intellect itself."[6] Modern people completely omitted the phrase at the end and acknowledged only the sentence, "Nothing dwells in the intellect that did not dwell earlier in the senses, " whereas Leibnitz clearly discerned that the intellect is something totally spiritual at work in the human being quite independently of all aspects of the physical corporeality.

As I have said, the intellect was active but did not recognize itself. Thus, it has been our experience that human beings are now in the transition to another phase of development in their life, and, so to speak, they carry nothing out with them into the night. For what is intellectually acquired is attained through the body and has no relationship to what is outside the body. People now have to work their way anew into the spiritual world. The possibility distinctly exists for them to look into this spiritual world. What people earlier had attained from their physical and etheric bodies as well as from their astral body in regard to an instinctive view of the cosmos can be attained again today. We can come to Imaginations and by means of them we can describe the world evolution from Saturn, Sun, Moon, to earth, and so on. We can behold what dwells in the nature of numbers, namely, the being of numbers. Through Inspirations, we can receive insight into how the world is shaped out of cosmic spirituality according to the laws of numbers. It is entirely possible that we can have insight into the world in this way through Imagination, Inspiration, and Intuition.

Most people will say: If we have not ourselves become clairvoyant, we can at most study these matters. Good and well, but one *can* study them, and it has been said again and again that the ordinary intellect can grasp them. Today, I shall add the reason why the ordinary intellect is able to grasp these matters. Assume that you are reading something like *An Outline of Occult Science.* Imagine that you try to place yourself into these descriptions with your ordinary intellect. You take it in with the intellect, which is only linked to the isolated human body. But you do take something in that you could not receive through this intellect, since throughout the past few centuries this intellect did not comprehend itself. Now you take something in that is incomprehensible on the basis of those concepts that the intellect derives from the external sense world. It does become comprehensible, however, when the intellect on its own makes the effort to understand it, initially neither agreeing nor disagreeing but only comprehending. After all, the emphasis is on understanding these things.

Initially, you need simply understand them. If you do, then you create something with the insight the ego has gained that extends into the night. Then, during the night, you no longer remain dull as is the case with the merely intellectual attitude towards the world; then, from the time of falling asleep until waking up, you dwell in a different content in the delicately filtered spirituality. Then, you awaken and find that the possibility has been added—small though it is each time—of inwardly acquiring what you have struggled to understand intellectually. With each passing night, every time we sleep, something of an inner relationship is added, we acquire an inward connection. Each time, upon falling asleep, we bear the aftereffect of our daytime comprehension with us into the world beyond corporeality. In this way, we acquire a relationship to the spiritual world, a relationship acquired completely out of reality. This, however, is the case only if the human being does not ruin this relationship by means of something with which he so frequently ruins it today. I have mentioned these means for ruining spirituality quite often. As you know, many people are intent on acquiring a certain state of sleepiness prior to going to sleep; they consume as many glasses of beer as it takes to have the necessary degree of sleepiness. This is a quite common practice, especially among "intelligent" people. In that case, the faculties I just mentioned certainly cannot develop.

Spirituality can be researched, however, and this spirituality can indeed be experienced as well in the manner just described. The human being has grown away from spirituality. He is capable of growing into it again. Today, we are only at the beginning of this process of growing into spirituality. In the past few centuries, from the fifteenth century into the nineteenth century when the intellect had reached its highest level, a certain spirituality has developed, in particular among the most progressive people in Europe, albeit a spirituality that has as yet no content. For it is only when we turn to Imagination that this spirituality receives its first content. This spirituality, which is filtered to the extreme, must first receive its content.

At this point in time, this content is being rejected by the majority of the people. The world wishes to remain with the filtered spirituality; it wishes to produce a content derived from the outer material world. People do not wish to struggle with their intellect to comprehend the results of insight into the spiritual world offered. The confessions that follow the Gospel are, after all, compromises between the intellect and ancient traditions; they have lost the connecting link. Ritual means nothing to them. This is why the latter has gradually disappeared within these confessions. People arrived at abstract concepts instead of a living comprehension of, for example, the Transubstantiation. At most, the simple stories can be told, but no meaning other than the one that is compatible with a materialistic theology can be connected with them, namely, that one is dealing with occurrences that can be linked to the humble man from Nazareth, and so forth. All this can no longer lead to a content; it is something that loses all connection with spirituality.

Thus, the situation in the world today is such that there is, first of all a faith that has rejected the intellect and did not strike any compromise. Due to this, in vast segments of the population a relationship has been retained, albeit an instinctive one, to the doctrines and dogmas, the content of which is no longer accessible to human beings but did flow out into these dogmas. This segment of the populace also has retained its living relationship to the cult, to the ceremonial ritual; it has retained its link to the sacraments. As depleted as all this is, the ancient spirituality—the spirituality to which there is still a connection through dogmas—did once dwell in what has become a skeleton, a shadow. Among the more recent Protestant confessions, where a compromise is being tried out, such a connection is no longer alive. And then we have those who call themselves quite enlightened and dwell only in the intellect, which is spiritual but does not wish to grasp the spirit.

These are the three streams we confront. In regard to the future, we cannot count on the fruitfulness of those streams that only tried to make an external compromise; we cannot count on mere intellectuality that cannot arrive at any content and therefore can only lose itself since it does not want to understand itself. We can only count on the direction in which these streams are gradually heading, and they are more and more clearly heading there, namely, we can count on what has been poured into ancient doctrines and is represented in the surviving Roman-Catholic Church. We can count on the attitude that takes the new intellectuality seriously and deepens it Imaginatively, Inspiratively, and Intuitively, thus arriving at a new spirituality. The modern world is becoming divided and estranged in these two contrasting directions. On the one hand stand people with their intellect. They are inwardly lazy and do not wish to utilize this intellect, but they need a content. So they refer to the dead dogmas. Particularly among intelligent people, who are, however, mentally indolent, who are in a certain respect intellectual and Dadaistic, a neo-Catholic movement is making itself felt that is trying to take hold of the old traditions that have rigidified in dogmas and that is trying to receive a content from outside, through historical phenomena but that rigidifies in historical forms. Based on the intellect, this trend tries desperately to make some sense of the ancient content; thus we have intellectual battles that, by means of the old content, try to prepare their rigidified doctrines in a new way for the use of human beings.

To cite an example, on many pages in the newest edition of the magazine *Tat*,[7] we can observe an intellectual, cramped tendency towards rigidified doctrines. After all, the publisher, Diederichs, does everything; he puts everything into categories and on paper. Thus, he has now dedicated a whole edition of *Tat* to the neo-Catholic movement. It allows us to discern how cramped people's thoughts are today, how people are developing inwardly cramped thinking so that they can avoid having to rouse themselves and can remain mentally lazy in order to grasp with the intellect whatever moves forward most indolently.

People experiment with all this in order to be able to reject this life-filled striving out of modern intellectuality towards spirituality, a striving that can and must be grasped. More and more, things will come to a head in such a way that a powerful movement with a fascinating, suggestive, hypnotic effect on all those wishing to remain lazy within the intellect permeates the world. A Catholic wave is even pervading the world of intelligent people who wish, however, to remain lazy within their intelligence. The drowsy souls just do not realize it. But it must remain unfruitful to strive for what Oswald Spengler described so vividly in his *Decline of the West*.[8] One can turn the Occident Catholic, but one will thereby slay its civilization. This Occident has to concern itself with waking up, with becoming inwardly active. Its intelligence must not remain lazy, for this intelligence can rouse itself; it can fill itself inwardly with an understanding for the new view of the spirit.

This battle is in preparation; in fact, it is here—and it is the main point. In the future, everything else concerning world views will become crushed between these two streams. We must turn our attention to this, for what is coming to expression conceals itself in any number of formulas and forms. Nobody is living fully in the present who believes that he can make progress with something that people were perhaps still dreaming about at the beginning of this century. He alone lives fully in the present who develops an eye for what dwells in the two streams described above. We have to be aware of this. For everything I have discussed a week ago when I said that nowadays a great number of people love evil and, purely due to their tendency towards evil, indulge in slander in the way I described—all this is what must come before our souls. We must bear in mind that inner untruthfulness, which expresses itself in the facts—as I told you—that people, who are supposed to be strengthened in their Catholic faith, are sent to the Catholic church in Stuttgart to attend a lecture by General von Gleich, and that this Catholic general concludes with a hymn by Luther! There, the two tendencies come together that care nothing about the confessions but only try to stream together in the proliferation of lies.

These things must be noticed today. If this is not done, then one is asleep and does not participate in what alone can make the human being today truly human.

LECTURE X
Dornach, April 29, 1921

In recent days, we have dealt with the development of European civilization and we shall try to add a number of considerations to what has been said. In this, it is always our intention to bring about an understanding of what plays into human life in the present age from the most diverse directions and leads to comprehension of the tasks posed by our time.

When you look at individual human life, it can indeed give you a picture of mankind's development. Nevertheless, you must naturally take into consideration here what has been mentioned in regard to the differences between the development of the individual and the overall development of humanity. I have repeatedly called attention to the fact that whereas the individual gets older and older, mankind as a whole becomes younger and younger, advancing, as it were, to the experience of younger periods of life. While keeping in mind that in this regard the life of the whole human community and that of the individual are direct opposites, at least for the sake of clarification, we can still say that individual human life can be a picture for us of the life of all humanity. If we then view the single human life in this way, we find that a quite specific sum of experiences belongs with each period of life. We cannot teach a six-year-old child something we can teach a twelve-year-old; in turn, we cannot expect that the twelve-year-old approaches things with the same comprehension as a twenty-year-old. In a sense, the human being has to grow into what is compatible with individual periods in life. It is the same in the case of humanity as a whole.

True, the individual cultural epochs we have to point out based on insight into humanity's evolution—the old Indian, the old Persian, the Egypto-Chaldean, the Greco-Roman epoch and then the one to which we ourselves belong—have quite specific cultural contents and the whole of mankind has to grow into them. But just as the individual can fall behind his potential of development, so certain segments of mankind can do the same. This is a phenomenon that must be taken into consideration, particularly in our age, since humanity is now moving into the evolutionary state of freedom. It is, therefore, left up to mankind itself to find its way into what this and the following epoch put forward. It is, as it were, left up to human discretion to remain behind what is posed as goals. If an individual lags behind in this regard, he is confronted by others who do find their way properly into their tasks of evolution. They then have to carry him along, in a manner of speaking. Yet, in a certain sense, this can frequently signify a somewhat unpleasant destiny for such a person when he has to become aware that in a certain way he remains behind the others who do arrive at the goal of evolution.

This can also take place in the life of nations. It is possible that some nations achieve the goal and that others remain behind. As we have seen, the goals of the various nations also differ from each other. First of all, if one nation attains its goal and the other falls short of what it is supposed to accomplish, then something is lost that could only have been achieved by this laggard nation. On the other hand, this backsliding nation will adopt much that is really not suitable for it. It appropriates contents it receives by imitating other nations that do attain their goal. Such things do take place in the evolution of mankind, and it is of particular significance for the present age to pay attention to them.

Today, we shall summarize a number of things, familiar to us from other aspects, and throw light on them from a certain standpoint. We know that the time from the eighth pre-Christian century until the fifteenth century A.D. is the time of the development of the intellectual or rational soul among the civilized part of humanity. This development of the intellectual or rational soul begins in the eighth pre-Christian century in southern Europe and Asia Minor. We can trace it when we focus upon the beginnings of the historical development of the Greek people. The Greeks still possess much of what can be termed the development of the sentient soul that was particularly suited to the third post-Atlantean age, the Egypto-Chaldean epoch. That whole period was devoted to the development of the sentient soul.

During those times, human beings surrendered to the impressions of the external world, and through these impressions of the outer world they received at the same time everything they then valued as insights and that they let flow into the impulses of their will. With all their being people were in a condition where they experienced themselves as members of the whole cosmos. They questioned the stars and their movements when it was a matter of deciding what to do, and so on. This experiencing of the surrounding world, this seeing of the spiritual in all details of the outer world, was the distinguishing feature of the Egyptians at the height of their culture. This is what existed in Asia Minor and enjoyed a second flowering among the Greeks. The ancient Greeks certainly possessed this faculty of free surrender to the outer surroundings, and this was connected with a perception of the elemental spirit beings within the outer phenomena.

Then, however, something developed among the Greeks, which Greek philosophers call "nous," namely, a general world intellect. This then remained the fundamental quality of human soul developments until the fifteenth century. It attained a kind of high point in the fourth Christian century and then diminished again. But this whole development from the eighth pre-Christian century up until the fifteenth century actually developed the intellect. However, if we speak of "intellect" in this period, we really have to disregard what we term "intellect" in our present age. For us, the intellect is something we carry within ourselves, something we develop within ourselves, by virtue of which we comprehend the world. This was not so in the case of the Greeks, and it was still not so in the eleventh, twelfth, and thirteenth centuries, when people spoke about the intellect. Intellect was something objective; the intellect was an element that filled the world. The intellect arranged the individual world phenomena. People observed the world and its phenomena and told themselves: It is the universal intellect that makes one phenomenon follow the other, places the individual phenomena into into a greater totality, and so forth. People attributed to the human brain no more than the fact that it shared in this general universal intelligence.

When we work out of modern physics and physiology and speak about light, we say that the light is within us. But even in his naive mind nobody would believe that light is only in our heads. Just as little as today's naive consciousness claims that it is dark outside and light exists only in the human head would a Greek or even a person of the eleventh or twelfth century have said that the intellect was only in his head. Such a person said, The intellect is outside, permeating the world and bestowing order on everything. Just as the human being becomes aware of light owing to his perceptions, so he becomes aware of the intellect. The intellect lights up in him, so to speak.

Something important was connected with this emergence of cosmic intelligence within the human cultural development. Earlier, when the cultural development ran its course under the influence of the sentient soul, people did not refer to a uniform principle encompassing the whole world. They spoke of the spirits of plants, of spirits that regulate the animal kingdom, of water spirits and spirits of the air, and so on. People referred to a multitude of spiritual entities. It was not merely polytheism, the folk religion, that spoke of this multitude. Even in those who were initiates, the awareness was definitely present that they were dealing with a multitude of actual beings in the world outside. Due to the dawn of the rational soul age, a sort of monism developed. Reason was viewed as something uniform that enveloped the whole world. It was not until then that the monotheistic character of religion developed, although a preliminary stage of it existed in the third post-Atlantean epoch. But what we should record scientifically concerning this era—from the eighth pre-Christian to the fifteenth century A.D.—is the fact that it is the period of the developing world intellect and that people had quite different thoughts about the intellect than we have nowadays.

Why did people think so differently about the intellect? People *thought* differently about the intellect because they also *felt* differently when they tried to grasp something by means of their intellect. People went through the world and perceived objects through their senses; but when they thought about them, they always experienced a kind of jolt. When they thought about something, it was as if they were experiencing a stronger awakening than they sensed in the process of ordinary waking. Thinking about something was a process still experienced as different from ordinary life. Above all, when people thought about something, they felt that they were involved in a process that was objective, not merely subjective. Even as late as the fifteenth century—and in its aftereffect even in still later times— people had a certain feeling in regard to the more profound thinking about things, a feeling people today do not have anymore. Nowadays human beings do not have the feeling that thinking about something should be carried out in a certain mood of soul. Up until the fifteenth century, people had the feeling that they produced only something evil if they were not morally good and yet engaged in thinking. In a sense, they reproached themselves for thinking even though they were bad persons. This is something we no longer experience properly. Nowadays people believe, In my soul I can be as bad as I want to be, but I can engage in thinking. Up to the fifteenth century, people did not believe that. They actually felt that it was a kind of insult to the divine cosmic intelligence to think about something while in an immoral soul condition. Hence, already in the act of thinking, they saw something real; in a manner of speaking, they viewed themselves as submerged with their soul in the overall cosmic intellect.

What was the reason for that? This came about because in this period from the eighth pre-Christian century to the fifteenth century A.D., and particularly in the fourth century, human beings predominantly employed their etheric body when they engaged in thinking. It was not that they decided to activate the ether body. But what they did sense—their whole soul mood—brought the etheric body into movement when thinking occurred. We can almost say: During that age, human beings thought with their etheric body. And the characteristic thing is that in the fifteenth century people began to think with their physical bodies. When we think, we do so with the forces the etheric body sends into the physical body. This is the great difference that becomes evident when we look at thinking before and after the fifteenth century. When we look at thinking prior to that time, it runs its course in the etheric body (see drawing, light-shaded crosshatching); in a sense, it gives the etheric body a certain structure. If we look at thinking now, it runs its course in the physical body (dark). Each such line of the ether body calls forth a replica of itself, and this replica is then found in the physical body.

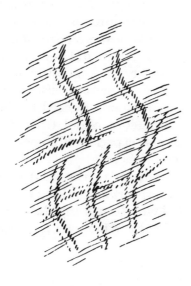

Since that time, what occurs in human beings when they think is, as it were, an impression of the etheric activity as though of a seal on the physical body. The development from the fifteenth to the nineteenth and twentieth centuries was mainly that human beings increasingly have taken their thinking out of the etheric body, that they adhere to this shadow image brought about in the physical body by the actual thought impulses originating in the etheric body. We therefore deal with the fact that in this fifth post-Atlantean epoch people really think with the physical body but that this is merely a shadow image of what was once cosmic thinking; hence, since that time, only a shadow image of cosmic thinking dwells in mankind.

You see, everything that has developed since the fifteenth century, all that developed as mathematics, as modern natural science and so on, is fundamentally a shadow image, a specter of former thinking; it no longer contains any life. People today actually have no idea of how much more alive an element thinking was in former times. In those ancient days, the human being actually felt refreshed while thinking. He was glad when he could think, for thinking was a refreshment of soul for him. In that age, the concept did not exist that thinking could also be something tiring. Human beings could become tired out by something else, but when they could truly think, they experienced this as a refreshment, an invigoration for the soul; when they could live in thoughts, they also experienced something of a sense of grace bestowed on them.

Now, this transition in the soul condition has occurred. In what appears as thinking in modern times, we are confronted with something shadowy. This is the reason for the difficulty in motivating a human being to any action through thinking—if I may put it like this. One can tell people all sorts of things based on thinking, but they will not feel inspired. Yet this is the very thing they must learn. Human beings must become aware of the fact that they possess shadow images in their current thinking. They have to realize that it must not be allowed to remain thus; that this shadow image, i.e. modern thinking, has to be enlivened so that it can turn into Imagination. It becomes evident, for example, in such books as my *Theosophy* or my *An Outline of Occult Science* that the attempt is always made to change modern thinking into Imagination, that pictures are driven everywhere into our thinking so that thinking can be aroused to Imagination, hence, to life. Otherwise, humanity would be laid waste completely. We can disseminate arid scholarliness far and wide, but this dry scholarliness will not become inflamed and rouse itself to will-filled action, if Imaginative life does not once more enter into this shadowy thinking, this ghost of thinking which has invaded mankind in recent times.

This is indeed the profound and fateful challenge for modern civilization, namely, that we should realize that, on the one hand, thinking tends to become a shadowy element into which human beings increasingly withdraw and that, on the other hand, what passes over into the will actually turns only into a form of surrender to human instincts. The less thinking is capable of taking in Imagination, the more will the full interest of what lives outside in society be abandoned to the instincts. Humanity of former times, at least in the epochs that bore the stamp of civilization—you have been able to deduce that from the previous lectures— possessed something, out of the whole human organism that was spiritual. Modern human beings only receive something spiritual from their heads; in regard to their will, they thus surrender to their impulses and instincts. The great danger is that human beings turn more and more into purely head-oriented creatures, that in regard to acting in the outer world out of their will, they abandon themselves to their instincts. This then naturally leads to the social conditions that are now spreading in the East of Europe* and also infect us here everywhere. This comes about because thinking has become but a shadow image. One cannot stress these things often enough.

It is on the basis of precisely such profound insight that the significant strivings of anthroposophically oriented spiritual science will be understood. Its aim is the shadow image once again become a living being, so that something will be available again to mankind that can take hold of the whole human being. This, however, cannot take place if thinking remains a shadow image, if Imaginations do not enter into this thinking once more. Numbers, for example, will have to be imbued again with life in the way I outlined when I pointed to the sevenfold human being, who is actually a nine-membered being, where the second and the third, the sixth and the seventh parts unite in such a way as to become in each case a unity, and where seven is arrived at when one sums up the nine parts. It is this inner involvement of what was once bestowed on man from within that must be striven for. We have to take very seriously what is characterized in this regard by anthroposophically oriented spiritual science.

From a different direction, an awareness came about of the fact that thinking is becoming shadow like; for

*Translator's note: This is a reference to what was happening in Russia.

that reason, a method was created in Jesuitism that from a certain aspect, brings life into this thinking. The Jesuit exercises are designed to bring life into this thinking. But they accomplish this by renewing an ancient form of life, above all, not by moving in the direction of and working through Imagination, but through the will, which particularly in Jesuit exercises plays an important role. We should realize—yet realize it far too little—how in a community such as the Jesuit order all aspects of the life of soul become something radically different from what is true of ordinary people. Basically, all other human beings of the present possess a different condition of soul than those who become Jesuits. The Jesuits work out of a world will; that cannot be denied. Consequently, they are aware of certain existing interrelationships; at most, such interrelationships are noticed also by some other orders that in turn are fought tooth and nail by the Jesuits. But it is this significant element whereby reality enters into the shadowy thinking that turns a Jesuit into a different kind of person from the others in our modern civilization. These think merely in shadow images and therefore are actually asleep mentally, since thinking no longer takes hold of their organism and does not really permeate their nervous system.

Nobody, I believe, has ever seen a gifted Jesuit who is nervous, whereas those imbued with modern scholarliness and education increasingly suffer from nervousness. When do we become nervous? When the physical nerves make themselves felt. Something then makes itself felt that, from a physical standpoint, has no right at all to make itself felt, for it exists merely to transmit the spiritual. These matters are intimately connected with the wrongness of our modern education. And from a certain standpoint of imbuing thinking with life—a standpoint we must nevertheless definitely oppose—Jesuitism is something that goes along with the world, even though, like a crab, it goes backwards. But at least it moves, it does not stand still, whereas the form of science in vogue today basically does not comprehend the human being at all.

Here, I would like to draw your attention to something. I have already mentioned repeatedly that it is actually painful to witness again and again that modern human beings, who can think all sorts of things and are so very clever, do not stand in a living manner with a single fiber of their lives in the present age, that they do not see what is going on around them, indeed, that they are unaware of what is happening around them and do not wish to participate in it. That is different in the case of the Jesuit. The Jesuit who activates his whole being is well aware of what vibrates through the world today. As evidence, I would like to read to you a few lines from a current Jesuit pamphlet from which you can deduce what sort of life pulsates in it:

> For all those who are serious about the fundamental Christian principles, those to whom the welfare of the people is truly a concern of the heart, whose soul was once profoundly touched by the words of the Savior, *"Miseror super turbam,"** for all those the time has now come when, borne by the ground swell of the Bolshevist storm tide, they can work with much greater success for the people and with the people. There is no room for timidity. Hence, as a matter of policy, we advocate the all out struggle against "capitalism, " against the exploitation of the people and profiteering at their expense,

---

*Translator's note: Latin for "I have compassion on the crowd" (Mathew 16:32).

stricter emphasis on the duty to work even for the higher classes, the procurement of decent housing for millions of fellow citizens, even if such procurement necessitates making use of palaces and larger houses, utilization of natural resources and energy gained from water and air for the general welfare, not for trusts and syndicates, enhancement and education of the masses of people, participation by all segments of the people in government and administration, utilization of the concept of the system of soviets for the purpose of developing class representation having equal rights alongside parliamentary mass representation in order to prevent "the isolation of the masses from the state apparatus" as censured justifiably by Lenin... God has given the goods of the earth to all human beings, not to a few so they can live on the fat of the land while millions languish in poverty, which is degrading both physically and morally...[1]

You see, this is the fiery mind that does sense something of what is happening. Here is a person who, in the rest of his book, sternly opposes Bolshevism and naturally wishes to have nothing to do with it. But, unlike somebody who has made himself comfortable in a chair today and is oblivious to the conflagration in the world all around him, he does not remain in such a position. Instead, he is aware of what is happening and knows what he wants because he sees what is going on.

People have gone so far as to merely think about the affairs of the world, and otherwise let things run their course. This is what has to be stressed again and again, namely, that the human being has more in him than mere thoughts with which to think about things while really not paying attention to the world's essential nature. As an example we need only indicate the Theosophical Society. It points to the great initiates who exist somewhere, and indeed, it can do so with justification. But it is not a matter of the initiates' existence; what is important is the manner in which those who refer to them speak of them. Theosophists imagine that the great initiates rule the world; in turn, they themselves sit down and produce good thoughts, which they let stream out in all directions. Then they talk of world rule, of world epochs, of world impulses. However, when the point is reached where something real, such as anthroposophy, has to live within the actual course of world events because it could not be otherwise, people find that uncomfortable since then they cannot really remain sitting on their chairs but have to experience what goes on in the world.

It must be strongly emphasized that the intellect has turned into a shadow in humanity, that it was earlier experienced in the etheric body and has now slipped, so to speak, into the physical body where it leads only a subjective existence. However, it can be brought to life through Imagination. Then it leads to the consciousness soul, and this consciousness soul can be grasped as a reality only when it senses the ego descends out of soul-spiritual worlds into incarnation and then passes through the gate of death into soul-spiritual worlds. When this inner soul-spiritual nature of the ego is comprehended, then the shadow image of the intellect can in fact be filled with reality. For it is through the ego that this has to be accomplished.

It is necessary to realize that living thinking exists. For what is it that people know since the fifteenth century? They know only logical thinking, not living thinking. This, too, I have pointed out repeatedly. What is living thinking? I shall take an example close at hand. In 1892, I wrote the *Philosophy of Freedom*. This book has a certain content. In 1903, I wrote *Theosophy*; again, it has a certain content. In *Theosophy*, mention is made of the etheric body, the astral body, and so on. In *Philosophy of Freedom*, there is no mention of that. Now those who are only familiar with the logical, dead thinking come and say, Yes, I read the *Philosophy of Freedom*; from it, I cannot extract any concept of the etheric and astral body; it is impossible; I cannot find these concepts from the concepts contained in the book. But this is the same as if I were to take a small, five-year-old boy and fashioned him into a man of sixty by pulling him upwards and sideways to make him taller and wider!

I cannot put a mechanical, lifeless process in place of something living. But picture the *Philosophy of Freedom* as something alive—which indeed it is—and then imagine it growing. From it, then develops what only a person who tries to cull or pick out something from concepts will not figure out. All objections concerning contradictions are based on just this, namely, that people cannot understand the nature of living thinking as opposed to the dead thinking that dominates the whole world and all of civilization today. In the world of living things, everything develops from within, A formerly black-haired person who has white hair has acquired the latter not because the hair has been painted white; it has turned white from within. Things that grow and wane develop from within, and so it is also in the case of living thinking. Yet, today, people sit down and merely try to form conclusions, try to sense outward logic. What is logic? Logic is the anatomy of thinking, and one studies anatomy by means of corpses. Logic is acquired through the study of the corpse of thinking. It is certainly justified to study anatomy by means of corpses. It is just as justified to study logic through the corpses of thinking. But one will never comprehend life by means of what has been observed on the corpse!

This is what is important today and what really matters if we wish with all our soul to take part in a living way in what actually permeates and weaves through the world. This side of the matter has to be pointed out again and again, because insofar as the positive world development and evolution of mankind are concerned, we need to invigorate a thinking that has become shadowy. This process of thinking becoming shadow-like reached its culmination in the middle of the nineteenth century. For that reason, the things that, so to say, beguiled humanity most of them fall into that period. Although in themselves these things were not great, if placed in the right location, they appear great.

Take the end of the 1850's. Darwin's *Origin of the Species*,[2] Karl Marx's *The Principles of Political Economy*,[3] as well as *Psycho-Physics* by Gustav Theodor Fechner,[4] a work in which the attempt is made to discover the psychic sphere by means of outward experiments, were published then. In the same year, the captivating discovery of spectral analysis by Kirchhoff[5] and Bunsen[6] is introduced; it demonstrates, as it were, that wherever one looks in the universe the same materiality is discovered. It is as if everything were being done in the middle of the nineteenth century to beguile human beings into believing that thinking must remain subjective and shadow-like, that it must not interfere in the world outside so that they could not possibly imagine that there might be reason, nous, in the cosmos, something that lives in the cosmos itself.

This is what caused this second half of the nineteenth century to be so unphilosophical. Basically, this is also what made it so devoid of deeds. This is what caused the economic relationships to become more and more complicated while commerce became enlarged into a world economy so that the whole earth in fact turned into *one* economic sphere, and particularly this shadow-like thinking was unable to grasp the increasingly complex and overwhelming reality. This is the tragedy of our modern age. The economic conditions have become more and more complex, weighty, and increasingly brutal; human thinking remained shadowy, and these shadows certainly could no longer penetrate into what goes on outside in the brutal economic reality.

This is what causes our present misery. Unfortunately, if a person actually believes that he is more delicately organized and has need of the spirit, he may possibly get into the habit of making a long face, of speaking in a falsetto voice and of talking about the fact that he has to elevate himself from brutal reality, since the spiritual basically can be grasped only in the mystical realm. Thinking has become so refined that it has to withdraw from reality, that it perishes right away in its shadowy existence if it tries to penetrate brutal reality. Reality in the meantime develops below in conformity with the instincts; it proliferates and brutalizes. Up above, we see the bloated ideas of mysticism, of world views and theosophies floating about; below, life brutally takes its course. This is something that must stop for the sake of mankind. Thinking must be enlivened; thought has to become so powerful that it need not withdraw from brutal reality but can enter into it, can live in it as spirit. Then reality will no longer be brutal. This has to be understood.

What is not yet understood in many different respects is that a thinking in which universal being dwells cannot but pour its force over everything. This should be something that goes without saying. But it appears as a sacrilege to this modern thinking if a form of thinking appears on the scene that cannot help but extend to all different areas. A properly serious attitude in life should be comprised of the realization: In thinking, we have been dealing with a shadow image, and rightly so, but the age has now arrived when life must be brought once again into this shadow image of thought in order that from this form of thought life, from this inner life of soul, the outer physical, sensory life can receive its social stimulus.

Tomorrow, we shall continue with this.

In the course of these lectures we have seen that the middle of the nineteenth century is an important time in the development of Western humanity. Attention was called to the fact that in a sense the culmination of the materialistic way of thinking and the materialistic world view occurred during this time. Yet it also had to be pointed out that this trend that has emerged in the human being since the fifteenth century was really something spiritual. Thus, it can be said that the characteristic of this developmental phase of recent human evolution was that simultaneously with becoming the most spiritual, the human being could not take hold of this spirituality. Instead, human beings filled themselves only with materialistic thinking, feeling, and even with materialistic will and activity. Our present age is still dominated by the aftereffects of what occurred in so many people without their being aware of it, and then reached its climax in mankind's development. What was the purpose of this climax? It occurred because something decisive was meant to take place in regard to contemporary humanity's attainment of the consciousness soul stage.

In focusing on the evolution of humanity from the third post-Atlantean epoch until approximately the year 747 (see sketch) before the Mystery of Golgotha, we find that a process runs its course that can be called the development of the sentient soul in humanity. Then the age of the rational or mind soul begins and lasts roughly

191

until the year 1413. It reaches its high point in that era of which external history has little to report. It must be taken into consideration, however, if European development is to be comprehended at all. This culmination point occurs approximately in the year 333 after Christ. Since the year 1413, we are faced with the development of the consciousness soul, a development we are still involved in and that saw a decisive event around the year 1850, or better, 1840.

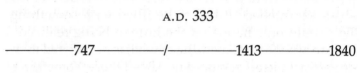

A.D. 333

————————747————————/————————1413————————1840

Sentient Soul   Rational Soul Consciousness Soul

For mankind as a whole, matters had reached a point around 1840 where, insofar as the representative personalities of the various nations are concerned, we can say that they were faced with an intellect that had already assumed its most shadowy form. (Following this, we shall have to consider the reaction of the individual nations.) The intellect had assumed its shadowlike character. I tried yesterday to characterize this shadow nature of the intellect. People in the civilized world had evolved to the extent that, from then on it was possible on the basis of the general culture and without initiation to acquire the feeling: We possess intellect. The intellect has matured, but insofar as its own nature is concerned, it no longer has a content. We have concepts but these concepts are empty. We must fill them with something.

This, in a sense, is the call passing through humanity, though dimly and inaudibly. But in the deep, underlying, subconscious longings of human beings lives the call, the wish to receive a content, substance, for the shadow nature of rational thinking. Indeed, it is the call for spiritual science.

This call can also be comprehended concretely. In the middle of the nineteenth century, the human organization, in the physical part of which this shadowy intellect is trained, had simply progressed to the point where it could cultivate this empty shadowy intellect particularly well. Now, something was required for this shadowy intellect; it had to be filled with something. This could only happen if the human being realized: I have to assimilate something of what is not offered to me on the earth itself and does not dwell there, something I cannot learn about in the life between birth and death. I actually have to absorb something into my intellect that, although it was extinguished and became obscured when I descended with the results of my former earth lives out of spiritual soul worlds into a physical corpo-reality, nevertheless rests in the depths of my soul. From there, I have to bring it up once again, I have to call to mind something that rests within me simply by vir-tue of the fact that I am a human being of the nineteenth century.

Earlier, it would not have been possible for human beings to have practiced self-awareness in the same manner. This is why they first had to advance in their human condition to the point where the physical body increasingly acquired the maturity to perfect and utilize the shadowy intellect completely. Now, at least among the most advanced human beings, the physical bodies had reached the point where one could have said, or rather, since then it is possible to say: I wish to call to mind what it is that I am seeking to bring up from the depths of my soul life in order to pour a content into this shadowy intellect. This shadowy intellect would have been filled with something and in this way the consciousness soul age would have dawned. Therefore, at this point in time, the occasion arose where the consciousness soul could have unfolded.

Now you will say: Yes, but the whole era prior to that, beginning with the year 1413, was the age of the consciousness soul. Yes, certainly, but at first it has been a preparatory development. You need only consider what basic conditions existed for such a preparation particularly in this period as compared to all earlier times. Into this period falls, for example, the invention of the printing press; the dissemination of the written word. Since the fifteenth century, people by and by have received a great amount of spiritual content by means of the art of printing and through writing. But they absorb this content only outwardly; it is the main feature of this period that an overwhelming sum of spiritual content has been assimilated superficially. The nations of the civilized world have absorbed something outwardly which the great masses of people could receive only by means of audible speech in earlier times. It was true of the period of rational development, and in the age of the sentient soul it was all the more true that, fundamentally speaking, all dissemination of learning was based on oral teaching. Something of the psycho-spiritual element still resounds through speech. Especially in former days, what could be termed "the genius of language" definitely still lived in words. This ceased to be when the content of human learning began to be assimilated in abstract forms, through writing and printed works. Printed and written words have the peculiarity of in a sense extinguishing what the human being brings with him at birth from his pre-earthly, heavenly existence.

It goes without saying that this does not mean that you should forthwith cease to read or write. It does mean that today a more powerful force is needed in order to raise up what lies deep within the human being. But it is necessary that this stronger force be acquired. We have to arrive at self-awareness despite the fact that we read and write; we have to develop this stronger faculty, stronger in comparison to what was needed in earlier times. This is the task in the age of the development of the consciousness soul.

Before taking a look at how the influences of the spiritual world have now started to flow down in a certain way into the physical, sensory world, let us pose the question today, How did the nations of modern civilization actually meet this point of time in 1840?

From earlier lectures we know that the representative people for the development of the consciousness soul, hence for what matters particularly in our age, is the Anglo-Saxon nation. The Anglo-Saxon people are those who through their whole organization are predisposed to develop the consciousness soul to a special degree. The prominent position occupied by the Anglo-Saxon nation in our time is indeed due to the fact that this nation is especially suited for the development of the consciousness soul. But now let us ask ourselves from a purely external viewpoint, How did this Anglo-Saxon nation arrive at this point in time that is the most significant one in modern cultural development?

It can be said that the Anglo-Saxon nation in particular has survived for a long time in a condition—naturally with the corresponding variations and metamorphoses—that could perhaps be described best by saying, Those inner impulses, which had already made way for other forms in Greek culture, were preserved in regard to the inner soul condition of the Anglo-Saxon people. The strange thing in the eleventh and tenth centuries B.C. is that the nations experienced what is undergone at different periods, that the various ages move, as it were, one on top of the other. The problem is that such matters are extraordinarily difficult to notice because in the nineteenth century all sorts of things already existed—reading, writing—and because the living conditions prevailing in Scotland and England were different from those in Homeric times.

And yet, if the soul condition of the people as a nation is taken into consideration, the fact is that this soul condition of the Homeric era, which in Greece was outgrown in the tragic age and changed into Sophoclism, has remained. This age, a kind of patriarchal conception of life and existence, was preserved in the Anglo-Saxon world up until the nineteenth century. In particular, this patriarchal life spread out from the soul condition in Scotland. This is the reason why the influence proceeding from the initiation centers in Ireland did not have an effect on the Anglo-Saxon nation. As was mentioned on other occasions, that influence predominantly affected continental Europe. On the British isle itself, the predominant influence originated from initiation truths that came down from the north, from Scotland. These initiation truths then permeated everything else. But there is an element in the whole conception of the human personality that, in a sense, has remained from primordial times. This still has aftereffects; it lingers on even in the way, say, the relationship between Whigs and Tories develops in the British Parliament. The fact is that fundamentally we are not dealing with the difference between liberal and conservative views. Instead, we have to do with two political persuasions for which people today really have no longer any perception at all.

Essentially, the Whigs are the continuation of what could be called a segment of mankind imbued with a general love of humanity and originating in Scotland. According to a fable, which does have a certain historical background, the Tories were originally Catholicizing horse thieves from Ireland. This contrast, which then expressed itself in their particular political strivings, reflects a certain patriarchal existence. This patriarchal existence retained certain primitive forces, which can be observed in the kind of attitude exhibited by the owners of large properties toward those people who had settled on these lands as their vassals.

This relationship of subservience actually lasted until the nineteenth century; nobody was elected to Parliament who did not possess a certain power by virtue of being a landowner. We only have to consider what this implies. Such matters are not weighed in the right manner. Just think what it signifies, for example, that it was not until the year 1820 that English Parliament repealed the law according to which a person was given the death penalty for having stolen a pocket watch or having been a poacher. Until then, the law decreed that such misdeeds were capital offenses. This certainly demonstrates the way in which particular, ancient, and elementary conditions had remained. Today, people observe life in their immediate surroundings and then extend the fundamental aspects of present-day civilization backwards, so to speak. In regard to the most important regions of Europe, they are unaware of how recently these things have developed from quite primitive conditions.

Thus, it is possible to say that these patriarchal conditions survived as the foundation and basis of a society that was subsequently infused with the most modern impulse, unimaginable in the social structure without the development of the consciousness soul. Just consider all the changes in the social structure of the eighteenth century due to the technological metamorphosis in the textile industry and the like. Note how the mechanical, technological element moved into this patriarchal element. Try to form a clear idea of how, owing to the transformation of the textile industry, the nascent modern Proletariat pushes into the social structure that is based on this patriarchal element, this relationship of landowner to subjects. Just think of this chaotic intermingling, think how the cities develop in the ancient countryside and how the patriarchal attitude takes a daring plunge, so to say, into modern, socialistic, proletarian life.

To picture it graphically, we can actually say that this form of life develops in the way it existed in Greece approximately until the year 1000B.C. (see drawing). Then it makes a daring jump and we suddenly find ourselves in the year A.D. 1820. Inwardly, the life of the year 1000B.C has been retained, but outwardly, we are in the eighteenth century, say 1770 (see arrows). Now everything that then existed in modern life, indeed, even in our present time, pours in. But it is not until 1820 that this English life makes the connection, finds it necessary to do so (see drawing); it is not until then that these matters even became issues, such as the abolition of the death penalty for a minor theft. Thus we can say that, here, something very old has definitely flown together with the most modern element. Thus, the further development then continues on to the year 1840.

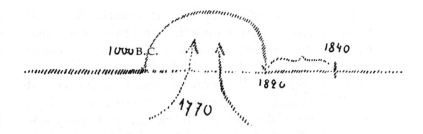

1000 B.C.   1840

1820

1770

Now, what had to occur specifically among the Anglo-American people during this time period, the first half of the nineteenth century? We have to recall that only after the year 1820, actually not until after 1830, it became necessary to pass laws in England according to which children under twelve years of age were not allowed to be kept working in factories for more than eight hours a day, no more than twelve hours a day in the case of children between thirteen and eighteen years of age. Please, compare that with today's conditions! Just think what the broad masses of working people demand today as the eight-hour day! As yet, in the year 1820, boys were put to work in mines and factories in England for more than eight hours; only in that year was the eight-hour day established for them. The twelve-hour day still prevailed, however, in regard to children between twelve and eighteen.

These things must certainly be considered in the attempt to figure out the nature of the elements colliding with each other at that time. Basically, it could be said that England eased its way out of the patriarchal conditions only in the second third of the nineteenth century and found it necessary to reckon with what had slowly invaded the old established traditions due to technology and the machine. It was in this way that this nation, which is preeminently called upon to develop the consciousness soul, confronted the year 1840.

Now take other nations of modern civilization. Take what has remained of the Latin-Roman element; take what has carried over the Latin-Roman element from the fourth post-Atlantean cultural period, what has brought over the ancient culture of the intellectual soul as a kind of legacy into the epoch of the consciousness soul. Indeed, what had remained of this life of the intellectual soul reached its highest point, its culmination, in the French Revolution at the end of the eighteenth century. We note that the ideals, *freedom, equality*, and *brotherhood* appear all at once in the most extreme abstraction. We see them taken up by skeptics such as Voltaire[1], by enthusiasts such as Rousseau;[2] we see them emerge generally in the broad masses of the people. We see how the abstraction, which is fully justified in this sphere, affects the social structure

It is a completely different course of events from the one over in England. In England, the vestiges of the old Germanic patriarchal life are permeated by what the element of modern technology and modern materialistic, scientific life could incorporate into the social structure. In France, we have tradition everywhere. We could say that the French Revolution has been enacted in the same manner in which a Brutus or a Caesar once acted in the most diverse ways in ancient Rome. Thus, here also, freedom, equality and brotherhood surfaced in abstract forms. Unlike in England, the old existing patriarchal element was not destroyed from the outside. Instead, the Roman juridical tradition, the adherence to the ancient concept of property and ownership of land, inheritance laws, and so on, what had been established in the Roman-juristic tradition was corroded by abstraction, driven asunder by abstraction.

We need only consider the tremendous change the French Revolution brought to all of European life. We only need remind ourselves that prior to the French Revolution those who, in a sense, distinguished themselves from the masses of the nation also had legal privileges. Only certain people could aspire to particular positions in government. What the French Revolution demanded based on abstraction and the shadowlike intellect was to make breaches into that system to undermine it. But it did bear the stamp of the shadowy intellect, the abstraction. Therefore, the demands that were being made fundamentally remained a kind of ideology. For this reason, we can say that anything that is of the shadowy intellect immediately turns into its opposite.

Then we observe Napoleonism; we watch the experimentation in the public and social realm during the course of the nineteenth century. The first half of the nineteenth century was certainly experimentation without a goal in France. What is the nature of the events through which somebody like Louis-Philippe, for example, becomes king of France, and so on—what sort of experimenting is carried out? It is done in such a way that one can recognize that the shadowy intellect is incapable of truly intervening in the actual conditions. Everything basically remains undone and incomplete; it all remains as legacy of ancient Romanism. We are justified in saying that even today the relationship to say, the Catholic Church, which the French Revolution had quite clearly defined in abstraction, has not been clarified in France in external, concrete reality. And how unclear was it time and again in the course of the nineteenth century! Abstract reasoning had struggled up to a certain level during the Revolution; then came experimentation and the inability to cope with external conditions. In this way, this nation encountered the year 1840.

We can also consider other nations. Let us look at Italy, for instance, which, in a manner of speaking, still retained a bit of the sentient soul in its passage through the culture of the intellect. It brought this bit of the sentient soul into modern times and therefore did not advance as far as the abstract concepts of freedom, equality, and brotherhood attained in the French Revolution. It did, however, seek the transition from a certain ancient group consciousness to individual consciousness in the human being. Italy faced the year 1840 in a manner that allows us to say, The individual human consciousness trying to struggle to the fore in Italy was in fact constantly held down by what the rest of Europe now represented. We can observe how the tyranny of Habsburg weighed terribly on the individual human consciousness that tried to develop in Italy. We see in the 1820's the strange Congress of Verona[3] that tried to determine how one could rise up against the whole substance of modern civilization. We note that there proceeded from Russia and Austria a sort of conspiracy against what the modern consciousness in humanity was meant to bring. There is hardly anything as interesting as the Congress of Verona, which basically wished to answer the question: How does one go about exterminating everything that is trying to emerge as modern consciousness in mankind?

Then we see how the people in the rest of Europe struggled in certain ways. Particularly in Central Europe, only a small percentage of the population was able to attain to a certain consciousness, experiencing in a certain manner that the ego is now supposed to enter into the consciousness soul. We notice attempts to achieve this at a certain high mental level. We can see it in the peculiar high cultural level of Goethe's age in which a man like Fichte was active;[4] we see how the ego tried to push forward into the consciousness soul. Yet we also realize that the whole era of Goethe actually was something that lived only in few individuals. I believe people study far too little what even the most recent past was like. They simply think, for example the Goethe lived from 1749 until 1832; he wrote *Faust* and a number of other works. That is what is known of Goethe and that knowledge has existed ever since.

Until the year 1862, until thirty years after Goethe's death, with few exceptions, it was impossible for people to acquire a copy of Goethe's works. They were restricted; only a handful of people somehow owned a copy of his writings. Hence, Goetheanism had become familiar only to a select few. It was not until the 1860's that a larger number of people could even find out about the particular element that lived in Goethe. By that time, the faculty of comprehension for it had disappeared again. An actual understanding of Goethe never really came about, and the last third of the nineteenth century was not suited at all for such comprehension.

I have often mentioned that in the 1870's Hermann Grimm gave his "Lectures on Goethe" at the University of Berlin.[5] That was a special event and the book that exists as Hermann Grimm's *Goethe* is a significant publication in the context of central European literature. Yet, if you now take a look at this book, what is its substance? Well, all the figures who had any connection with Goethe are listed in it but they are like shadow images having only two dimensions. All these portrayals are shadow figures, even Goethe is a two-dimensional being in Hermann Grimm's depiction. It is not

Goethe himself. I won't even mention the Goethe whom people at the afternoon coffee parties of Weimar called "the fat Privy Councillor with the double chin." In Hermann Grimm's *Goethe*, Goethe has no weight at all. He is merely a two-dimensional being, a shadow cast on the wall. It is the same with all the others who appear in the book; Herder—a shadow painted on a wall. We encounter something a little more tangible in Hermann Grimm's description of those persons coming from among the ordinary people who are close to Goethe, for example, Friederike von Sesenheim who is portrayed there so beautifully, or Lilli Schoenemann from Frankfurt—hence those who emerge from a mental atmosphere other than the one in which Goethe lived. Those are described with a certain "substance." But figures like Jacobi and Lavater are but shadow images on a wall. The reader does not penetrate into the actual substance of things; here, we can observe in an almost tangible way the effects of abstraction. Such abstraction can certainly be charming, as is definitely the case with Hermann Grimm's book, but the whole thing is shadowy. Silhouettes, two-dimensional beings, confront us in it.

Indeed, it could not be otherwise. For it is a fact that a German could not call himself a German in Germany at the time when Hermann Grimm, for example was young. The way one spoke of Germans during the first half of the nineteenth century is misunderstood, particularly at present. How "creepy" it seems to people in the West, those of the Entente, when they start reading Fichte's *Addresses to the German Nation* today and find him saying: "I speak simply to Germans, to Germans as such." In the same way, the harmless song "Germany, Germany above all else"* is interpreted foolishly, for

---

*Translator's note: "Deutschland, Deutschland über alles," the German national anthem.

this song means nothing more than the desire to be a German, not a Swabian, a Bavarian, an Austrian, a Franconian, or Thuringian. Just as this song referred only to Germans as such, so Fichte wished simply to address himself to Germans, not to Austrians, Bavarians, those from the province of Baden, Wuerttemberg, Franconia, or Prussia; he wanted to speak "to Germans." This is naturally impossible to understand, for instance, in a country where it has long since become a matter of course to call oneself a Frenchman. However, in certain periods in Germany, you were imprisoned if you called yourself German. You could call yourself an Austrian, a Swabian, a Bavarian, but it amounted to high treason to call yourself a German. Those who called themselves Germans in Bavaria expressed the sentiment that they did not wish to look up merely to the Bavarian throne and its reign within Bavaria's clearly defined borders, but implied that they also wished to look beyond the borders of Bavaria. But that was high treason! People were not permitted to call themselves Germans.

It is not understood at all today that these things that are said about Germans and Germany, refer to this unification of everything German. Instead, the absurd nonsense is spread that, for example, Hoffmann's song refers to the notion that Germany should rule over all the nations of the world although it means nothing else but: Not Swabia, not Austria, not Bavaria above all else in the world, but Germany above all else in the world, just as the Frenchman says: France above all else in the world. It was, however, the peculiar nature of Central Europe that basically a tribal civilization existed there. Even today, you can see this tribal culture everywhere in Germany. A Wuerttembergian is different from a Franconian. He differs from him even in the formulation of concepts and words, indeed, even in the thought forms disseminated in literature. There really is a marked difference, if you compare, say, a Franconian, such as cloddy Michael Conrad—using modern literature as an example—with something that has been written at the same time by a Wuerttembergian, hence in the neighboring province.

Something like this plays into the whole configuration of thoughts right into the present time. But everything that persists in this way and lives in the tribal peculiarities remains untouched by what is now achieved by the representatives of the nations. After all, in the realm commonly called Germany something has been attained such as Goetheanism with all that belongs to it. But it has been attained by only a few intellectuals; the great masses of people remain untouched by it. The majority of the population has more or less maintained the level of central Europe around the year A.D. 300 or 400. Just as the Anglo-Saxon people have stayed on the level of around the year 1000 B.C., people in Central Europe have remained on the level of the year A.D. 400. Please do not take this in the sense that a terrible arrogance might arise with the thought that the Anglo-Saxons have remained behind in the Homeric age, and we were already in the year A.D. 400. This is not the way to evaluate these matters. I am only indicating certain peculiarities.

In turn, the geographic conditions reveal that this level of general soul development in Germany lasted much longer than in England. England's old patriarchal life had to be permeated quickly with what formed the social structure out of the modern materialistic, scientific, and technological life first in the area of the textile industry, and later also in the area of other technologies.

The German realm and Central Europe in general opposed this development initially, retaining the ancient peculiarities much longer. I might say, they retained them until a point in time when the results of modern technology already prevailed fully all over the world. To a certain extent, England caught up in the transformation of the social structure in the first half of the nineteenth century. Everything that was achieved there definitely bypassed central Europe.

Now, Central Europe did absorb something of abstract revolutionary ideas. They came to expression through various movements and stirrings in the 1840's in the middle of the nineteenth century. But this region sat back and waited, as it were, until technology had infused the whole world. Then, a strange thing happened. An individual—we could also take other representatives—who in Germany had acquired his thinking from Hegelianism, namely, Karl Marx, went over to England, studied the social structure there and then formulated his socialist doctrines. At the end of the nineteenth century, Central Europe was then ready for these social doctrines, and they were accepted there. Thus, if we tried to outline in a similar manner what developed in this region, we would have to say: The development progressed in a more elementary way even though a great variety of ideas were absorbed from outside through books and printed matter.

The conditions of A.D. 400 in central Europe continued on, then made a jump and basically found the connection only in the last third of the nineteenth century, around the year 1875. Whereas the Anglo-Saxon nation met already the year 1840 with a transformation of conditions, with the necessity of receiving the consciousness soul, the German people continued to dream. They still experienced the year 1840 as though in a dream. Then they slept through the grace period when a bridge could have been built between leading personalities and what arose out of the masses of the people in the form of the proletariat. The latter then took hold of the socialist doctrine and thereby, beginning about the year 1875, exerted forcible, radical pressure in the direction of the consciousness soul. Yet even this was in fact not noticed; in any case it was not channeled in any direction, and even today it is basically still evaluated in the most distorted way.

In order to arrive at the anomalies at the bottom of this, we need only call to mind that Oswald Spengler, who wrote the significant book *The Decline of the West*, also wrote a booklet concerning socialism of which, I believe, 60,000 copies or perhaps more have been printed. Roughly, it is Spengler's view that this European, this Western civilization, is digging its own grave. According to Spengler, by the year 2200, we will be living on the level of barbarism. We have to agree with Spengler concerning certain aspects of his observations; for if the European world maintains the course of development it is pursuing now, then everything will be barbarized by the time the third millennium arrives. In this respect Spengler is absolutely correct. The only thing Spengler does not see and does not want to see is that the shadowy intellect can be raised to Imaginations out of man's inner being and that hence the whole of Western humanity can be elevated to a new civilization.

This enlivening of culture through the intentions of anthroposophical spiritual science is something a person like Oswald Spengler does not see. Rather, he believes that socialism—the real socialism, as he thinks, a socialism that truly brings about social living—has to come into being prior to this decline. The people of the Occident, according to him, have the mission of realizing socialism. But, says Oswald Spengler, the only people called upon to realize socialism are the Prussians. This is why he wrote the booklet *Prussianism and Socialism*. Any other form of socialism is wrong, according to Spengler. Only the form that revealed its first rosy dawn in the Wilhelminian age, only this form of socialism is to capture the world. Then the world will experience true, proper socialism.

Thus speaks a person today whom I must count among the most brilliant people of our time. The point is not to judge people by the content of what they say but by their mental capacities. This Oswald Spengler, who is master of fifteen different scientific disciplines, is naturally "more intelligent than all the writers, doctors, teachers, and ministers" and so on. We can truly say that with his book about the decline of the West he has presented something that deserves consideration, and that, by the way, is making a most profound impression on the young people in Central Europe. But next to it stands this other idea that I have referred to above, and you see precisely how the most brilliant people can arrive today at the strangest notions. People take hold of the intellect prevalent today and this intellect is shadowy. The shadows flit to and fro, one is caught up in one shadow, then one tries to catch up with another—nothing is alive. After all, in a silhouette, in a woman's shadow image cast on the wall, her beauty is not at all recognizable. So it is also with all other matters when they are viewed as shadow images. The shadow image of Prussianism can certainly be confused with socialism. If a woman turns her back to the wall and her shadow falls on it, even the ugliest woman might be considered beautiful. Likewise, Prussianism can be mistaken for socialism if the shadowlike intellect inwardly pervades the mind of a genius.

This is how we must look at things today. We must not look at the contents, we must aim for the capacities; that is what counts. Thus, it has to be acknowledged that Spengler is a brilliant human being, even though a great number of his ideas have to be considered nonsense. We live in an age when original, elementary judgments and reasons must surface. For it is out of certain elementary depths that one has to arrive at a comprehension of the present age and thus at impulses for the realities of the future.

Naturally, the European East has completely slept through the results of the year 1840. Just think of the handful of intellectuals as opposed to the great masses of the Russian people who, because of the Orthodox religion, particularly the Orthodox ritual, are still deeply immersed in Orientalism. Then think of the somnolent effect of men like Alexander I, Nicholas I, and all the other "I's" who followed them! What has come about today was therefore the element that aimed for this point in which the consciousness soul was to have its impact on European life.

We shall say more about this tomorrow.

LECTURE XII
Dornach, May 1, 1921

Yesterday I tried to outline the various preparations of different nations for the significant point in humanity's development in the middle of the nineteenth century that then, in a sense, flowed from that time on into our present age. All this can be illustrated through descriptions of the connections between external phenomena and the inner spiritual course of development. Today, we shall bring together several facts that can throw some light on the actual underlying history of the nineteenth century. After all, it is true that the middle of that century is the point when intellectual activity completely turned into a function, an occupation, of the human physical body. Whereas this activity of the intellect was a manifestation of the etheric body during the whole preceding age; from the eighth century B.C. until the fifteenth century A.D., it has increasingly become an activity of the physical body since that time. This process reached a culmination in the middle of the nineteenth century. Along with this, the human being has in fact become more spiritual than was previously the case.

The insights into the spiritual world that had come about earlier and had diminished since the beginning of modern times were derived, after all, from the more intensive union of the physical body with the etheric body. Simply because they were now in a position to carry out something completely nonphysical with their physical body, namely, intellectual activity, human

211

beings thus became completely spiritual beings in regard to their activity. But as I already pointed out yesterday, they denied this spirituality. People related what they grasped mentally only to the physical world. And as I attempted to characterize it yesterday, the different nations were prepared in different ways for this moment in the development of modern civilization.

From this earlier characterization, the fundamental difference between the soul condition of the Roman-Latin segment of Europe's population and that of the Anglo-Saxon part will have become clear. A radical difference does indeed exist in regard to the inner soul constitution. This radical difference can best be characterized if certain spiritual streams that have run their course in humanity's evolution since ancient times and have been recognized long ago are juxtaposed to the contrast between France, Spain, Italy, and the inhabitants of the British Isles and their American descendants. This can be characterized in the following way. Everything that was part of the Ahura-Mazdao cult in the ancient Persian culture, mankind's looking up to the light, encountered in a diminished form in the Egypto-Chaldean civilizations and, even more diminished, in Greek culture, finally became abstract in the Roman culture. All this left residual traces in what has been preserved throughout the Middle Ages and the modern era in the Romance segment of the European population. The last offshoot of the Ormuzd or Ahura-Mazdao culture has remained behind, as it were, whereas, on the other hand, the stream that was considered the ahrimanic one in the ancient Persian world view emerges as modern culture. Indeed, like Ormuzd and Ahriman, these two cultures confront each other in recent times. We find poured into this Ormuzd stream everything that comes from the Roman Church. The forms Christianity assumed by enveloping itself with the Roman-juristic forms of government, by turning into the papal church of Rome, are the last offshoots. We have indicated much else from which these forms originated, but together with all these things they are the last offshoots of the Ormuzd cult. These last traces can still be detected in the offering of the Mass and all that is present in it. A proper understanding of what lies at the basis of these traces will be attained only if less value is placed on insignificant aspects as compared to the great streams of humanity, only if in studying these matters the true value is sought in the forms of thought and feeling that hold sway.

In regard to external civilization, modern impulses came to expression in a tumultuous way in the French Revolution at the end of the eighteenth century. As I indicated yesterday, there lived in it though in abstractions, the appeal addressed to the individual, the conscious human being. We might actually say, like a counterblow against what continued to survive in Romanism, these abstractions of freedom, equality, and brotherhood came into being out of the world of ideas. We must distinguish between what found its way into the Roman forms of thought and feeling out of ancient spiritual streams, and the element that originated from human nature. After all, we must always distinguish the essence of a single nationality from the ongoing stream of humanity in general. We shall see how a light that clearly points to the characteristic moment in humanity's evolution in that century also takes shape precisely in the French civilization later on in the nineteenth century. But the national element in the French, Spanish, and Italian cultures contains in itself the continuation of the Ormuzd element in those times in which this element—naturally transformed through the Catholicity of Christianity—appears as a shadow of an ancient civilization. Therefore, we see that despite all aspirations towards freedom Romanism became and has remained the bearer of what the Roman Church in its world dominion represents.

You really do not understand much of the course of European development, if you do not clearly realize in what sense Roman ecclesiasticism continues to live in Romanism to this day. Indeed even the thought forms employed in the struggle against the institutions of the Church are in turn themselves derived from this Roman Catholic thinking. Thus, we have to distinguish between the general stream of humanity's evolution, which has assumed abstract character and flows through the French Revolution, and the particular national, the Roman-Latin stream, which is actually completely infected with Roman Catholicity.

Out of this stream of Roman Catholicity, a remarkable phenomenon arises in the beginning of the nineteenth century. This phenomenon and its significance for the development in Europe is given far too little attention. Most people who spend their lives being asleep to the phenomena of civilization know nothing of what has been living in the depths of European culture since the beginning of the nineteenth century and is still fully grounded in Roman Catholicity. All this is concentrated, I should say, in the first third of the nineteenth century in the activities of a certain personality, namely, de Maistre.[1] De Maistre is actually the representative of the Catholicity borne by the waves of Romanism, Catholicity that has the aspiration to lead the whole of Europe back into its bosom. With de Maistre, a personality of the greatest imaginable genius, of compelling spirituality but Roman Catholic through and through, appears on the scene.

Let us now give some consideration to something that is completely unfamiliar to those who think along Protestant lines, yet is present in a relatively large number of people in Europe. It is not commonly known that a spiritual stream does in fact exist that is quite unknown to what has otherwise developed since the beginning of the fifteenth century, but that is itself well-acquainted with the effects of this new mentality of the fifth post-Atlantean epoch.

Let us try to characterize the world view in the minds of those for whom de Maistre was a brilliant representative in the first third of the nineteenth century. He himself has long since died, but the spirit that inspired him lives on in a relatively large number of people in Europe. Our present is the time in which it is coming to life again, assuming new forms and seeking to gain larger and larger dimensions. We shall characterize the world view at its roots in a few sentences. This view holds that since the beginning of the fifteenth century the course of human life on earth is going downhill. Since that time, only dissipation, godlessness, and vapidity have proliferated in European civilization; the mere intellect focusing on usefulness has gripped humanity. Truth, on the other hand, which is identical with the spirituality of the world, expresses something different since time immemorial. The problem is that modern man has forgotten this ancient, sacred truth. This primordial, sacred truth implies that man is a fallen creature. The human being has cause to appeal to his conscience and remorse in his soul so that he can lift himself up, so that his soul will not fall prey to materiality. But inasmuch as European humanity utilizes materiality since the middle of the fifteenth century, the European civilization is falling into ruin and with it the whole of mankind.

That is the world view whose main exponent is de Maistre. According to this view all of humanity falls into two categories, one representing the kingdom of God, the other representing the kingdom of this world. The followers of this view look upon the earth's population and distinguish those who they say belong to the kingdom of God. They are the ones who still believe in the ancient truths, who, in fact, have vanished in their true form since the beginning of the fifteenth century. Their noblest aftereffects can still be detected in the views of Augustine,[2] who also differentiates between human beings who are predestined to salvation and those predestined to damnation. The adherents of de Maistre claim that when one encounters a person in this world, he either belongs to the kingdom of God, or to the kingdom of this world. It only appears as though human beings were all mixed together. In the eyes of the spiritual world they are strictly separated from one another, and they can be distinguished from one another. In antiquity, those who belonged to the kingdom of the world, worshiped superstition, that is, they fashioned for themselves false images of the deity; since the beginning of the fifteenth century, they cling to unbelief. That is what de Maistre and his followers say. They know very well what the majority of the European population has slept through, namely, the new age that has in fact dawned since the beginning of the fifteenth century. They indicate this point in time; they indicate it as that moment in time when humanity forgot the source, the actual source of divine truth. The put it like this:

Through sole use of the shadowy intellect, human beings found themselves in a position where the connecting link between them and the source of eternal truth was severed. Since that time, Providence no longer extends mercy to mankind, only justice, and this justice will hold sway on the day of Judgment.

If one relates something like this, it is like telling people a fairy tale; nevertheless, there are those in Europe who cling to this view that since the beginning of the fifteenth century divine world rule has assumed a quite different position in regard to earth humanity. They cling to this tenet just as modern scientists adhere to the law of gravity or something like that. Despite the fact that the existence of this view of life is of fundamental significance particularly for the present, people today do not wish to pay any heed to something like this. De Maistre sees the most pronounced defection from ancient truth in the French Revolution. He does not view it in the way we considered it, namely, as the arising in abstract form of what is supposed to direct human beings to the consciousness soul. Instead, he views this Revolution as the fall into unbelief, the worst thing that could have happened to modern humanity. The French Revolution in particular signifies to him that the seal has now been set on the fact that the divine world power no longer has any obligation to extend mercy in any form on the human being but merely justice, which will be sure to prevail on the Day of Judgment. It is assumed in these circles that those who will fall prey to the powers of doom are already predestined, and also already preordained are those who are the children of the Kingdom of God, who are destined to save themselves because they still cling to ancient wisdom that enjoyed its special bloom in the fourth century A.D.

Such an impulse pervades the text *Observations About France* de Maistre wrote in 1796 when he still lived in Piermont. Already then he reproached France, the France of the Revolution, for its long list of sins. Already then, he referred to the foundations of Romanism that still retain what has come down from ancient times. This sentiment is expressed even more strongly in de Maistre's later writings, and the latter are connected with the whole mission in world history de Maistre ascribed to himself.[3]

After all, he chose Petersburg as the setting for his activity; his later writings proceeded from there. De Maistre had the grandiose idea to tie in with Russianism, particularly with the element that had found its way since ancient times from Asia into the Orthodox Catholic, Russian religion. From there, he wished to create a connection to Romanism. He tried to bring about the great fusion between the element living in the Oriental manner of thinking in Russian culture, and the element coming from Rome. The article he wrote in Petersburg in 1810, "Essay Concerning the Creative Principle of Political Constitutions," is already imbued with this view. We can discern from this text how de Maistre refers back to what Christianity was in regard to its metaphysical view prior to the scholastic age, what it was in the first centuries and what was acceptable to Rome. De Maistre aimed for Roman, for Catholic, Christianity as a real power, but in a certain sense he even rejected what the Middle Ages had already produced as an innovation on the basis of Aristotle's philosophy. In a certain sense, de Maistre tried to exclude Aristotle, for the latter was to him already the preparation for what has appeared since the fifteenth century in the form of the modern faculty of reason. Through human faculties other than logic, de Maistre wanted to attain to a relationship with spirituality.

The essay he wrote in the second decade of the nineteenth century, "Concerning the Pope," moves particularly strongly in the direction of this concept of life. We might say that it is a text that exudes a classic spirit in its composition, a spirit that belongs, in a manner of speaking, to the finest times of French culture under Louis XIV. At the same time, it had as penetrating an effect as any inspired writing. The Pope is presented as the rightful ruler of modern civilization, and it is significant that this is being stated in Petersburg. The manner of presentation is such that one is supposed to distinguish between the temporal, namely, the corruption that has come into the world through a number of Popes, the objectionable elements in regard to some of the Popes, and the eternal principle of Roman Papacy. In a sense, the Pope is represented as incarnation of the spirit of the earth that is to rule over this earth. One is moved to say: All the warmth that lives in this essay about the Pope is the shining forth of Ormuzd's spirit that very nearly sees Ahura-Mazdao himself incarnated in the Roman Pope and therefore makes the demand that the Roman Catholic Church in its fusion with all that found its way from the Orient into Russia—for this is implied in the background—will rule supreme, that it will sweep away all that the intellectual culture has produced since the beginning of the fifteenth century.

De Maistre was really brilliantly effective in this direction. In 1816, his translation of Plutarch was published.[4] In it he tried to demonstrate the sort of power that Christianity possessed; a power, so he thought, that had insinuated itself as thought form into Plutarch's dissertations although the latter was still a pagan. Finally, the last work from de Maistre's pen, again proceeding from Petersburg, *Twilight Hours in St. Petersburg*, was published in two volumes.[5] First of all, everything I have already characterized appears in them in an especially pronounced form; in particular he depicts the radical struggle of Roman Catholicism against what appears on the British Isles as its counterpart.

If, on the one hand, we see how Roman Catholicism crystallizes in all this in a certain direction, if we note what is connected in the form of Roman Catholicism with personalities like Ignatius of Loyola, [6] Alfonso di Liguori, [7] Francis Xaverius, [8] and others and relate this to the brilliant figure of de Maistre; if we observe everything that is present here, then, in a manner of speaking, we see the obsolete, archaic light of Ormuzd. On the other hand, we note what de Maistre sees arising on the British Isles and what he then assails cuttingly with the pungent acid of his penetrating mind. This struggle by de Maistre against the true essence of the Anglo-Saxon spirit is one of the most grandiose spiritual battles that has ever taken place. In particular, he aims at the personality of the philosopher Locke[9] and sees in him the very incarnation of the spirit that leads mankind into decline. He opposes Locke's philosophy brilliantly to excess.

We need only recall the significance of this philosophy. In the background, on the one hand, we must note the Roman principles of initiation that express themselves like a continuing Ormuzd worship. We must be aware of everything that flowed into this from somebody like Ignatius of Loyola, Bossuet, [10] and in such grand manner from de Maistre himself. On the other hand, in contrast to everything that has its center in Roman Catholicism in Rome itself, yet is based on initiation and, I might say, is certainly the newest phase of the Ormuzd initiation, we have to observe all the secret societies that spread from Scotland down through England and of which English philosophy and politics are an expression. From a certain, different viewpoint, I have described that on another occasion. De Maistre is just as well informed about what makes itself felt out of an ahrimanic initiation principle as he is knowledgeable about what he is trying to bring to bear as the Ormuzd initiation in the new form for European civilization. De Maistre knows how to evaluate all these things; he is intelligent enough to recognize them esoterically, inasmuch as he attacks the philosopher Locke who in a sense is an offspring, an outward, exoteric offspring, of this other, ahrimanic initiation. He is attacking an important personality, the one who made his appearance with the epochal book *Concerning Human Reason*, which then greatly influenced French thinking. Subsequently, Locke was indeed revered by Voltaire.[11] His influence was such that Madam de Sevigné[12] remarked concerning an Italian writer who made Locke palatable in a literary sense for Italy, that the latter would have like to consume Locke's rhetorical embellishments in every bowl of boullion.

Now de Maistre took a close look at Locke and said: It is impossible that Voltaire, for example, and other Frenchmen could have even read this Locke! In his book *Twilight Hours in St. Petersburg* de Maistre discusses in detail how writers actually gain world fame. He demonstrates that it is quite possible that Voltaire had never read Locke; he really could not have read him, otherwise he would have been smart enough not to defend Locke as he did.

Even though de Maistre sees a veritable devil in Voltaire, he still does him justice by saying this of him. And in order to substantiate this, he offers long essays on how individuals like Locke are written and spoken about in the world, individuals who are viewed as great men. This is notwithstanding the fact that in reality people are not concerned with gaining firsthand knowledge about them, but instead familiarize themselves with such individuals by means of secondary sources. It is as if humanity were imprisoned in error—this is how Locke affects these people. The whole modern way of thinking that, according to de Maistre's view, then led to the catastrophe of the French Revolution actually proceeds from Locke; in other words Locke is the exponent, the symptom, the historical symptom for this. From the point from which Locke proceeded, this way of thinking dominates the world. De Maistre scrutinizes Locke, and he says that there were few writers who had such an absolute lack of a sense of style as did Locke, and he demonstrates this in detail. He tries to prove in every instance that Locke's statements are so trivial, so matter of fact, that one need not reckon with them at all, that it is quite unnecessary to trouble one's thoughts with them. He states that Voltaire said Locke always clearly defined everything, but, asks de Maistre, what are these definitions by Locke? Nothing but truisms, "nonsensical tautologies," to use a modern term, and ridiculous. According to him, all of Locke's pen pushing is supposedly a joke without style, without brilliance, full of tautologies and platitudes.

This is how de Maistre characterized something that became most valuable for modern mankind, namely, that people today see greatness in platitude, in popular style, in the lack of genius and style, in what can be found in the streets but passes itself off as philosophy.

Yet, de Maistre is actually a person who in all instances pays attention to the deeper spiritual principles, to the spiritually essential. It is most difficult for matters such as these encountered here to be made comprehensible to a person today. For the way a personality like de Maistre thinks is really quite foreign to present day human beings who are accustomed to the shadowy intellect. De Maistre not only observes the individual person; he sees the spiritual element working through that individual. What Locke wrote must be characterized in de Maistre's sense in the way I have just described it. However, de Maistre expresses this with extraordinary brilliance and geniality. At the same time, he says: If, in turn, I consider Locke as a person he was indeed a quite decent fellow; one can have nothing against him as a person. He is the corrupter of Western European humanity, but he is a decent person. If he would be born again today and would have to watch how human beings make use of this triviality that he himself recognized as such after death, he would cry bitter tears over the fact that people have fallen for his platitudes in this manner.

All this is expressed by de Maistre with tremendous forced and plausible emphasis. He is imbued with the impulse thus to annihilate what appears to him as the actual adversary of Roman Catholicism and what, according to his view, thrives especially on the other side of the Channel. I would like to read to you one passage verbatim from the "Petersburg Twilight Conversations," where he speaks of the—to his view wretched—effect of Locke on politics: "These dreadful seeds"—so he says—"perhaps would not have come to fruition under the ice of his style; animated in the hot mud of Paris, they have produced the monster of the Revolution that has engulfed Europe."

After having uttered such words against the spirit working through Locke, he again turns to Locke as a person. This is something that is so difficult to impress on people of our age who constantly confuse the external personality with the spiritual principle that expresses itself through that human being and see it as a unit. De Maistre always distinguishes what reveals itself as actual spirituality from the external human being. Now he turns again to the outward personality and says: He is actually a man who had any number of virtues, but he was gifted with them about as well as was that master of dance who, according to Swift, [13] was so accomplished in all the skills of dance and had only one fault—he limped. Thus, says de Maistre, Locke was gifted with all virtues. Yet, de Maistre truly sees him as an incarnation of the evil principle—this is not my figure of speech, de Maistre himself uses this expression—that speaks through Locke and holds sway supersensibly since the beginning of the fifteenth century. One really gains some respect for the penetrating spirituality that imbued de Maistre. One must also be aware, however, that there really exist people who are gaining influence today and are on the verge now of winning back their influence over European civilization, who are definitely inspired by that spirituality that de Maistre represented on the highest level.

De Maistre still retained something of the more ancient, instinctive insights into the relationship between world and man. This is particularly evident from his discourse about the Sacrifice Offering and the ritual of the Sacrifice. He had somewhat of an awareness of the fact that what is linked to the physical body in regard to the consciousness soul must make itself felt independently in the human being and that it is embodied in the blood. Basically, it was de Maistre's view that the divine element had only been present in human evolution up to the fourth Christian century. He did not wish to acknowledge the Christ Who works on continuously. Above all, he tried to extinguish everything existing since the fifteenth century. He longed to return to ancient times. Thus, he acquired his particular view of the Christ, a view that possessed something of the ancient Yahweh, indeed of the old pagan gods, for he really went back to the cult of Ormuzd. And he gathered from this viewpoint that the divine element can only be sought far beyond the human consciousness soul, hence, beyond the blood. Based on such profound depths of his world view de Maistre expressed the thought that the gods—namely the gods of whom he spoke—have a certain distaste for the blood, and in the first place have to be appeased by the blood sacrifice. The blood has to offer itself up in sacrifice.[14]

It goes without saying that this is something the supremely enlightened modern human being laughs at. Yet it is something that has passed on from de Maistre to those who are his followers and who represent a segment of humanity that must be taken seriously, but who are also intimately connected with everything proceeding today from Roman ecclesiasticism. We must not forget that in de Maistre we confront the finest and most brilliant representative of what infused France from Romanism and what indeed has come to expression in French culture, I would say, in an ingenious but folk-oriented form. It is this that lives in French culture and has constantly brought it about that clericalism played a significant role in everything motivating French politics throughout the whole nineteenth century.

In France, the abstract impulses of freedom, equality, and brotherhood clashed with what existed there as Roman Catholicism. Actually, we must vividly feel what imbued a person such as Gambetta[15] when, at a decisive moment, the deep sigh escaped from him: *"Le clericalisme, voila l'ennemi!"* ("Clericalism, that is the enemy!"). He sensed this clericalism that pulsed up from everything in the art of social experimentation during the first half of the nineteenth century. It lived in Napoleon III; it was something even the Commune[16] had to struggle against. It was an element that survived into later times, permeating the Boulangism[17] of the 1880's and the conflicts around the personality of Dreyfus;[18] it is something that is alive even today.

An element is present in France that stands in an inner, spiritual, and absolutely radical difference to all that exists on the other side of the Channel in Great Britain and is basically embodied in the elements that remained behind from something else, from the various Masonic orders and lodges. Whereas, on the one hand, we are dealing with initiated Roman Catholicism, on the other hand we encounter the movements of secret societies, which I have already characterized here from another viewpoint and which represent the ahrimanic stream. There is a tremendous difference in the way the modern question of one person's individual status is expressed, say, in the elections to Parliament in France, or over in Great Britain. In France, everything proceeds from a certain theory, from certain ideologies. In England, everything emerges directly from the practical relationships of commercial and industrial life and collides, as I pointed out yesterday, with the ancient patriarchal conditions that prevailed particularly in the landowners' lifestyle. Just look at the way things take place in France. You find everywhere what you might call spiritual battles. There are struggles for freedom, for equality and brotherhood; people fight for the separation of school and church. People struggle to push the church back. But it is not possible to do so, for the church dwells in the depths of the soul's existence. Everything runs its course, in a manner of speaking, in the domain of certain dialectics, of certain arguments.

Over in England, these matters run their course as questions of power. There, we find a certain spiritual movement that is typical of the Anglo-Saxon people. I have often pointed out that as the middle of the nineteenth century approached, certain people came to the conclusion that things could not be allowed to go on in the same way any longer; human beings had to be made aware of the fact that a spiritual world does exist. The merely shadowlike intellect did not suffice. Yet people could not make up their minds to bring this inclination towards the spirit to the attention of the world in a manner other than through something that is "super-materialistic," namely, through spiritism. This spiritism, which in turn has a greater impact than one would think, has its origins there. Spiritism, out to grasp the spirit externally, so to speak, just as one grasps matter, is therefore super-materialistic, is more materialistic than materialism itself. Locke lives on, so to say, in this super-materialism. And this element that in a sense, dwells in the inner sphere of the modern cultural development, expresses itself outwardly. It is certainly again and again the same phenomenon.

We encounter a tendency toward that spiritual stream de Maistre opposes so radically in the 1840's across the Channel: The tendency to comprehend everything by means of material entities. Locke basically referred to the intellect in such a manner that he deprived the intellect of its spiritual nature. He made use of the most spiritual element in the human being in order to deny the spirituality in the human being, indeed, in order to direct human beings only to matter. Similarly people in the nineteenth century referred to the spirit and tried to demonstrate it through all sorts of material manifestations. The intention was to make the spirit comprehensible to human beings through materialism. The element, however, that imbued the initiates of the various fraternities then passed over into the external social and political conditions.

One is inclined to say: By fighting for the abolition of the grain tariff in 1846 and succeeding in that endeavor, the cotton merchant Cobden and the Quaker Bright[19] were the outward agents of the inner spiritual stream in the political life in the same way as the two most inept individuals who ever existed in politics, Asquith and Grey in the year 1914.[20] Certainly, Cobden and Bright were not as blind as Asquith and Grey, but basically it is the same symptom, presented to the world in outward phenomena such as the abolition of the grain tariff in 1846 when industry was victorious over the ancient patriarchal system, only on a new stage. Yesterday, I listed the other stages preceding this one. Then we can observe, so to speak, stage following upon stage. We see the workers organizing themselves. We note that the Whigs increasingly become the party concerned with industry, that the Tories turn into the party of the landowners, of the old patriarchal system. But we also see that this ancient patriarchal element could no longer resist the abrupt clash with modern technology—I characterized the manner of that yesterday—and that, all at once, modern industrialism pushed its way in. Thus, centuries, indeed millennia, were skipped, and England's mental condition that dated back to pre-Christian eras and existed well into the nineteenth century simply merged with what has developed in recent times.

Then we see the right to vote increasingly extended, the Tories calling for the support of a man, who only a short while ago certainly would not have been counted among them, Disraeli, Lord Beaconsfield, who was of Jewish extraction, an "outsider."[21] We watch the Upper House finally becoming a shadow and the year 1914 approaching in which a quite new England emerges. Only future historiography will be able to evaluate this emergence of the new England correctly.

You see, this is the course of the major events in the development of the nineteenth century. We see the various moments flashing up, indicating how significant a point in humanity's evolution has actually appeared. Only the most enlightened minds, however, can discern the light flashes that are the most important. I have frequently called attention to a phenomenon that is highly significant for the comprehension of the development in the nineteenth century. I have called attention to the moment in Goethe's house in Weimar when, having heard of the July revolution in France, Eckermann appeared before Goethe and Goethe said to him: "In Paris, unheard-of things have occurred, everything is in flames!" Naturally, Eckermann believed that Goethe was referring to the July revolution. That was of no interest at all to Goethe; instead, he said: "I don't mean that; that is not what interests me. Rather, in the academy in Paris, great controversy between Cuvier and Geoffroy de Saint-Hilaire has broken out concerning whether the individual types of animals are independent or whether the one type passes over into the next." Cuvier claimed the first, namely, that one is dealing with firm, rigid types that cannot evolve into other types. Geoffroy held that one has to view a type as being changeable, that one type passes over into the next.[22] For Goethe, this was the major world event of modern times!

In fact, this was true. Goethe, therefore, had a profound, tremendously alive sensitivity. For what did Geoffroy de Saint-Hilaire argue against Cuvier? The former sensed that when human beings look into their inner being, they can animate this shadowy intellect, that it is not merely logic, which is passively concerned with the external world, but that this logic can discover something like living truth about the things in this world within itself. In what imbued Geoffroy de Saint-Hilaire, Goethe sensed the assertion of the living intellect, something that arose, I might say, in the occult development of modern humanity and reached its culmination in the middle of the nineteenth century. Goethe really sensed something of great significance.

Cuvier, the great scholarly scientist, claimed that one had to be able to differentiate between the individual species and had to place them side by side. He stated that it was impossible to transform one type into the next, least of all, for example, the bird species into that of the mammals, and so on. Geoffroy de Saint-Hilaire, on the other hand, claimed that it was possible to do so.

What sort of confrontation was that? Ordinary truth and sublime error? Oh no, that is not the case. With ordinary, abstract logic, with the shadow-intellect, one can just as easily prove the correctness of what Cuvier claims as of what Geoffroy de Saint-Hilaire has stated. On the basis of ordinary reason, which still prevails in our science today, this question cannot be resolved. This is why it has come up again and again; this is why we see Geoffroy de Saint-Hilaire confront Cuvier in Paris in 1830 and in a different manner Weissmann[23] and others confront Haeckel.[24] These questions cannot be determined by way of this external science. For here, the element that has turned into the shadowlike intellect since the beginning of the fifteenth century, something that de Maistre detests so much, is really aiming at abolishing spirituality itself.

De Maistre pointed to Rome, even to the fact that the Pope—except for the temporal, passing papal personalities—sits in Rome as the incarnation of what is destined to rule over modern civilization. The culmination point of these discourses by de Maistre was reached in the year 1870, when the dogma of the Pope's infallibility was proclaimed. By way of the outmoded Ormuzd worship, the element that should be sought in spiritual heights was brought down into the person of the Roman Pope. What ought to be viewed as spirituality became temporalized matter; the church was turned into the secular state. This was subsequent to the fact that the church had already for a long time been successful in fitting the secular states into the form it had assumed itself when it had turned into the state religion under Constantine.

Therefore, in Romanism, we have on the one hand something that turns into the modern state inasmuch as the legal principle itself rebels and brings about its own polarity, so to speak, in the French Revolution; on the other hand, we have the outdated Ormuzd worship. Then we confront the element arising from the economic sphere, for all the measures that are taken on the other side of the English Channel originate from that sphere. In de Maistre we encounter the last great personality who tries to imprint spirituality into the judicial form of the state, who tries to carry the spirit into earthly materiality. This is what anthroposophically oriented spiritual science has to oppose. It wishes to establish supersensible spirituality. It tries to add to the prolonged Ormuzd worship, to the ahrimanic worship, something that will bring about a balance, it wishes to make the spirit itself the ruler of the earth.

This cannot be accomplished other than in the following manner. If, on the one hand, the earthly element is imprinted into the structure of political laws and, on the other hand, into the economic form, this spiritual life, in turn, is established in such a way that it does not institute the belief in a god who has become secular but rather inaugurates the reign of the spirit itself that flows in with each new human being incarnating on earth. This is the free spiritual life that wishes to take hold of the spirit that stands above all that is earthly. Once again, the intention is t bring to bear what one might call the effusion of the Spirit.

In A.D. 869, during the general ecumenical council, the view of the spirit was toned down in order to prevent human beings from arriving at the acknowledgment of the spirit that rules the earth from heaven, at the beginning of the fifteenth century, in order to make possible the appearance of a man such as de Maistre as late as the nineteenth century.

This is what is important: Rather than appealing to the spirit believed to be incarnated in an earthly sense, a Christ-being believed to be living on in an earthly church, we must appeal to the spiritual entity that is indeed connected with the earth, yet must be recognized and viewed in the spirit. But since everything human beings must attain in the earthly domain has to be acquired within the social order, this cannot come about in any other way but by acknowledging the free right of the spirit descending with each new human life in order to acquire the physical body, the spirit that can never become sovereign in an earthly personality and dwells in a supersensible being.

The establishment of the dogma of infallibility is a defection from spirituality; the last point of what had been intended with that council of 869 had been reached. We must return to the acknowledgment, belief in, and recognition of the spirit. This, however, can only come about if our social order is permeated with the structure that makes possible the free spiritual life alongside other things—the earth-bound political and economic life.

This is how the insight human beings must acquire today places itself into the course of civilization. This is how it has to be experienced within the latter. If we fail to do that, we cannot arrive at the essence of what is actually trying to come to expression in the "Threefold Social Organism," of what tries to work for the salvation of a civilization that otherwise must fall victim to decline in the manner described by Spengler.

LECTURE XIII
Dornach, May 5, 1921

The fourth post-Atlantean epoch, the epoch of the development of humanity's intellect, was guided by the Greek mystery centers. Initially, the mysteries provided the basis of this intellectual or mind culture for the general population of Asia Minor and southern Europe. The secret of human life and its connection with the sun played a major role in these mysteries. We know from the descriptions given in my book *Theosophy* how the ego lights up within man's intellectual or mind soul, after which it is meant to attain to its full inner power through the consciousness soul. Now, insofar as man's ego was destined to be developed during the age of the intellectual culture, the mysteries of that age had to be occupied with the secrets of the sun's life and particularly the sun's links with the human ego. You also know from my description in *Riddles of Philosophy* that the Greeks still perceived their ideas and concepts in the outer world, just as we today perceive colors, sounds, and so on. For the ancient Greeks, the element that dwells in concepts was not something merely created within the mind. It was something they beheld with the objects. In this respect, Goethe definitely possessed something of a Greek nature. He made this evident in the famous conversation with Schiller. When he heard Schiller say that his mental images—something conceptual and ideal—were not perceptions but ideas, Goethe replied that in this case he *saw* his ideas just as he saw external perceptions around him.

The Greeks' relationship to concepts was associated with a quite definite sensation the Greeks experienced when they directed their glance upon the outer world. In fact, they regarded the conceptual content that shone forth to them everywhere as the offspring of the sun's life. When the sun rose in the morning, they sensed the rising of conceptual life in space. With the setting sun they experienced the disappearance of the life of thought. We cannot understand the evolution of nations if we do not take into consideration this change in the soul life.

That faculty, my dear friends, has actually been lost from the soul life of human beings, namely, the faculty to sense and experience the spirituality of the whole environment. Today, a person sees the rise of the sun's round globe and only has an awareness of what is encountered there in the way of colored and shining atmospheric phenomena; it is the same when the sun is viewed as it disappears in the red glow of a sunset. The Greeks had the feeling that in the morning the world arose and bestowed on them their world of ideas. It vanished in the evening and a world then appeared that withdrew from them their world of ideas. In the darkness of night, they felt bereft of their ideas. When they looked up at the sky, which appears blue to us, but for which they used the same term as for "darkness," they actually felt that the boundaries of space consisted of what was beyond conceptual life.

Where the Greeks saw the universe reaching a boundary, there ended for them the world of ideas with which the human being is endowed. Beyond this universe, the Greeks divined the existence of other worlds, the thought worlds of the gods. Those worlds seemed to them closely linked to what they designated as light.

They were revealed to them concentrated, as it were, in the sun's life, whereas, otherwise, they withdrew into the expanse of the dark cosmic firmament. We have to have insight into this quite different world of sensations if we are to understand the way in which this manner of perception in all its inner vitality affected the evolution of the human being for some time. We have to realize what the most advanced representatives of mankind felt when they could no longer experience the spiritual reflection of the sun's life in the cosmos upon them. And especially the most advanced representatives of humanity who had received their education in the Greek mysteries then experienced the Mystery of Golgotha as a salvation inasmuch as it once again brought about the possibility of enkindling this light within their being. The light such individuals had actually experienced earlier as a divine element they now wished to experience by means of participating with their soul and spirit in the events of the Mystery of Golgotha.

We do not acquire an actual knowledge of what has come to pass in mankind in the course of millennia when we merely study these things with the intellect. We have to focus on the transformation of the whole human mind and soul life. Living since the beginning of the fifteenth century in the age of the consciousness soul development, we have retained only the shadowy nature of our inner intellectual activity, of the spirituality of reason that existed in the fourth post-Atlantean period. I have outlined this here during the past few weeks. Now, once again, we have to struggle to attain an awareness of what can permeate our form of shadowy intellect with a living perception of the universe. It was precisely because of the modern culture of the shadowy intellect that the human being, in a manner of speaking, has been fettered to the earth. Today we actually consider only what the earth offers to us, particularly when we allow ourselves to be infected by the constantly expanding, purely scientific culture. People have no idea that they belong not only to the earth with their whole being but to the whole extraterrestrial universe as well. This knowledge of their connection with the cosmos beyond earth is something mankind must acquire once again.

We simply take earthly life today as the basis of our ideas and concepts and construe a view of the whole universe in accordance with conditions on earth. The resulting picture of the universe is then not much else than the transference of earthly conditions to extraterrestrial ones. Thus, by means of the tremendous achievements of modern science, through spectral analysis and other methods, a view of the sun was developed that is really modeled entirely upon earthly conditions. A conception is formed of what a luminous body of gas might look like. This conception is then transferred to what meets our eye as the sun in the cosmos. We must once again learn to use the materials of spiritual science to arrive at a conception of the sun. The physicist believes that the sun would present itself to him as a luminous sphere of gas if he were able to travel out into space. Yet, despite the fact that it reflects the cosmic light to us in its own way in the manner it receives it, the sun is a spiritual entity through and through. We are not dealing with a physical entity that moves about somewhere out there in the universe but with a completely spiritual being.

The Greeks still had the right feeling when they experienced the light, shining down upon them from the sun, as something that must be brought into a connection with their ego development insofar as this ego development is tied to the conceptual nature of the intellect. The sun's rays were to the Greeks something that enkindled their ego within them. It is therefore obvious that the Greeks still had a feeling for the spirituality of the cosmos. To them, the sun being was substantially a being related to the ego. The element the human being becomes aware of when he says "I" to himself, the force that works in him and enables him to say "I" to himself, this is what the Greeks looked at. They felt called upon to address the sun in the same way they addressed their ego, to regard the sun with the same feelings they had for their ego.

Ego and sun are the inner and the outer aspects of the same being. What orbits out there through space as the sun is the cosmic *I*. What lives within me is the human *I*.

One is inclined to say that this sensation is still faintly perceptible to those who have a somewhat deeper feeling of affinity for nature. The basis of such an experience has already vanished to a large degree. Yet, something is still alive in the human being today that is attuned to the rise of the sun in springtime, that can still experience the spirituality of the sunbeam and can feel how the ego is imbued with new life when the rays of the sun illuminate the earth with greater intensity. Yet, it is but a last, faint sensation that, even in this external manner, is dying out in mankind. It is about to disappear in the abstract, shadowy culture of the intellect that has gradually become prevalent in the whole of civilized life today. However, we must once again reach the point where some recognition can be gained of humanity's relationship with supersensible existence. In this respect I want to point out a number of things today.

By bringing together all the references found here and there in anthroposophical literature, we shall be able, first of all, to comprehend once more the sun's connection with the ego. We shall be able to perceive the significant contrast between the forces radiating from the sun to the earth and those forces that are active in what we term the moon. Sun and moon are in a certain respect total opposites. Complete polarity exists between them. When we study the sun by means of spiritual science, we find that the sun sends down to us everything that fashions us into bearers of our ego. We owe to the rays of the sun what in fact bestows on us the human form and, in the latter, molds us into an image of the ego. What works in the human being from outside and determines his form from without even as early as the embryonic stage are influences from the sun. When the human embryo is developing in the womb, a great deal more is taking place than what present-day science is dreaming about, namely, that forces originate from the impregnated mother that then develop the human being. No, the human embryo merely rests in the mother's body; it is given form by the sun's forces. It is true, however, that we must bring these sun forces into connection with the moon's forces that have opposite effects. The moon forces become evident, above all, as the inner influence in the lower, metabolic nature of man. In drawing an outline, we may therefore say: The sun's forces are the element molding the human being from outside. What develops in the metabolic processes from within are the moon's forces, positioning themselves within the human organism and radiating outward from the center.

This does not contradict the fact that these moon forces also play a part, for instance, in forming the

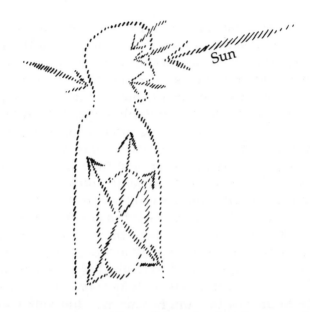

Sun

human countenance, They shape the face because the effects that proceed from the center, from the lower, metabolic system, exert an attracting power, as it were, from outside on the development of the human face. The moon forces have a differentiating effect on this development due to adding their influence to that of the sun's forces while counteracting the latter from within the human being. For this reason, the organism connected with human reproduction depends on the moon forces, which bestow the form. On the other hand, the result of procreation depends on the sun forces. With their whole being human beings are placed into the polarity between sun forces and moon forces.

In seeking the moon forces within the inner human organism, we have to distinguish them in the metabolic process from the forces originating within this process itself. The moon forces play into the metabolism but the latter possesses its own forces. These are the earth forces. The forces contained in food substances, in vegetables and other foods, work in the human being by virtue of their own nature. Here, they are active as earth forces. Metabolism is primarily a result of the earth's forces, but elements of the moon's forces work into them. If the human being possessed only the metabolic process with its forces, if only the substances of his foods would unfold their forces in his body after having been consumed, then he would have nothing but a chaotic play of all kinds of forces. The fact that these forces continuously work to renew the human being from within does not depend at all on the earth; it is due to the moon that is added to earth. The human being is shaped from within outwards by the moon, from without inwards by the sun. Inasmuch as the sun's rays are received through the eye into the human head organization, they also have an inward effect; nevertheless, they still work from outside in.

Thus, on the one hand, in regard to his whole ego development the human being depends on the influence of the sun; without the sun he could not be an ego dwelling solidly on the earth. On the other hand, there would be no human race, no propagation, if the moon were not the earth's companion. It is possible to say that it is the sun that firmly places the human being as a personality, as an individual, on the earth. It is the moon that conjured human beings in their multitude, in their whole evolution, upon the earth. The human race in its physical succession of generations is the result of the moon forces, which stimulate human beings. Man as a single being, an individuality, is the product of the sun forces. Therefore, if we wish to study the human being as well as the human race, we cannot study merely the conditions of earth. Geologists seek in vain to investigate the earth's conditions in order to comprehend the human being; they study in vain the other forces of earth so as to arrive at this understanding. Human beings are not primarily a creation of the earth. They are formed out of the cosmos; they are the offspring of the world of the stars, above all, of sun and moon. From the earth, only those forces are derived that are contained in matter itself. They are effective outside man and then continue their effects when, through eating and drinking, they have entered into the human being, but there they are received by something that is of an unearthly nature.

The processes that take place within the human being are by no means merely earthly ones; they are definitely something provided for out of starry worlds. It is this insight that human beings have to struggle to attain once again.

When we observe the human being further, we can take into consideration, first of all, that he is a physical body. This body absorbs the external foods. They in turn extend their forces into this physical body. But the latter is also taken hold of by the astral body, and in it the moon's influence is active in the manner I have just described. The sun's effect also plays into this astral body. Imbuing it with their forces, sun and moon permeate the astral body, and the latter works in the manner I have outlined above. The etheric body stands in the middle between physical and astral body.

When we study the forces coming from foodstuffs, we find, to begin with, that they are active in the physical body, and, in the manner I described earlier, are then taken hold of by the astral body containing the sun and moon influences. But in between the physical and astral bodies we find something else that is active in the etheric body. It, too, is not derived from the earth but from the whole surrounding cosmos. When we study the earth with its products in relation to the human being, the substances composed of solid, liquid, or aeriform ingredients, we see that they are consumed by the human being and then worked upon by the forces of sun and moon. In addition, there are also active in man forces that stream in from all directions of the universe. The forces active in the foodstuffs come from the earth. Those streaming into the human being from all corners of the universe are the etheric forces. They also take hold of the foodstuffs, but in a much more uniform manner, and transform them in such a way that they become inwardly capable of life. In addition, the etheric forces turn these foodstuffs into something that can inwardly experience the etheric element as such, namely, light and warmth. Thus, we can say that because of his physical body the human being is part of the earth, because of his etheric body he is related to the whole surrounding sphere, and because of his astral body man in connected above all with the effects of moon and sun.

Now, these effects of moon and sun contained in the astral body are in turn modified. They are modified to the extent that a powerful difference exists between the effects upon the upper human organization and those on the lower human organism.

Let us refer today to the part of the human being that is permeated by the bloodstream flowing upwards toward the head as "upper human organization"; let us refer to what lies below the heart as "lower human organism." In viewing the human being thus, we have, first of all, the upper part including his head and whatever is organically connected with it. Its formation is dependent mainly on the sun's effects and also develops first during embryonic life. Already in the embryo, the sun's effects work on this organization in a quite special way, but these effects then continue after birth when the human being is present physically in the life between birth and death. Roughly speaking, what lies in this part of the human organism above the heart—a more detailed description would have to trace the blood circulation above the heart—is then modified in regard to the astral influences by Saturn, Jupiter, and Mars (see outline p. 248).

According to the Copernican world view, Saturn has forces it develops in its orbit around the sun and then sends down to the earth. It possesses those forces that are effective in the whole human astral body, particularly in the part belonging to the above mentioned upper organism of man. Saturn possesses the forces that stream into this astral body. As these forces penetrate and enliven the latter, they essentially determine the extent to which the astral body places itself in a proper relationship to the physical body. When a person cannot sleep well, for example, when his astral body does not properly emerge from the etheric and physical bodies, when it does not correctly reenter them upon awakening, or in some other way does not fit itself properly into the physical body, then this is an effect, but an irregular one, of the Saturn forces. Saturn is chiefly that celestial body that, by way of the human head, brings about a correct relationship of the astral body to the human physical and etheric bodies. By means of this, on the other hand, it is the Saturn forces that produce the connection between astral body and ego because of Saturn's relation to the sun. This relationship of Saturn to the sun's effect is expressed in regard to space and time in the fact that Saturn completes its orbit around the sun in a period of thirty years.

In the human being this relationship of Saturn to the sun comes to expression in the ego achieving an appropriate relationship to the astral body, and above all, in the proper incorporation of the astral body into the whole human organization. Thus, we can say Saturn possesses a relationship to the upper part of the whole human astral body. This relationship was definitely an important factor for people in ancient times. Even in Egypto-Chaldean times, going back to the third and fourth millennium prior to the Mystery of Golgotha, we would find that among the teachers, the sages in the mysteries, every individual was judged according to how he had determined his relationship to Saturn by the date of his birth. For these wise men knew quite well that depending on whether a person was born during one or another of Saturn's celestial positions, he was one who could use his astral body in the physical body in a more efficient or less efficient manner. Insight into such things played an important role in ancient times. The progress of mankind's evolution, however, is denoted precisely by the fact that in our age, which, as you know, began in the fifteenth century, we are freeing ourselves of the influences affecting us there.

My dear friends, do not misunderstand this. It does not mean that Saturn is not active in us today. It works in us just as it did in antiquity; the point is that we have to free ourselves from it. And do you know in what this freeing ourselves in the proper way from the Saturn influences consists? You free yourself most poorly from the Saturn influences if you follow the shadowy intellect of the present time. In doing so you actually permit the Saturn effects to run riot within yourself, to shoot hither and thither, and actually to turn you into what is nowadays called a nervous person. A nervous condition in a person is caused mainly by the fact that the astral body does not fit properly into the whole physical configuration. The nervousness of our age is due to this. Human beings must be induced to strive for real perception, for Imagination. If they remain with abstract conception, they will become more and more nervous, for they are actually growing out of the Saturn activity, which is nevertheless within them, shooting back and forth, pulling the astral body out of the nerves, thus making people nervous. In a cosmic sense, the nervousness of our age has to be recognized as an effect of Saturn.

Just as Saturn is chiefly involved with the upper part of the whole astral body inasmuch as the latter is connected with the whole organism through the nervous system, so Jupiter is active in thinking (see outline p. 248).

Human thinking, after all, is also based in a certain way on a partial activity of the astral body. I should say, a smaller part of the astral body is active in thinking than in sustaining the whole human being. It is Jupiter's effect that works in our astral body and, above all, strengthens our thinking. The effect of Jupiter deals mainly with the astral permeation and organization of the human brain.

Now, Saturn's effects actually extend over the whole of adult human life after the first three decades of our life. For our whole life and health depend on how we develop in our astral body during the periods of growth, and in fact, they only cease after age thirty. That is why Saturn requires thirty years to circle around the sun. This completely fits the human being. The thinking that develops in us has to do with the first twelve years of life. After all, what orbits out there in space is not without a connection to the human being.

Just as Jupiter has to do with thinking, so Mars has to do with speech.

Saturn—upper part of the whole astral body
Jupiter—thinking
Mars—speech

Mars separates a still smaller part of the astral body from its incorporation into the remaining human organization than the one that comes into play in regard to thinking. And it depends on the Mars effects within us that the forces can unfold that then pour into speech. The small revolution of Mars also has a bearing on this. A human being acquires the first sounds of speech within a time span that corresponds roughly to half the Martian orbit around the sun.

Ascending and descending development! We see how this whole development is linked with the forces of Saturn, Jupiter, and Mars insofar as it is tied to the region of the human head.

We have thus considered the outer planets' activity in the human astral body. Whereas the sun is connected more with the ego, these three cosmic bodies, Saturn, Jupiter, and Mars, have to do with the development of what is tied to the astral body, namely, speech, thinking, and the whole conduct of the human soul in the human organism.

Besides the sun, which has to do with the actual ego, we also have in addition those planets called the inner planets. They are the ones that are closer to earth than to the sun, having their place between earth and sun, whereas, seen from the earth, the other planets, Saturn, Jupiter, and Mars, are on the other side of the sun. When we focus on these inner planets, we likewise arrive at a consideration of the connections between their forces and the human being. To begin with, we shall consider Mercury.

Similar to the moon, Mercury has its target points more in the inner being of man, working from outside only on the human countenance. In the part lying below the region of the heart, its forces are effective by taking hold inwardly of the human organization and, in turn, streaming forth from there. Mercury's chief task is to bring the astral body's activity into all breathing and circulation processes of the human being. Mercury is the intercessor between the astral body and the rhythmic processes in man. Thus, we are able to say that its forces intercede between the astral element and the rhythmic activity (see outline on p. 250). Due to this, similar to the moon forces, the Mercury forces also intervene in the whole human metabolism, but only insofar as the metabolism is subject to rhythm, reacting upon rhythmic activity.

Then there is Venus. Venus is active especially in the human etheric body, in what works out of the cosmos in the human etheric body and its activities.

Finally we have the moon, which we have already mentioned. It is the element in the human being that is the polar opposite of the sun forces. From within, it leads substances into the realm of life and therefore is also connected with reproduction. In the fullest sense, the moon stimulates inner reproduction as well as the procreative process of reproduction.

You realize now that what actually takes place in the human being is becoming evident to you in its dependence on the surrounding cosmos. On the one hand, with the physical body, the human being is tied to the earthly forces. On the other hand, he is linked to the

Saturn	upper part of the whole astral body
Jupiter	thinking
Mars	speech
Sun	ego
Mercury	leading the astral elements into the rhythmic activity of the human being
Venus	activity of the human etheric body
Moon	stimulator of reproduction

whole cosmic environment with his etheric body. In that body, differentiations occur in the manner I have just outlined, and inasmuch as the differentiation proceeds primarily from man's astral body, the forces of Saturn, Jupiter, Mars, Mercury, Venus and moon integrate themselves into this body. By way of the ego, the sun is also active in man. Now take into consideration that due to the fact that the human being is integrated into the cosmos in this manner, it makes a difference whether a person stands at a given spot on the earth, and Jupiter, for instance, shines down on him from the sky, or whether he is in a location where Jupiter is covered by the earth. In the first case, Jupiter's effects on the person are direct ones; in the second case, the earth is placed in between. This results in a significant difference.

We have said that Jupiter is connected with thinking. Let us assume a person receives the direct Jupiter influence during the period when his physical organ of thinking is in the stage of major development after birth. His brain will be formed into a quite special organ of thinking; the person receives a certain predisposition to thinking. Assume that a person spends these years in a place where Jupiter is on the opposite side of the earth, the latter thus hindering Jupiter's influences. Such a person's brain is less developed into an organ for thinking. If, on the other hand, the earth with its substances and forces is active in a person and everything proceeding from them is transformed, say, by the moon influences, which, in a certain sense, are always present, such a person turns into a dull dreamer, one who is barely aware. Between these two possibilities we find any number of variations.

Let us take the case of an individual possessing forces from his former incarnation that predestine his thinking to develop in a pronounced way in the earth life on which he is about to embark. He is on the verge of descending to earth. Since Jupiter has its set time for completing its orbit, he chooses the moment when he is to appear on earth, when he is to be born, so that Jupiter sends down its rays directly.

In this manner, the starry constellation provides the setting into which the human being allows himself to be born, depending on the conditions of his former incarnations.

Today, in the age of the consciousness soul, the human being must free himself increasingly from what is becoming evident to you here. It is a matter, however, of freeing oneself from these forces in the proper manner, of actually doing something I have indicated in regard to the Saturn effects, namely of trying to turn once again from the mere shadowy, intellectual developing of thoughts to a pictorial, concrete one. What is developed out of spiritual science in the way I described it in *Knowledge of the Higher Worlds* is also a guideline for human beings to become independent in the right way from the cosmic forces that are nevertheless active in them.

It depends on the starry constellations how a human being finds his way into earth life as he allows himself to be born. Yet, he has to equip himself with forces that make him independent in the right way from this starry constellation.

It is to such insights that our civilization must attain once again, insights concerning the relationship of the human being with the cosmos beyond the earth. Human beings must acquire an attitude that makes them realize that it is not only the ordinary forces of heredity acknowledged by today's science that are active in the human organization. In regard to the actual facts it is sheer nonsense, for example, to believe that the forces transmitted through heredity are contained in the structure of the female organism. Nowadays, heredity is an unclear, mystical concept; it is thought that the above forces then develop a heart, a liver, and so on. There would be no heart in the human organism if the sun did not incorporate it into the latter, and proceeding from the head at that. There would be no liver if Venus would not incorporate it into the human organism. And so it is with each single organ. They are certainly connected with extraterrestrial effects. The Jupiter forces are active in the human brain. The Saturn forces influence the healthy or pathological way in which the astral body is fitted into the physical organization. Human beings learn to speak because the Mars forces work in them; they become evident through speech.

These are matters humanity must once again learn to understand. We must realize that human beings cannot be explained by a science that merely considers earthly phenomena. Then, the connection between the human being and the earth will also become better known. After all, the other beings dwelling in our surroundings are also not merely creatures of the earth. To begin with, only the minerals are earth beings. Yet, in the minerals, too, changes have taken place that in turn were dependent upon forces in the earth's cosmic environment. Insofar as they are crystallized, all our metals owe their shape to extraterrestrial forces. They were formed when the earth had not yet evolved its own forces intensely but when forces from outside the earth were still active in it. Healing properties contained in minerals and particularly in metals are connected with the way the metals developed within the earth through cosmic forces.

When we go back in the post-Atlantean age to the first epoch, when the ancient Indian culture was at its prime, we see that the human being definitely experienced himself in the whole universe, as a citizen of the cosmos. Although he had not yet developed the faculties mankind is so proud of today, he was Man in the true sense of the word.

Subsequently, the human being was more or less diverted from the cosmic forces. Still, in the whole Chaldean epoch and early Greek time, we see that human beings looked up at least to the sun. In a certain sense, they were still like a kind of amphibian, a being that was happy when the rays of the sun poured down upon it and it no longer had to burrow in the earth's dankness. The human being had turned into an amphibian. Now, inasmuch as he believes he is related only to the earth's forces, one cannot even say any longer that man is like a mole. At most, he is really an earthworm that is aware of the return of something that rose in the first place from earth into space, namely, of rain water. This is the only thing the human being still perceives of extraterrestrial forces. But even earthworms perceive that—you could have seen it this morning if you had set foot in the streets! In his materialism, the human being today has basically turned into an earthworm. Once again, we must overcome this earthworm nature. We can do that only when we develop to the point of recognizing our connection with the cosmos outside the earth.

Therefore, my dear friends, the point is that we must bring it about in our age to lift ourselves out of our civilization and this earthworm-state to a new spirituality.

LECTURE XIV
Dornach, May 13, 1921

The lectures I have just given on the nature of color and the lecture last Thursday preceding the ones on color may have served to show that we can approach the true nature of man only if we consider the human being in connection with the whole universe. Yet, when asking about the nature of the human being, we must at length learn to look up from the earth to what is extra-terrestrial. Our age in particular stands in need of this. For, as we have seen, the human intellect has grown more and more shadowlike. Particularly since the developments of the nineteenth century it is no longer rooted in reality.

All this indicates to us that human beings absolutely have to think of receiving new impulses into their soul life. All this will become even clearer to us as we turn our minds today again to certain incisive cosmic events; having studied them already from outer points of view, we shall bring these cosmic events once more before our souls.

You will no doubt remember and probably also know from your reading of my *Occult Science* that one of those mighty events that intervened in the earth's evolution was the moon's withdrawal from the earth being. The moon we see shining down upon us from the cosmos was once united with the earth. It separated from the earth and has been circling it ever since as its satellite.

We know of the profound changes in human evolution that are connected with this separation of the moon from the earth. You know that we have to go far back—far beyond the Atlantean flood—to reach that time when the moon departed from earth existence.

Today, we will only consider what became manifest on earth with respect to the human being and the surrounding kingdoms of nature through the moon's separation from the earth. We have already seen that the variously colored minerals basically derive their colors from this relationship of the moon to the earth. This insight has enabled us to bring these cosmic events together with an artistic conception of existence. Very important other things are also connected with this. The human being, as we know, has brought his nature with him from the preceding metamorphoses of earth existence, from the Saturn, Sun, and Moon nature. Now, while he evolved as a Saturn, Sun, and Moon being, no mineral kingdom existed as yet in his environment. The mineral kingdom and everything of a mineral nature appeared only during earth evolution. Hence, what is now considered mineral matter permeated the human being only during the earth age. During the ancient Saturn, Sun, and Moon age, the human being contained nothing of a mineral element. Nor was he as yet a being who depended on spending his existence on earth. On the contrary, he was a being who, through his very constitution, belonged to the whole cosmos.

Prior to the moon leaving the earth, before the mineral kingdom in its multicolored nature developed within the earth, the human being was as yet not adapted at all to the earth. And, if we may so express ourselves, the question of what to do with man was indeed a very real one for the spiritual beings guiding this earth evolution. Should he be placed upon the earth or should he spend his existence outside and beyond it? We can actually call it a decision on the part of the beings who guide the evolution of mankind that the moon was separated and that the whole earth and man along with it were changed. For through the fact that the crude moon substance was separated from the earth the human being acquired the organization that enabled him to become an earth being. Hence, through this event—through the moon separation and the incorporation of the mineral kingdom into earth—the human being became an earthly being. Basically, it was this that gave man his earthly weight. On the other hand, he would never have become a being capable of inner freedom if he had not received this earthly weight. Earlier, he was not a personality in the proper sense. He became a personality due to the fact that the forces intended to form his body drew together. This densification took place because of the moon separation and the incorporation of the mineral kingdom. The human being became a personality and thus accessible to freedom.

This evolution of man on earth since the departure of the moon has gone through the most diverse stages. One can say that as long as nothing else had occurred except that the moon had left the earth, it was always possible for the human being to receive images of ancient clairvoyance due to his whole organization and nature of body and soul.

The human being was not deprived of this faculty of having clairvoyant images by the moon's separation. He beheld the world in images, something we have often described. If nothing else had taken place, human beings would be living in that world of images to this day. But as we know, evolution went still further. The human being did not remain in a condition that merely fetters him to the earth. He was in turn induced to a regressive development, as it were, and the nineteenth century was the culmination point of this development. I have characterized this repeatedly in my recent lectures. Already in ancient times it had come about that although in a sense man was earth-bound, weighted down in his metabolic system, in his head system he was enabled to cosmic existence. Human beings developed their intellect. The images of ancient clairvoyance condensed into this intellect, something that continued up until the fourth century A.D. It was only then, and particularly after the fifteenth century, that the human intellect became more and more shadowy. Though it is something entirely spiritual, this human intellect has no real existence at all; basically, it possesses only what would have to be described as a picturelike existence. When a person thinks today merely by means of his intellect, his thoughts are not rooted in reality. Human thoughts only move about in a shadowy existence and this is becoming more and more the case. This development reached an extreme in the nineteenth century and today human beings altogether lack a sense of reality. They live in a spiritual element but are materialists. With their spiritual thoughts that are, however, only shadow thoughts, they think only in terms of material existence.

Thus this second event came to pass. The human being has again become more spiritual, but the spiritual contents bestowed on him by matter in earlier times no longer ensoul him. He has become more spiritual; yet, with what is spiritual he merely thinks of things material.

Now you know that one day the moon will reunite with the earth. The point in time when this reunion of moon and earth will occur is placed by astronomers and geologists who live in abstractions, many, many thousands of years in the future; that, however, is an illusion. In reality, we are not so very far away from that point in time. As you know, humanity as such is becoming younger and younger. It is becoming more and more the case that the development of body and soul only continues up to a certain point in life. At the time of the death of the Christ when the event of Golgotha took place, mankind in general was capable of physical and soul development until age thirty-three. Today, people are able to develop only until age twenty-seven. In the fourth millennium A.D., a time will come when human beings will be capable of development only until age twenty-one. Again, in the seventh millennium, a time will come when their bodily nature will be capable of development only until the fourteenth year of life. Then, women will cease to be fertile; an entirely different form of living on earth will come about. That will be the time when the moon will again approach the earth and will be incorporated into it.

You see, my dear friends, human beings must now begin to pay attention to such extraterrestrial events. They must not go on dreaming, vaguely and abstractly, of something divine. They must begin to focus on the events connected with their evolution. They must know: The moon once separated from the earth; the moon will reunite with the earth again. And just as this moon separation had a tremendous impact, so will the moons reentry. It is true that we will still be inhabiting the earth then as human beings, but we shall no longer be born in the ordinary way. We shall be connected with the earth in a way other than through birth. We shall have evolved in a certain manner by the time this point is reached. We must now learn to connect what is happening today—the increasing shadowiness of the intellect—with what will occur one day in earth evolution as an incisive event, namely, the moon's whirling back into earth's matter.

Our intellect is becoming more and more shadowy. If this were to go on, if men were never to make up their minds to receive what can come to them from spiritual worlds, the human being would gradually become completely absorbed in the shadowy cast of his intellect.

Try to realize what this shadowlike intellect actually contains. It cannot really understand the human being himself; it comprehends the minerals. That, after all, is the only thing the shadowy intellect can understand to a certain degree. Already the life of the plant remains a riddle for it; this is true even more so of the life of the animals, and its own life becomes completely obscure for it. Thus people go on evolving views of the world that, in reality, are but questions, because all they contain is unable to approach the nature of plant and animal, least of all that of the human being. Yet, this forming of pictures will increase more and more unless we make up our minds to receive what is being given us by way of new Imaginations in which the existence of the world is described. Into our shadowy intellectual concepts the living wisdom that spiritual science is able to give must be received. The shadow images of the intellect must in this way be called to life.

This calling to life of the shadow images of the intellect is not only a human event, it is a cosmic event. Remember what I described in my *Occult Science*—how once upon a time human souls migrated up to the planets and afterward returned to earth existence. I outlined in my *Occult Science* how the human beings of Mars,

Jupiter, and so on came down again to earth. Now, a most important event took place—it can only be described from the facts that are confirmed as truths in the spiritual world—a very important event occurred at the end of the seventies of the nineteenth century. Whereas in ancient Atlantean times these *human* beings descended to earth from Saturn, Jupiter, Mars, and the other planets—and it was therefore a matter of *human* soul beings entering the earth existence then—now a time is beginning when beings who are *not human* are coming down to earth from cosmic regions beyond. These beings are not human but depend for the further development of their existence on coming to earth and on entering here into relationships with men.

Thus, since the eighties of the nineteenth century, heavenly beings are seeking to enter this earth existence. Just as the Vulcan men were the last to come down to earth,* so Vulcan beings are now actually entering this earth existence. Heavenly beings are already here in our earth existence. And it is thanks to the fact that beings from beyond the earth are bringing messages down into this earthly existence that it is possible at all to have a comprehensive spiritual science today.

Taken as a whole, however, how does the human race behave? If I may say so, the human race behaves in a cosmically rude way toward the beings who are appearing from the cosmos on earth, albeit, to begin with, only slowly. Humanity takes no notice of them, ignores them. It is this that will lead the earth into increasingly tragic conditions. For in the course of the next few centuries, more and more spirit beings will move among us

* Translator's note: This occurred during the Atlantean age.

whose language we ought to understand. We shall understand it only if we seek to comprehend what comes from them, namely, the contents of spiritual science. This is what they wish to bestow on us. They want us to act according to spiritual science; they want this spiritual science to be translated into social action and the conduct of earthly life.

Since the last third of the nineteenth century, we are actually dealing with the influx of spirit beings from the universe. Initially, these were beings dwelling in the sphere between moon and Mercury, but they are closing in upon earth, so to say, seeking to gain a foothold in earthly life through human beings imbuing themselves with thoughts of spiritual beings in the cosmos. This is another way of describing what I outlined earlier when I said that we must call our shadowy intellect to life with the pictures of spiritual science. That is the abstract way of describing it. The description is concrete when we say: Spirit beings are seeking to come down into earth existence and must be received. Upheaval upon upheaval will ensue, and earth existence will at length arrive at social chaos if these beings descended and human existence were to consist only of opposition against them. For these beings wish to be nothing less than the advance guard of what will happen to earth existence when the moon reunites once again with earth.

Nowadays it may appear comparatively harmless to people when they think only those automatic, lifeless thoughts that arise through comprehension of the mineral world itself and the mineral element's effects in plant, animal, and man. Yes, indeed, people revel in these thoughts; as materialists, they feel good about them, for only such thoughts are conceived today. But imagine that people were to continue thinking in this way, unfolding nothing but such thoughts until the eighth millennium when moon existence will once more unite with the life of the earth. What would come about then? The beings I have spoken about *will* descend gradually to the earth. Vulcan beings, Vulcan supermen, Venus supermen, Mercury supermen, sun supermen, and so on will unite themselves with earth existence. Yet, if human beings persist in their opposition to them, this earth existence will pass over into chaos in the course of the next few thousand years. People will indeed be capable of developing their intellect in an automatic way; it can develop even in the midst of barbaric conditions. The fullness of human potential, however, will not be included in this intellect and people will have no relationship to the beings who wish graciously to come down to them into earthly life.

All the beings presently conceived so incorrectly in people's thoughts—incorrectly because the mere shadowy intellect can only conceive of the mineral, the crudely material element, be it in the mineral, plant, animal or even human kingdom—these thoughts of human beings that have no reality all of a sudden will become realities when the moon and the earth will unite again. From the earth, there will spring forth a horrible brood of beings. In character they will be in between the mineral and plant kingdoms. They will be beings resembling automatons, with an over-abundant intellect of great intensity. Along with this development, which will spread over the earth, the latter will be covered as if by a network or web of ghastly spiders possessing tremendous wisdom. Yet their organization will not even reach up to the level of the plants. They will be horrible spiders who will be entangled with one another. In their outward movements they will imitate everything human beings have thought up with their shadowy intellect, which did not allow itself to be stimulated by what is to come through new Imagination and through spiritual science in general.

All these unreal thoughts people are thinking will be endowed with being. As it is covered with layers of air today, or occasionally with swarms of locusts, the earth will be covered with hideous mineral-plant-like spiders that intertwine with one another most cleverly but in a frighteningly evil manner. To the extent that human beings have not enlivened their shadowy, intellectual concepts, they will have to unite their being, not with the entities who are seeking to descend since the last third of the nineteenth century, but instead with these ghastly mineral-plant-like spidery creatures. They will have to dwell together with these spiders; they will have to seek their further progress in cosmic evolution in the evolutionary stream that this spider brood will then assume.

You see, this is something that is very much a reality of earth humanity's evolution. It is known today by a large number of those human beings who hold mankind back from receiving spiritual scientific knowledge. For there are those who are actually conscious allies of this spidery entangling of human earth existence. Today, we must no longer recoil from descriptions such as these. For descriptions of this kind are behind what is said to this day by many people who, based on ancient traditions, still have some awareness of things like these, and who would like to surround these ancient traditions with a certain veil of secrecy. The evolution of earthly humanity is not such that it can be veiled in secrecy any longer. However great the resistance in hostile quarters, these things must be said; for, as I have stated again and again, the acceptance or rejection of spiritual scientific knowledge is a serious matter facing mankind. It is not something that can be decided on the basis of more or less indifferent sympathies or antipathies; we are dealing with something that definitely affects the whole configuration of the cosmos.

We are dealing with the question of whether humanity at the present time will resolve to grow gradually into what benevolent spirits, wishing to ally themselves with human beings, bring down from the universe, or whether mankind will seek its continued cosmic existence in the gradual entanglement, in the spider-brood of its own, merely shadowy thoughts. It does not suffice today to set down in abstract formulas the need for spiritual scientific knowledge. It is necessary to show how thoughts become realities. This is what is so dreadful about all abstract theosophists who appear on the scene and place abstractions before people, for example: Thoughts will become realities in the future. But it does not occur to them to present the full and actual implications of these matters. For the concrete implication is that the intellectual, shadow-like thoughts, spun inwardly by human beings today, will one day cover the earth like a spider's web. Human beings will become entangled in it if they are not willing to rise above these shadowy thoughts.

The path of the ascent, my dear friends, is indeed outlined. We must take profoundly serious thoughts such as the one with which I concluded my lectures on color last Sunday where I said: The point is to lift the comprehension of color out of the abstractions of physics into a region where the creative fancy, the feeling of the artist who understands the being of color, will harmonize effectively with a spiritual scientific insight into the world. We have seen how the beings and nature of color can be taken hold of, how the artistic element, which physics with its dreadful diagrams lets slide down into the ahrimanic sphere, can be lifted up. Thus, a theory of color can be founded; it would be remote from the established thought habits of modern science, yet can provide a basis for artistic creativity, if we will only imbue ourselves with its insight. Such thoughts must certainly be taken seriously.

Another thought must be earnestly considered. What do we witness today throughout the civilized world? Our young people are sent into the hospitals and to the scientific faculties of the universities; there the human being is explained to them. They become acquainted with the human skeleton and with the human organism by studying the corpse. They learn to put together the human being logically in abstract thoughts.

Yet, my dear friends, this is no way to comprehend the human being; in this way, one only gets to know the mineral aspect of man. What we learn about the human being through such a science is something that simply and solely has significance from the moon's separation until its return, something that out of the spider thoughts of today will then turn into spider beings. A knowledge must be prepared that takes hold of the human being quite differently, and this can be done only if science is lifted into artistic vision. We must admit that science in the present-day sense of the word can reach only to a certain level. It reaches only as far as the mineral element in the mineral, plant, and human kingdoms. Already in the plant kingdom science must change into art; still more so in the animal. It is sheer nonsense to try to understand the animal form in the way the anatomists and physiologists do. And as long as we do not admit that it is nonsense, the shadowy intellect cannot really be transformed into a living, spiritual grasp of the world.

What our young people are taught in so wretchedly abstract a form in the universities must everywhere turn into an artistic comprehension of the world. For nature around us creates artistically. Unless it is understood that nature around us is an artistic creation and can be grasped only with artistic concepts, no good will come of our world conceptions. The idea should take hold that the torture chambers in medieval castles, where people were locked into the "Iron Maiden," for instance, and them pierced through with spears, remind us of a procedure that, though more physical and concrete, is the same as the one that occurs when young people today are introduced to anatomy and physiology and told that this will make them understand something of human nature. No, they comprehend nothing but what has been produced by a soul-spiritual element of torture: The human being torn limb from limb, the mineralized human being—that part of man that one day will be woven into the spider-cover of the earth.

Is it not sad that the power of civilization belongs now to those who consider the thoughts of truth itself, which most inwardly and intimately relate to the salvation and whole mission of mankind's development in the world, nonsense! It is tragic and we must be mindful of this tragedy. For only if we place this clearly and objectively before our soul's eye, shall we perhaps bestir ourselves to resolve to do what we can so that the intellect, shadowy as it has become, may find the way to admit the spiritual world that is approaching from the heavenly realms. Then, this shadowy intellect will be made fit for the potential it is to achieve. After all, this shadowy intellect should not be cast back into the realm beneath the plant kingdom, into a spider brood that will spread over the earth. No, it is intended that the human being shall be lifted up, in that time when women will no longer be fertile, when the eighth millennium will have arrived and the moon will unite again with the earth. The earthly shall then remain behind, and the human being only direct it from outside—like a foot stool. It will be something he is not supposed to take along with him into his cosmic existence. Human beings should prepare themselves so that they need not become one with what will someday have to develop on the surface of this earth in the manner described above.

Mankind entered from a pre-earthly existence into this physical existence. At the time of the departure of the moon, physical birth commenced. The human being began to be born of woman. Just as this came to pass, so in the future the human being will no longer born of woman. For that is only a passing episode in the whole of cosmic evolution. It is the episode that is to bring to man the feeling of freedom, the consciousness of freedom, the integrated wholeness of individuality and personality. It is an episode that must not be disdained, an episode that was necessary in the whole cosmic process, but it must not be retained. Human beings must not give themselves up to the indolence of merely looking up to an abstract divine principle; they must concretely behold everything connected with their evolution. For they can attain a true inner revitalization of the whole soul-spirit being only if they comprehend that great period of time—but in its concrete evolutionary configuration—through which they will live in successive earth incarnations.

This is what a true spiritual science tells us today. Yet, such a spiritual science encounters opposition. We are threatened by a conscious will that would exclude us from spirituality and unite us with the spider web of the earth. This conscious will dwells in some people, for they believe that it will be to their advantage if they train only themselves spiritually and leave the others to live in ignorance. In most cases, however, this is done in ignorance; basically, people do not have the remotest idea of the appalling earthly destiny they are approaching by uniting themselves with what an ancient spiritual knowledge called the sixteen paths of human perdition. For, my dear friends, just as there are many ways in which we can turn with the shadowy intellect toward what can come to us as a message from the spiritual worlds, so there are variations of the shadowy intellect itself, various ways of uniting ourselves through this intellectual activity with the elements of spidery incrustation that will be spun over the whole earth in the future. In that time, the intellect will hold sway objectively in the manifold limbs these spider creatures will possess. They will entwine and wind themselves around one another; in doing so, in these convolutions reminiscent of the caduceus, they will produce the most marvelous, clever, the most ingenious formations — ingenious in todays's sense of the word. However, by again acquiring an understanding of the artistic from within, human beings will be able to show understanding for what goes beyond the mineral and is expressed in the formation of the plant.

It is symptomatic that in the course of mankind's evolution it was Goethe who discovered the teaching of metamorphosis—Goethe, who was artistically inclined. All the pedants around him considered it to be dilettantism, and they think so even today. In Goethe, however, the artistic conception of the world and his clarity of mind in general combined with the power of vision that recognizes, even in nature herself, nature as the artist. He was not yet capable of seeing the animal kingdom in the same way, except for the formation of the vertebra and the skull. That wondrous transmutation of a previous existence of man, where the present shape of the head develops from the form of the earlier remainder of the body, that marvelously artistic transformation of the long bones of the limbs into the spherical bones of the skull—only when this will truly be perceived will a real inner comprehension of the difference between the head and the whole remaining human form result. Such is the insight we must attain if we would plastically connect the head with the remainder of the human organism.

Yet, as art, this is at the same time true science, for all science that does not rise to the level of art is a deceptive science, a science casting humanity into cosmic misfortune. Thus, we see, on the one hand, that a true spiritual science shows us the way to an artistic grasp of things. Like a great hymn, I might say, this dwelled in Goethe's soul, when, as early as 1780, he wrote "Nature" his hymn in prose: "Nature, we are surrounded and encompassed by her..." The whole hymn weaves a tapestry of thoughts such that one would like to say: It is like the unfolding of a mighty longing to receive spirit beings from the whole universe. Indeed, to pursue and develop further the thoughts living in Goethe's hymn "Nature" would be to provide a dwelling place for those beings who are seeking to descend from the cosmos to the earth. On the other hand, the torturous concepts developed in the nineteenth century concerning human physiology, biology, the system of plants, and so on, actually have nothing to do with the true being of the plants, something we had occasion to point out during our reflections on color. These inartistic concepts neither provide real insight nor do they penetrate to the human level. Therefore, what is held to be science today is essentially a product of Ahriman; it leads mankind to earthly doom and does not allow the human being to reach the sphere that, if I may say so, is brought toward him since the last third of the nineteenth century by beings from the cosmos.

The cultivation of spiritual science, my dear friends, is no abstract pursuit. It implies opening doors to cosmic influences that have been trying to enter upon the earth since the last third of the nineteenth century. It is a real, cosmic event to cultivate spiritual science. We need to become conscious of this fact.

Thus we may say, we overlook the whole span of time from the moon's departure until its return. This moon, which reflects the sunlight to us, has indeed a profound connection to our existence. It separated from the earth in order that the human being might become free. Humanity, however, must make use of this period so as not to provide for the moon, when the latter will have returned again, the material that can be bound up with the moon existence in the earth in that new kingdom of nature, of which I have now told you a little in a more or less graphic form.

We can say that now and then there arises in human beings some kind of forboding of what is to come. I do not know what meaning has been attached by readers to what Nietzsche describes in the chapter on the ugliest man in the valley of death in his *Zarathustra*. It is a touching, tragic description. Of course, Nietzsche had no vision of the valley of death into which earth existence will be transformed when the above-mentioned spider brood will cover the earth. Nevertheless, at the time when this fantasy of the valley of death arose in Nietzsche, there lived in him subconsciously something of this picture of the future. Therefore, he placed the ugliest of human beings into this vale of death. It was indeed some sort of foreboding of the time to come when human beings will be carried along in the most hideous shapes by the moon existence as it sinks down upon the earth, if they continue to cultivate only their shadowy thoughts. As the ugliest of men, they will fall into this swarm of spiders and be united with it.

What would be the use of keeping these things secret today, as many people would have us do? It would mean pulling the wool over people's eyes. After all, a large part of what is disseminated as spirituality today is nothing else but throwing dust in people's eyes. Occasionally one encounters people who realize what this means, namely, not to comprehend a single historical event as it is in reality. How many people are there today who know that events of fundamental importance are taking place in our days? I have already drawn attention to these things. How few are prepared really to enter into them? People would like to close their eyes to them. They would like to say: Well, these things are really not of so much importance. Yet, the signs of the times are there, and should be understood by human beings.

This is what I wished to add to my considerations on the world of color and man's relationship with the cosmos beyond the earth. We shall continue with these studies in the future.

LECTURE XV
Dornach, June 2, 1921

In the past few weeks, I have repeatedly spoken of the great change that took place in Western civilization during the fourth century A.D. When such a matter is discussed, one is obliged to point out one thing again and again, that has already been the subject of discussion here many times. Yet it is necessary to focus on it time and again. I am referring to the metamorphoses of human development, markedly differing from each other on the soul level. When speaking of such a major point in human evolution as the one in the fourth century, one has to pay heed to the fact that the soul life of humanity changed in a sense with one great leap.

This view is not prevalent today. The prevailing opinion holds that the human race has undergone a certain history. This history is traced back to about the third or fourth millennium along the lines of the most recent documented records. Then, going back further, there is nothing for a long time; finally, one arrives at animalistic-human conditions. But in regard to the duration of the historical development, it is assumed that human beings have in the main always thought and felt the way they do today; at most, they formerly adhered to a somewhat more childish stage of scientific pursuit. Finally, however, human beings have struggled upward to the level of which we say today that it is splendid how far we have come in the comprehension of the world. To be sure, a reasonably unbiased consideration of human life arrives at the opposite view. I have had to indicate to you

273

the presence of a mighty transition in the fourth Christian century; I outlined the other change in the whole human soul life at the beginning of the fifteenth century. Finally, I described how a turning point in human soul life occurred also during the nineteenth century.

Today, we shall consider one detail in this whole development. I would like to place before you a personality who illustrates particularly well that human beings in the relatively recent past thought completely differently from the way we think today. The personality, who has been mentioned also in earlier lectures, is John Scotus Erigena,[1] who lived in the ninth century A.D. at the court of Charles the Bald in France.[2] Erigena, whose home was across the Channel, who was born approximately in the year 815 and lived well into the second half of the ninth century, is truly a representative of the more intimate Christian mode of thinking of the ninth century A.D. It is, however, a manner of thinking that is still completely under the influence of the first Christian centuries. John Scotus Erigena apparently was intent on immersing himself in the prevalent scholarly and theological culture of his time. In his age, scholarly and theological knowledge were one and the same. And such learning was most readily acquired across the British Channel, particularly in the Irish institutions where Christianity was cultivated in a certain esoteric manner. The Franconian kings then had ways of attracting such personalities to their courts. The Christian knowledge permeating the Franconian kingdom, even spreading from there further east into western Germany, was mainly influenced by those who had been attracted from across the Channel by these Franconian kings.

John Scotus Erigena also immersed himself into the contents of the writings by the Greek Church Fathers, studying also the texts of a certain problematic nature within Western civilization, namely, the texts by Dionysius the Areopagite.[3] As you know, the latter is considered by some to be a direct pupil of Paul. Yet, these texts only surfaced in the sixth century, and many scholars therefore refer to them as pseudo-Dionysian writings composed in the sixth century by an unknown person, which were then accredited to Paul's disciple.

People who say that are ignorant of the way spiritual knowledge was passed on in those early centuries. A school like the one in which Paul himself taught in Athens possessed insights that initially were taught only orally. Handed down from generation to generation, they were finally written down much, much later on. What was thus recorded at a later time, was not necessarily anything less than genuine for that reason; it could preserve to some extent the identity of something that was centuries old. Furthermore, the great value that we place on personality today was certainly not attached to personality in those earlier ages. Perhaps we will be able to touch upon a circumstance in this lecture that must be discussed in connection with Erigena, namely, why people did not place much value on personality in that age.

There is no doubt about one thing: The teachings recorded in the name of Dionysius the Areopagite were considered especially worthy of being written down in the sixth century. They were considered the substance of what had been left from the early Christian times, which were now in particular need of being recorded. We should consider this fact as such to be significant. In the times prior to the fourth century, people simply had more confidence in memory working from generation to generation than they had in later periods. In earlier ages, people were not so eager to write everything down. They were aware, however, that the time was approaching when it would become increasingly necessary to write down things that earlier had been passed on by word of mouth with great ease; for the things that were then recorded in the writings of Dionysius were of a subtle nature.

Now, what John Scotus Erigena was able to study in these writings was certainly apt to make an extraordinarily profound impression on him. For the mode of thinking found in this Dionysius was approximately as follows. With the concepts we form and the perceptions we acquire, we human beings can comprehend the physical sensory world. We can then draw our conclusions from the facts and beings of this sensory world by means of reasoning. We work our way upward, as it were, to a rational content that is then no longer visually perceptible but is experienced in ideas and concepts. Once we have developed our concepts and thoughts from the sensory facts and beings, we have the urge to move upward with them to the supersensory, to the spiritual and divine.

Now, Dionysius does not proceed by saying that we learn this or that from the sensory things; he does not say that our intellect acquires its concepts and then goes on to deduce a deity, a spiritual world. No, Dionysius says, The concepts we acquire from the things of the senses are all unsuitable to express the deity. No matter how subtle the concepts we form of sensory things, we simply cannot express what constitutes divinity with the aid of these concepts. We must therefore resort to negative concepts rather than positive ones. When we encounter our fellowmen, for example, we speak of personality. According to this Dionysian view, when we speak of God, we should not speak of personality, for the concept of personality is much too small and to lowly to designate the deity. Rather we should speak of super-personality. When referring to God, we should not even speak of being, of existence. We say, a man *is*, an animal, a plant *is*. We should not ascribe existence to God in the same sense as we attribute existence to us, the animals, and the plants; to Him, we ought to ascribe a super-existence. Thus, according to Dionysius, we should try to rise from the sensory world to certain concepts but then we should turn them upside down, as it were, allowing them to pass over into the negative. We should rise from the sense world to positive theology but then turn upside down and establish negative theology. This negative theology would actually be so sublime, so permeated by God and divine thinking that it can only be expressed in negative predicates, in negations of what human beings can picture of the sensory world.

Dionysius the Areopagite believed he could penetrate into the divine spiritual world by leaving behind, so to speak, all that can be encompassed by the intellect and thus finding the way into a world transcending reason.

If we consider Dionysius a disciple of Paul, then he lived from the end of the first Christian century into the second one. This means that he lived a few centuries prior to the decisive fourth century A.D. He sensed what was approaching: The culmination point of the development of human reason. With a part of his being, Dionysius looked back into the days of antiquity. As you know, prior to the eighth century B.C., human beings did not speak of the intellect in the way they did after the eighth century. Reason, or the rational soul was not born until the eigth century B.C., and from the birth of the rational soul originated the Greek and Roman cul-

277

tures. These then reached their highest point of development in the fourth century A.D. Prior to this eighth century B.C. people did not perceive the world through the intellect at all; they perceived it directly, through contemplation. The early Egyptian and Chaldean insights were attained through contemplation; they were attained in the same manner in which we acquire our external sensory insights, despite the fact that these pre-Christian insights were spiritual insights. The spirit was perceived just as we today perceive the sensory world and as the Greeks already perceived the sensory world. Therefore, in Dionysius the Areopagite, something like a yearning held sway for a kind of perception lying beyond human reason.

Now, in his mind, Dionysius confronted the mighty Mystery of Golgotha. He dwelled in the intellectual culture of his time. Anybody studying the writings of Dionysius sees—regardless of who Dionysius was— how immersed this man was in all that the intellectual culture of his time had produced. He was a well educated Greek but at the same time a man whose whole personality was imbued with the magnitude of the Mystery of Golgotha. He was a man who realized that regardless of how much we strain our intellect, we cannot comprehend the Mystery of Golgotha and what stands behind it. We must transcend the intellect. We have to evolve from positive theology to negative theology.

When John Scotus Erigena read the writings of this Dionysius the Areopagite, they made a profound impression on him even in the ninth century. For what followed upon the fourth Christian century had more of an Augustine character and developed only slowly in the way I described in the earlier lectures. The mind of such a person, particularly of one of those who had trained themselves in the schools of wisdom over in Ireland, still dwelled in the first Christian centuries; he clung with all the fibers of his soul to what is written in the texts of Dionysius the Areopagite. Yet, at the same time, John Scotus Erigena also had the powerful urge to establish by means of reason, by what the human being can attain through his intellect, a kind of positive theology, which, to him, was philosophy. He therefore diligently studied the Greek Church Fathers in particular. We discover in him a thorough knowledge, for example of Origen,[4] who lived from the second to the third century A.D.

When we study Origen, we actually discover a world view completely different from the Christian view, that is from what appeared later as the Christian view. Origen definitely still holds the opinion that one has to penetrate theology with philosophy. He believes that it is only possible to examine the human being and his nature only if he is considered as an emanation of the deity, as having had his origin in God. Then, however, man lowered himself increasingly; yet through the Mystery of Golgotha, he has gained the possibility of ascending once again to the deity in order once more to unite with God. From God into the world and back to God—this is how one could describe the path that Origen perceived as his own. Basically, something like this also underlies the Dionysian writings, and then was passed on to such personalities as John Scotus Erigena. But there were many others like him.

One could say that it is a sort of historical miracle that posterity came to know the writings of John Scotus Erigena at all. In contrast to other texts of a similar nature from the first centuries that have been completely lost, Erigena's writings were preserved until the eleventh, twelfth, a few even until the thirteenth century. At that time, they were declared heretic by the Pope; the order was given to find and burn all copies. Only much later, manuscripts from the eleventh and thirteenth century were rediscovered in some obscure monastery. In the fourteenth, fifteenth, sixteenth, and seventeenth centuries, people knew nothing of John Scotus Erigena. His writings had been burned like so many other manuscripts[5] of a similar content from that period. From Rome's point of view the search was more successful in the case of other manuscripts: all copies were fed to the flames. Yet, of Erigena's works, a few copies remained.

Now, considering the ninth century and also taking into account that in John Scotus Erigena we have an expert in the wisdom and insights of the first Christian centuries, we must conclude the following. He is a characteristic representative of what extended form an earlier age, from the time preceding the fourth century, into later periods. One could say that in these later times, all knowledge had ossified in the dead Latin language. All the wisdom of the spiritual world that had been alive earlier became ossified, dogmatized, rigid, and intellectualized. Yet, in people like Erigena lived something of the ancient aliveness of direct spiritual knowledge that had existed in the first Christian centuries and was utilized by the most enlightened minds to comprehend the Mystery of Golgotha.

For a time, this wisdom had to die out in order for the intellect of man to be cultivated from the first third of the fifteenth century until our era. While the intellect as such is a spiritual achievement of the human being, initially it turned only to the material realm. The ancient wealth of wisdom had to die so that the intellect in its shadowy nature could be born. If, instead of immersing ourselves in a scholarly, pedantic manner into his writings, we do so with our whole being, we will notice that through Scotus Erigena something had spoken out of soul depths other than those from which people spoke later on. There, the human being had still spoken out of mental depths that subsequently could no longer be reached by human soul life. Everything was more spiritual, and if human beings spoke intellectually at all, they spoke of matters in the spiritual realm.

It is extremely important for one to scrutinize carefully what the structure of Erigena's knowledge was like. In his mighty work on the divisions of nature that has come down to posterity in the manner I described, he divided what he had to say concerning the world in four chapters. In the first, he initially speaks of the uncreated and the created world (see outline below). In the way Erigena believed himself able to do it, the first chapter describes God and the way He was prior to His approaching something like the creation of the world.

Ancient Legacy:

3. post-Atlantean Age:	I. Uncreated and created world: *Theology*
2. post-Atlantean Age:	II. Created and creating world: *Ideal World*
1. post-Atlantean Age:	III. Created and noncreating world: *Pneumatology* Cosmology, Anthropology
Living Striving:	IV. Uncreated and noncreating world: *Soteriology, Eschatology* Materialistic Natural Science

The Human Being

Existence: Father
Wisdom: Son
Life: Holy Spirit

1. *is* as a mineral being.
2. lives and thrives as plant.
3. feels as animal
4. judges and draws conclusions as human being.
5. perceives as angel
6. intuits as archangel

John Scotus Erigena clearly describes this in the way he learned through the writings of Dionysius. He describes by means of developing the most refined intellectual concepts. At the same time, he is aware that with them he only reaches up to a certain limit beyond which lies negative theology. He therefore merely approaches the actual true being of the spirit, of the divine. Among other topics, we find in this chapter the beautiful discourse about the Trinity, instructive even for our age. He states that when we view the things around us, we initially discover existence as an overall spiritual quality (see above). Existence embraces everything. Now, we should not attribute existence as possessed by things to God. Yet, looking upward to existence transcending existence, we cannot but speak summarily of the deity's existence.

Likewise, we find that things in the world are illuminated and permeated by wisdom. To God, we should not merely ascribe wisdom but wisdom beyond wisdom. But when we proceed from things, we arrive at the limit of wisdom-filled things. Now, there is not only wisdom in all things. They live; there is life in all things. Therefore, when Erigena calls to mind the world, he says: I see existence, wisdom, life in the world. The world appears to me in these aspects as an existing, wisdom-filled, living world. To him, these are three veils, so to speak, that the intellect fashions when it surveys all things. One would have to see through these veils, then, to see into the divine-spiritual realm. To begin with, Erigena describes these veils: When I look upon existence, this represents the Father to me; when I look upon wisdom, it represents the Son to me; when I look upon life, it represents the Holy Spirit in the universe.

As you can see, John Scotus Erigena certainly proceeds from philosophical concepts and then makes his way up to the Christian Trinity. Inwardly, proceeding from the comprehensible, he still experiences the path from there to the so-called incomprehensible. Indeed, of this he is convinced. Yet, from the way he speaks and presents his insights we can see that he has learned from Dionysius. Precisely when he arrives at existence, wisdom, and life, which to him represent the Father, the Son, and the Holy Spirit, he would really like to have these concepts dissolve in a general spiritual element into which the human being would then have to rise by transcending concepts. However, he does not credit the human being with the faculty of arriving at a state of mind that goes beyond the conceptual.

In this, John Scotus Erigena was a product of the age that developed the intellect. Indeed, if this age had understood itself correctly, it would have had to admit that it could not enter into the realm transcending the conceptual level.

The second chapter then describes something like a second sphere of world existence, the created and the creating world (see p. 281). It is the world of the spiritual beings where we find the angels, the archangels, the Archai, and so on. This world of spiritual beings, men tioned already in the writings of Dionysius the Areopagite. is creative everywhere in the world. Yet this hierarchical world is itself created; it is begun, hence created, by the highest being and in turn is active creatively in all details of existence surrounding us.

In the third chapter, Erigena then describes as a third world the created world that is noncreating. This is the world we perceive around us with our senses. It is the world of animals, plants, and minerals, the stars, and so on. In this chapter, Erigena deals with almost everything we would designate as cosmology, anthropology, and so forth, all that we would call the realm of science.

In the fourth chapter, Erigena deals with the world that has not been created and does not create. This is again the deity, but the way it will be when all creatures, particularly all human beings, will have returned to it. It is the Godhead when it will no longer be creating, when, in blissful tranquility—this is how John Scotus Erigena imagines it—it will have reabsorbed all the beings that have emerged from it.

Now, in surveying these four chapters, we find contained in them something like a compendium of all traditional knowledge of the schools of wisdom from which Scotus Erigena had come. When we consider what he describes in the first chapter, we deal with something that can be called theology in his sense, the actual doctrine of the divine.

Considering the second chapter, we find in it what he calls in terms of our present-day language the ideal world. The ideal is pictured, however, as existing. For he does not describe abstract ideas but angels, archangels, and so forth. He pictures the whole intelligible world, as it was called. Yet it was unlike our modern intelligible world; instead it was a world filled with living beings, with living, intelligible entities.

As I said, in the third chapter Erigena describes what we would term science today, but he does so in a different way. Since the days of Galileo and Copernicus, who, after all, lived later, we no longer possess what was called cosmology or anthropology in Scotus Erigena's age. Cosmology was still described from the spiritual standpoint. It depicted how spiritual beings direct and also inhabit the stars, how the elements, fire, water, air, and earth are permeated by spiritual beings. What was described as cosmology, was indeed something different. The materialistic way of viewing things that has arisen since the middle of the fifteenth century did not yet exist in Erigena's time, and his form of anthropology also differed completely from what we call anthropology in our materialistic age.

Here, I can point out something extraordinarily characteristic for what anthropology is to John Scotus Erigena. He looks at the human being and says: First, man bears existence within himself. Hence, he is a mineral being, for he contains within himself a mineral nature (see outline p. 281). Secondly, man lives and thrives like a plant. Third, man feels as does the animal. Fourth, man judges and draws conclusions as man. Fifth, man perceives as an angel.

It goes without saying that in our age this would be an unheard-of statement! When John Scotus Erigena speaks of judgment and conclusions, something that is done, for instance, in a legal court where one pronounces judgment over somebody—then, so he says, human beings do this as human beings. But when they perceive, when they penetrate the world in perception then human beings do not behave as human beings but as angels! The reason for pointing this out is that I am trying to show you that for that period anthropology was something different from what it is for our present age. For it is true that you could hardly hear anywhere, not even in a theological seminar, that human beings perceive as angels. Therefore, one is forced to conclude that our science no longer resembles what Erigena describes in the third chapter. It has turned into something different. If we wanted to call Erigena's science by a word that is no longer applicable to anything existing today, we would have to say that it was a spiritual doctrine of the universe and man, pneumatology.

Now to the fourth chapter: This contains, first of all, Erigena's teaching of the Mystery of Golgotha and the doctrine concerning what the human being has to expect in the future, namely, entrance into the divine-spiritual world, hence, what in modern usage would be called soteriology. "Soter," after all, means savior; the teaching of the future is eschatology. We find that Erigena here deals with the concepts of the Crucifixion and Resurrection, the emanation of Divine Grace, man's path into the divine-spiritual, world, and so on.

There is one thing that truly holds our attention, if we study attentively a work such as the *De divisione naturae* by John Scotus Erigena about the divisions of nature. The world is definitely discussed as something that is perceived in spiritual qualities. He speaks of something spiritual as he observes the world. But what is not contained in this work? We have to pay attention, after all, to what is not included in a universal science such as Erigena is trying to establish there.

In John Scotus Erigena's work, you discover as good as nothing of what we call sociology today, social science, and things of that kind. One is almost inclined to say it appears from the way Erigena pictures human beings that he did not wish to give mankind social sciences, no more so than any animal species, say the lion, the tiger, or any bird species, would come out with a sociology if it produced some sort of science. For a lion would not talk about the way it ought to live together with the other lions or how it ought to acquire its food and so on; this is something that comes instinctively. Just as little could we imagine a sociology of sparrows. Surely sparrows could reveal any number of the most interesting cosmic secrets from their viewpoint, but they would never produce any teaching about economics, for sparrows would consider this a subject that goes without saying, something they do because their instinct tells them to do it.

This is what is remarkable: Because we discover as yet nothing like this in Erigena's writings, we realize that he still viewed human society as if it produced the social elements out of its instincts. With his special kind of insight, he points to what still lived in the human being in the form of instincts and drives, namely, the impulses of social living. What he describes transcends this social aspect. He describes how the human being had emerged from the divine, and what sort of beings exist beyond the sense world. Then, in a form of pneumatology, he shows how the spirit pervades the sensory world, and he presents the spiritual element that penetrated into the world of the senses in his fourth chapter on soteriology and eschatology. Nowhere is there a description, however, of how human beings ought to live together. I should say, everything is elevated above the sensory world. It was generally a characteristic of this ancient science that everything was elevated beyond the sense world.

Now, if we contemplate writings such as John Scotus Erigena's teaching in a spiritual scientific sense, we discover that he did not think at all with the same organs humanity thinks with today. We simply do not understand him if we try to understand him with the thinking employed by mankind today. We understand him only when, through spiritual science, we have acquired an idea of how to think with the etheric body, the body that, as a more refined body, underlies the coarse sensory corporeality.

Thus Erigena did not think with the brain but with the etheric body. In him, we simply have a mind who did not yet think with the brain. Everything he wrote down came into being as a result of thinking with the etheric body. Fundamentally speaking, it was only subsequent to his age that human beings began to think with the physical body, and only since the beginning of the fifteenth century did people think totally with the physical body. It is normally not recognized that during this period the human soul life has truly changed, and that if we go back into the thirteenth, twelfth, and eleventh centuries, we encounter a form of thinking that was not yet carried out with the physical but with the etheric body. This thinking with the etheric body was not supposed to extend into later ages when, dialectically and scholastically, people discussed rigid concepts. This former thinking with the etheric body, which certainly was the form of thinking employed during the first Christian centuries, was declared to be heretical. This was the reason for burning Erigena's writings. Now, the actual soul condition of a thinker in that age becomes comprehensible.

Going back to earlier times, we find a certain form of clairvoyance in all people. Human beings did not think at all with their physical body. In past ages, they thought with their etheric body and carried on their soul life even with the astral body. There, we should not speak of thinking at all, since the intellect only originated in the eighth century B.C., as I have pointed out. However, certain remnants of this ancient clairvoyance were retained, and it is particularly true of the most outstanding minds that with the intellect, which had already come into being, they tried to penetrate into the knowledge that had been handed down through tradition from former ages. People tried to comprehend what had been viewed in a completely different manner in past times. They tried to understand, but now had to have the support of abstract concepts such as existence, wisdom, life. I would say that these individuals still knew something of an earlier spirit-permeated insight and at the same time felt quite at home within the purely intellectual perception.

Later on, when the intellectual perception had turned into a shadow, this was not felt anymore. Earlier, however, people felt that in past ages insights had existed that permeated human beings in a living way out of spiritual worlds, it was not something merely thought up. Erigena lived in such a divided state. He was only capable of thinking, but when this thinking arrived at perception, he sensed that there was something of the ancient powers that had permeated the human being in the ancient manner of perception. Erigena felt the angel, the angelos, within himself. This is why he said that human beings perceive as angels. It was a legacy from ancient times, extending into his age of intellectual knowledge, that made it possible for a mind like Scotus Erigena's to say that man perceives like an angel. In the days of the Egyptian, Chaldean, and the early ages of the Hebrew civilization, nobody would have said anything else but: The angel perceives within me; as a human being, I share in the knowledge of the angel. The angel dwells within me, he cognizes, and I take part in what he perceives.

This was true of the era when reason did not yet exist. When the intellect had appeared, it became necessary to penetrate this older knowledge with reason. In Scotus Erigena, however, there still existed an awareness of this state of permeation with the angel nature.

Now, it is a strange experience to become involved in this work of Erigena's and to try and understand it completely. You finally arrive at a feeling of having read something most significant, something that still dwells very much in spiritual regions and speaks of the world as something spiritual. But then, in turn, the feeling arises that everything is basically mixed up. You realize that with this text you find yourself in the ninth century when the intellect had already brought much confusion. And this is truly the case. For if you read the first chapter, you are dealing with theology. But it is a theology that is certainly secondary even for John Scotus Erigena, a theology which evidently points back to something greater and more direct. I shall now speak as if all these matters were hypotheses, but what I now develop as a hypothesis can be established by spiritual science as a fact. A condition must once have existed, and we look back on it, when as yet theology was not addressed in such an intellectual manner but was considered to be something one delved into in a living way. Without doubt, it was that kind of theology the Egyptians spoke of, those Egyptians of whom the Greeks—I mentioned it above—report that Egyptian sages told them: You Greeks are like children;[6] you have no knowledge of the world's origin, we do possess this sacred knowledge of the world's beginnings.

Obviously, the Greeks were being referred to an ancient, living theology. Thus, we have to say: During the time of the third post-Atlantean period, which begins in the fourth millennium and ends in the first millennium B.C. in the eighth pre-Christian century, approximately in the year 747B.C., there existed a living theology. It now needed to be penetrated by Erigena's intellect. It was obviously present in a much more vital form to the personality who must be recognized as Dionysius the Areopagite. Dionysius had a much more intense feeling for this ancient theology. He felt that it was something that existed but could no longer be approached, that becomes negative as one tries to approach it. Based on the intellect, so he thought, one can only arrive at positive theology. Yet, with the term, negative theology, he was really referring to an ancient theology that had disappeared.

Again, when we consider what appears in the second chapter as the ideal world, we could believe that it is something modern. That, however, is not the case, That ideal world actually is identical with a true idea of what appears in the ancient Persian epoch, just as I described it in my *Occult Science*, hence in the second post-Atlantean period. Among Plato and the Platonists, this ancient Persian living world of angels, the world of the Amshaspands, and so on, had already paled into the world of ideals and ideas due to a later development. Yet, what is actually contained in this ideal world and is clearly discernible in Scotus Erigena goes back to this second ancient Persian age.

What appears in Erigena's book as pneumatology, as a kind of pantheism is not vague and nebulous such as is frequently the case today, but a pantheism that is alive and spiritual, though dimmed in Erigena's writing.

This pneumatology is the last remnant, the very last vestige filtered out of the first post-Atlantean, ancient Indian period.

And what about the fourth chapter? Well, it contains Erigena's living perception of the Mystery of Golgotha and the future of humanity. We hardly speak of this anymore today. As an ancient tradition, it is still mentioned by theologians, but they know of it only in rigidified dogmas. They even deny that man could attain such insight through living knowledge. But it did originate from what was thus cultivated as soteriology and eschatology. You see, the theology of former times was handed over, as it were, to the councils; there, it was frozen into dogmas and incorporated into Christology. It was not to be touched anymore. It was viewed as impenetrable to perception. It was removed, so to speak, from what was carried out in schools by means of knowledge. As it was, exoteric matters were already being preserved like nebulous formations from ancient times. But at least the activities in schools were to be linked with thoughts that emerged in the age of thinking. They were to be connected, after all, with the Mystery of Golgotha and the future of mankind. There, one spoke of the Christ being's rule among human beings; one spoke of a future day of judgment. The concepts that people could come up with were used for that.

Thus, we see that Scotus Erigena actually records the first three chapters as though they had been handed down to him. Finally, he applies his own intellect to the fourth chapter but in such a manner that he speaks of things that far surpass the physical, sensory world, yet have something to do with this world. We realize that he took pains to apply the intellect to eschatology and soteriology. After all, we know the kind of scholarly disputes and discussions Scotus Erigena was involved in. For example, he was involved in discussions of the question whether in Communion, that is, in something that was related to the Mystery of Golgotha, human beings confront the actual blood and the actual body of Christ. He took part in all the discussions of human will, its freedom and lack of freedom in connection with divine grace. Hence, he honed and schooled his intellect in regard to everything that was the subject of his fourth chapter. This is what people discussed then.

We could say that the content of the first three chapters was an ancient tradition. One did not change it much but simply communicated it. The fourth chapter, on the other hand, was a living striving; there, the intellect was applied and schooled.

What became of this intellect that was schooled there? What happened to the concepts of soteriology and eschatology arrived at by people like Scotus Erigena in the ninth century? You see, my dear friends, since the middle of the fifteenth century this has become our science, the basis of the perception of nature. Once, people employed the intellect in order to consider whether bread and wine in the Sacrament are transformed into the body and blood of Christ. They pondered whether grace is bestowed on man in one way or another. This same intellect was later used to consider whether the molecule consists of atoms and whether the sun's body consists of one form of substance or another, and so on. It is the continuation of the theological intellect that inhabits natural science today. Precisely the same intellect that stimulated Scotus and the others who were involved with him in the dispute over Communion—and the discussions were indeed very lively in those days—survived in the teachings of Galileo and Copernicus. It survived in Darwinism, even, say, in Strauss's materialism. It has lived on in a straight line. You know that the old is always preserved alongside the new. Therefore, the same intellect that in David Friedrich Strauss hatched the book *The Old and the New Faith*, which preaches total atheism, occupied itself in those days, with soteriology and eschatology; it continues in a straight line.

We could therefore say that if this book had to be written today based as much on modern conditions as Scotus Erigena based what he wrote on the conditions of his age, then, here (referring to outline on p. 281), total atheism would not appear, but rather our natural science. For, naturally, complete atheism would contradict the first chapter. In the ninth century soteriology and eschatology still appeared there, for then the intellect was applied to other things. But here, (see p. 281), materialistic science would emerge today. History reveals to us nothing else but this. Now, we can perhaps see what becomes evident from the whole conception of this work.

Basically, what is listed here (outline on p. 281) would have to appear in a different sequence. The third chapter would have to read: world view of the first post-Atlantean age. The second chapter, would have to read: world view of the second post-Atlantean age, and the first chapter: world view of the third post-Atlantean age. In the sense of Scotus Erigena—who lived in the fourth post-Atlantean age that only came to an end in the fifteenth century—the last chapter applies to the fourth post-Atlantean epoch. The sequence (in the outline) would therefore have to be: III, II, I, IV. This is what I meant when I said earlier that one receives the impression that things are actually mixed up. Scotus Erigena simply possessed bits of the ancient legacy but he did not list them in accordance with their sequence in time. They were part of the knowledge of his age, and he mentioned them in the order in which they were most familiar to him. He listed the nearest at hand as the highest; the others appeared so nebulous to him that he considered them to be inferior.

Yet, the fourth chapter is nevertheless most remarkable. Let us try to understand from a certain viewpoint what it should actually be. Let us go back into pre-Christian times. If we were to seek among the Egyptians a representative mind such as Scotus Erigena was for the ninth century, such a person would still have known something concerning theology in a most lively way. He would have had even more alive concepts of the ideal or angelic world, of the sphere that illuminates and permeates the whole world with spirit. He would still have known all that and would have said: In the very first age, there once existed a human world view that beheld the spirit in all things. But then, the spirit was abstractly lifted up into the heights. It became the ideal world, finally the divine world. Then, the fourth epoch arrived. It was supposed to be even more spiritualized than the theological epoch. This Greco-Latin period was really supposed to be more spiritualized than the third epoch. And above all, the fifth which then followed, namely our time, would have to be an even more spiritualized era, for with materialistic science in place of soteriology or eschatology it would have to be listed in fourth place, or we would have to add a fifth listing with our natural science, and the latter would have to be the most spiritual view.

Yet, in fact, my dear friends, matters are buried. We hear Scotus Erigena saying that man exists as a mineral being, lives and thrives as a plant, feels as an animal, judges and draws conclusions as a human being, perceives as an angel—something Erigena still knew from ancient traditions. Now, we who aspire to spirit knowledge would have to go even further. We would have to say: Right, human beings exist as mineral beings, live and thrive as plants, feel as animals, judge and draw conclusions as human beings, perceive as angels and, sixth, human beings behold—namely, imaginatively, the spiritual world—as archangels. When we speak of the human being since the first third of the fifteenth century, we would have to ascribe to ourselves the following. We perceive as angels and develop the consciousness soul by means of soul faculties of vision—to begin with, unconsciously, but yet as consciousness soul—as archangels.

Thus, we face the paradox that in the materialistic age human beings actually live in the spiritual world, dwelling on a higher spiritual level than they did in earlier times. We can actually say: Yes, Scotus Erigena is right, the angel experience is awakening in man, but the archangel experience is also awakening since the first third of the fifteenth century. We should rightfully be in a spiritual world.

In realizing this, we could really look back also to a passage in the Gospels that is always interpreted in a most trivial way, namely, the one saying: The end of the world is near and the kingdoms of heaven are at hand. Yes, my dear friends, when we have to say of ourselves that in us the archangel is developing vision so that we can receive the consciousness soul, then there results a strange view of this approach of the heavens. It appears that it is necessary to revise such conceptions of the New Testament once more from the standpoint of spiritual science. These views are very much in need of revision, and we really have two tasks: First, to understand whether our age is not actually meant to to be different than the age when Christ walked on earth and whether the end of the world of which Christ spoke might not be something we have behind us already? This is the one task we confront. And if it is true that we have the so-called end of the world behind us and we therefore already face the spiritual world, then we would have to explain why it has such an unspiritual appearance, why it has become so material, arriving finally at that terrible, astounding life that characterizes the first third of the twentieth century? Two mighty and overwhelming questions place themselves before our soul. We shall continue speaking about that tomorrow.

LECTURE XVI
Dornach, June 3, 1921

Yesterday, we concluded with two significant questions resulting from considering the position of a personality such as John Scotus Erigena. In him, we discover a world view, dating from the first centuries of Christianity that throws its light into the ninth century. Based on everything we have learned recently, we can say that the manner of perception, the whole way of thinking, differed in the first centuries A.D. from what it was later on. As we already know, a great change occurred in the fourth Christian century. From the middle of that century onward, people simply thought much more rationally than they had done earlier. One could say that until that time all perception, all forming of concepts had sprung far more from a form of inspiration than later on when human beings became increasingly conscious of the fact that they themselves were working with thoughts. What we have found to be the consciousness of human beings prior to the fourth century A.D. is still echoed in statements such as that by Scotus Erigena that man makes judgments and draws conclusions as a human being but perceives as an angel. This idea Scotus Erigena brings up as an ancient legacy, as a kind of reminiscence, was acknowledged by anyone who thought at all prior to the fourth century A.D. It never occurred to people in those days to attribute to the human being thoughts that transmit knowledge or perception. They ascribed those to the angel working within man. An angel inhabited the body of human beings; the angel perceived, and human beings shared in this knowledge.

Such a direct consciousness had faded away altogether after the fourth century. In men like Scotus Erigena it emerged once again, drawn forth from the soul with effort, as it were. This proves that the whole way of looking at the world had changed in the course of these centuries. That is why it is so difficult for people today to turn their minds back to the mode of thinking and conceiving prevalent in the first centuries after Christ. Only with the help of spiritual science can this be done again. We have to arrive once more at views that will truly correspond to what was thought in the first centuries A.D.

Already in the days of John Scotus Erigena controversies such as the one over Communion and man's predestination began. These were unmistakable indications of the fact that what was earlier more like an inspiration people did not argue about had now moved to the level of human debate. This came about because, as time went on, many things were simply no longer understood at all.

Among the things that were no longer understood, for example, is the beginning of the Gospel of St. John in the form generally known. If we take this beginning of the Gospel of John seriously, it actually states something that is no longer present in subsequent centuries in the general consciousness of those who profess Christianity. Consider that this Gospel starts with the words: "In the beginning was the Word"—and then it says further that through the Logos all things were made, that is, everything came into being that belongs among created things, and nothing was created except through the Logos.

If we take these words seriously, we have to admit: They signify that all visible things, all the things of the world, came into being through the Logos and that the Logos is therefore the actual creator of all things. In the Christian thinking after the fourth century A.D. the Logos, rightly identified with Christ in the sense of the Gospel of John, was certainly not regarded as the creator of all visible things. Instead, Christ is contrasted with the Creator as the Father, as God the Father. The Logos is designated as the Son, but the Son is not considered the Creator; it is the Father Who is made into the Creator. This doctrine has persisted through the centuries and completely contradicts the Gospel of St. John. You cannot take this Gospel seriously and not regard Christ as the Creator of all things visible, and instead view the Father God as the Creator. You can see, my dear friends, how little this Gospel was taken seriously in later Christian times.

In our mind, we have to place ourselves in the whole mode of thinking of the first Christian centuries, which, as I have said, experienced a change at the point in time indicated above. This way of thinking was in turn structured on the basis of insights into the spiritual world left behind from ancient pagan times. In particular, we have to understand clearly how people viewed the Last Supper, which then continued in the Christian Sacrifice of the Mass. We have to understand the view concerning Communion, the main content of which is contained in the words: "This is my body" — pointing to the bread — and "This is my blood" — pointing to the wine. This content of Communion was truly comprehended during the first Christian centuries; it was even understood by people who were by no means educated but simply gathered together in remembrance of Christ in the Sacrament of Communion. But what did people actually mean by that? They referred to the following.

Throughout antiquity, people were in possession of a religious doctrine of wisdom. Fundamentally speaking, the further back we go in time, the more we find this religious teaching of wisdom based on the being of the Father God. When we consider the religions of very ancient times, preserved in decadent form in later religious faiths, they exhibit in all instances a certain worship of what had remained behind from the ancestor of a tribe or a people. In a sense, human beings worshiped the ancestral father of a tribe. You know from Tacitus' *Germania*[1] how even those tribes who then invaded the Roman empire and made possible the new civilization, definitely retained such memories of tribal deities although in many cases they had already changed to a different form of worship, namely, to that of local gods—something I have mentioned in the public lectures of the last course.[2] They believed that while generation after generation had passed since a certain ancient ancestor had lived who had established the tribe or nation, the soul, the soul-spiritual element of this tribal father, still held sway in the most recent generations.

This presence was believed to be connected with the physical community of the bodies in the tribe. After all, these bodies were all related to each other. They all had the same ancestry. The common blood flowed through their veins. The body and the blood were one. As people looked up in religious devotion to the soul-spiritual element of the tribal father, they also experienced the presence of the deity to whom the tribal father had returned, the god through whom this ancestral father now affected the whole tribe or nation by means of his soul-spiritual nature. The rule of this deity was seen in the bodies, in the blood that ran down through the generations. A profound mystery was sensed in the mysterious forces of the body and the blood.

In those ancient pagan times, people actually beheld the forces of the deity in what held sway in the body and circulated in the blood. Therefore, it is possible to say that when a follower of such an ancient world view saw an animal's blood or, what was more, human blood run out, he beheld in this blood the corporeality of the deity. In the bodies of his race or tribe, which were built up by the blood, he beheld the forms, the image, of the deity. People today no longer have any idea of how the divine-spiritual was worshiped then at the same time as the material substance.

Truly, through the blood of the generations flowed the power of the deity; through the bodies of the generations the deity formed its image. The soul and spirit of the ancestor rose up to this deity and hence worked upon the descendants with divine power and was worshiped as the ancestral god. Not only in regard to these ancient beliefs, but above all in regard to actual truth, the elements working in the human body depend on the forces of the earth. As you know, the body's origins lie in much more ancient times but the forces of the earth are active in the human body as it is today—containing the mineral kingdom—and in the blood.

In the human blood, for example, not only those forces are active that enter the human being through foods but also those that are effective in the whole planet earth. For instance, due to the fact that a person lives in a region rich in red soil, hence a region possessing certain geological characteristics and certain metallic inclusions in the soil, an effect proceeds from the earth to the blood. In turn, the formation, the body, of man is dependent on the earth. The body develops one way in

303

warmer, another way in colder regions of the earth. The corporeality and the elements active in the blood depend on the forces working in the earth. This truth, which we are approaching once again today through spiritual scientific research, was immediately clear to people in antiquity due to their instinctive perception. They know that the earth forces pulsate in the blood.

Today we say that when we connect a telegraph machine in station A by wire to one in station B, we connect the machines one-sidedly. We transmit the electrical current through the wire but the circuit must be closed. It is closed when we make the so-called ground connection. You probably know that if we have a telegraph machine at one station, we guide the wire over the telegraph poles. Yet the circuit is then not closed and it must be closed. We transmit the current into the plate sunk into the ground at one station and do the same at the other station but do nothing more. We could run a different wire there, but we do not do that; we mount an earth-wire plate on both ends of the wire, and the earth takes care of the rest. We know this today as a result of science. We have to presume that electricity, the electric current, works within the earth.

Now people in antiquity knew nothing of electricity and electric currents. Instead, they know something about their blood. They stood on the earth and knew that something was in the earth that also lived in the blood. They looked at the matter differently; they did not speak of electricity but of an earthly element that dwelled in their blood. We no longer know that the earth's electricity lives in the blood. We only speak out of attempts to grasp the matter outwardly through mathematical and mechanistic conceptions. This is why human beings linked their conception of God to the earth's body as such. They realized that the divine element worked in the blood and in the body through the earth. This was what appeared in the concept of the Father God because people considered the primal ancestor, the father, of the tribe or their folk as the point of departure for the influence of the divine element. The primal ancestor was believed to be working through the earth as his means, and the effects of the earth in the blood and the whole human body were seen to be the effects of the divine.

Now these people of old had still another conception. They said, The human being is not only affected by the earthly element. It would be fine if only the earth influenced mankind, but that is not the case. The neighbor of the earth, the moon, works together with the earth's forces. Therefore, they said, it really is not the earth alone but earth and moon together that are effective. With this combination of earth and moon forces, they now linked conceptions of not only one uniform deity of the earth, but many subordinate deities who were then present in the pagan world. All the conceptions that existed of the deity, the elements that affected the human being through the body and blood, all these were the primal source that fed any view of God in this ancient period.

It is not surprising that all search for insight turned in antiquity to the earth, the moon, and the earth's influences and therefore people had to figure out what affected the earth. Thus, a most sophisticated form of science was developed. An echo of this science of the Father God still influenced the first three books by John Scotus Erigena I spoke about yesterday. Basically though, he was not really familiar any more with this primal wisdom, for he lived as late as the ninth century, but bits of this science had been handed down and been pre-served. They referred to the insight that the Father God, Who was not created but creates, dwells in everything surrounding the human being on earth, that the other deities, who have been created but also create, live in it as well. They are then the various entities of the hier-archies. Furthermore, the visible world is spread out around man, the created as well as the noncreating. Finally, human beings are to await the world in which the deity as a noncreating and not created, hence, as a resting divinity, holds sway and receives all else into its bosom. This is what is contained in Scotus Erigena's fourth book.

As I have told you, this fourth book deals mainly with soteriology and eschatology. It presents the history of Christ Jesus, the Resurrection and the gifts of grace, but also the end of the world and the entering into the rest-ing Godhead. The first three chapters of the great book by Scotus Erigena clearly show us a reflection of ancient world views, for basically only the fourth chapter is really Christian. The first three chapters are permeated with a number of Christian concepts but what predomi-nates in them really dates from ancient pagan times. We also find this unchanged pagan wisdom in the Church Fathers of the first Christian centuries. We can say that through nature, through what the human being saw in the creatures surrounding him, he beheld the region of the Father God. He saw a world of ideals behind nature; he saw certain forces in nature. He also saw the rule of the Father God in the sequence of generation, in the development of mankind in individual tribes and nations.

In the first Christian centuries, another insight had joined this knowledge, which has been almost completely lost. The first Christian Church Fathers referred to something their later critics thoroughly eradicated. They said it was true that the Father God worked in the element flowing in the blood through the generations and expressed in the bodies, but He did so in constant conflict and together with His opponent powers, the nature spirits. This was a particularly vivid conception in the first Christian centuries, namely, that the Father God had never been quite successful in exerting His influence exclusively. Rather, He was waging a constant battle with the nature spirits who rule in any number of things in the outer world. Therefore, these first Christian Church Fathers said, The ancients of pre-Christian times believed in the Father God, but they really could not distinguish Him from the nature spirits, they actually believed in a kingdom of the Father God that included the domain of nature. They believed that the whole visible world has its source in it. This, however, is not true, so they said. All these spiritual beings, these various nature deities, do work together in nature, but first of all they crept into the things of the earth. Now, these earthly things we see around us with our senses, the things that have come about on earth, neither originate from these nature spirits nor from the Father God Who actually expressed His creative being only in the metamorphoses preceding the earth. What we see as earth does not originate from the Father God nor from the nature spirits. It comes from the Son, from the Logos, whom the Father God let spring forth from Himself so that the earth might be created by the Logos. And the Gospel of St. John, a mighty, significant monument was written in order to indicate: No, it is not as the people of old believed; the earth was not created by the Father God. The Father God made the Son come forth from

Him; and the Son is the creator of·the earth.

This is what the Gospel of John was supposed to state. This was basically what the Church Fathers of the first Christian centuries struggled for. This then became so hard to grasp for the developing human intellect that Dionysius the Areopagite preferred to say: Everything the intellect creates is positive theology and does not penetrate into the regions containing the actual mysteries of the universe. We can enter into them only if we negate all predicates, if we do not speak of the existence of God but of God's existence transcending existence, if we do not refer to the personality but the personality transcending personality. Hence, human beings only enter into them if they transpose everything into its negative. Then, through negative theology, he takes hold of the actual secret of existence. So Dionysius and his successors, such as John Scotus Erigena, who was already completely imbued with the intellect, did not believe that the human being was at all capable of explaining these mysteries of the universe with human intellect.

Now, what is implied by saying that the Logos is the creator of everything? We need to recall what was present in all the ancient pre-Christian times and endured in diminished form until the time of the Mystery of Golgotha. People believed that the deity works through the blood and through the body. This led them to believe that when the blood flows through the veins of the human being or the animals, it is really taken away from the gods. It is the rightful possession of the gods. Therefore, human beings can approach the gods if they return blood to them. The gods really wish to keep the blood for themselves; humans have taken possession of it. In turn, human beings must give the blood back to the gods, hence the blood sacrifice of ancient times.

Then came Christ and said: This is not what counts; this is not the way to approach earthly things. They do not originate from those gods who desire the blood. Look upon what works in the human being prior to the earth's influence on him; take bread, something that nourishes human beings, and look at how they initially partake of it. They partake of it by means of the sense of taste. The food in human beings goes to a certain point before it is transformed into blood. For it is only changed into blood after having passed through the walls of the intestines into the organism. Only there does the earth's influence begin; as long as the food has not been taken hold of by the blood, the earth's influence has not yet begun. Therefore, do not view blood as something corresponding to the god; behold that in the bread before it turns into blood and in the wine before it enters the blood. There is the divine element; there is the incarnation of the Logos. Do not look upon the element that flows in the blood, for that is an ancient legacy from the Moon age, the pre-earthly time. Before it turns into blood, food has to do with what is earthly in the human being. Therefore, do away with the conceptions of blood, body, and flesh. Instead, turn your thinking to what has not yet become blood nor flesh; direct your minds to what is prepared out there on earth, to what is of the earth without the moon having had an influence on it, to what comes from the sun's influence. For we behold the things through the light of the sun; we eat bread and drink wine, and in them we eat and drink the force of the sun. The visible things have not come about through the Father God, they have come into being through the Logos.

With this, the whole realm of human thought was directed to something that could not be attained from the whole of nature int he way people in the past had done. It could be attained only by looking upon what the sun lets shine forth upon the earth. Human thinking had been turned to something purely spiritual. Human beings were not supposed to extract the divine element from the physical things of the earth; they were supposed to behold this divine element in the purely spiritual, the Logos. The Logos was contrasted to the ancient conceptions of God the Father. That is, people's minds were directed toward a purely spiritual element. In pre-Christian times, people beheld the deity only through what was in a manner of speaking, organically brewed up in them and then arose within them somewhat like a vision. They did indeed behold the divine arising out of the blood. Now they sought to grasp it in the purely spiritual element. They were to view the visible things around them as a result of the Logos and not of what had only slipped into them, as the result of a god who had been creative in pre-earthly times.

Only by thinking in this manner do we actually approach the concepts of the first Christian centuries. Human beings had been told not to use any force other than that of their consciousness to attain the concepts with which to arrive at the comprehension of the deity. Human beings were being directed toward the spirit. Therefore, what could be said to them? They could be told: Formerly, the earth was so powerful that it bestowed upon you the concepts of the divine. That has ceased. The earth no longer gives you anything. Through your own efforts you must come to the Logos and to the creative principle. Up to now, you have basically worshipped something that was creative in

310

pre-earthly conditions; now you must revere the creative principle in the earthly realm. But you can grasp this only through the power of your *I,* your spirit.

The first Christians expressed this by saying: The end of the world is near. They meant the end of the earth condition that bestows insights on man without his working on these insights with his consciousness. In fact, a profound truth is expressed in these words concerning the end of the world, for human beings had formerly been children of the earth. They had given themselves up to the forces of the earth. They had relied on their blood to give them their knowledge. This, however, was no longer possible, The kingdoms of the heavens drew near, the kingdoms of the earth ceased to be. Henceforth, man can no longer be a son of the earth. He has to turn into the companion of a spiritual being, a being that has come down to earth from the spiritual world, the Logos, the Christ.

The end of the world was prophesied for the fourth century A.D.: the end of the earth, the beginning of a new kingdom, the dawn of that age when man is to experience himself living as spirit among spirits. This is probably the most difficult to picture for people of our present age, namely, that our present manner of dwelling as human beings would not have been considered by people of the early Christian centuries as living in an earthly manner. It would have been seen as life in the spirit realm, after the destruction of the earth as it was when it still bestowed faculties upon the human being. If we properly understood the first Christians' way of thinking, we would not say that they superstitiously believed in the end of the world, which did not take place. As the first Christians saw it, this end did occur in the fourth century A.D.

The way we live today would have been considered by the first Christians as the New Jerusalem, the kingdom where the human being lives as spirit among spirits. However, they would have said: According to our view, the human being has actually entered heaven, but he is so worthless that he does not realize it. He believes that in heaven everything overflows with milk and honey, that there are no evil spirits against whom he has to defend himself. The first Christians would have said: Formerly, these evil spirits were contained in the things of nature; now they have been let loose, flit about invisibly, and human beings must withstand them.

Hence, in the sense of the first Christian centuries, the end of the world definitely did occur, but people simply did not comprehend this. It was not understood that instead of the god dwelling in the earth, a god whose presence is announced through events on the earth, now the supersensory Logos was present who must be recognized in the supersensory realm and to whom human beings must adhere by means of super-sensory faculties. Now, assuming this, we can comprehend why in the ninth, tenth, and eleventh centuries, a feeling of the end of the world was present again in civilized Europe. Again, people awaited the world's end. They did not know what the first Christians had meant by it. Out of this frame of mind of anticipating the end of the world, which spread over all of civilized Europe during these centuries, something developed that caused people to seek Christ in a more physical manner than they ought to have looked for him. People should realize that we are to find the Logos in the spirit, not based on nature's phenomena. This search for the Logos in the spirit is something that these people, who once again were in a mood of expecting the end of the world, did not understand. Instead, they set about this search in a more materialistic way. Thus, this mood gave rise to the Crusades, the material quest for Christ in his tomb in the Orient. People adhered to Christ in this mood of the world's end, in the misunderstood mood of the end of the world.

However, Christ was not found in the Orient. People received approximately the same answer his disciples had received when they sought him tangibly in his tomb—He whom you seek is no longer here—for He must be sought in the spirit.

Now, in the twentieth century, once again a mood of the world's end prevails—and these phenomena will increase—although people have become so lethargic and indifferent that they do not even notice this anticipation of the end of the world. But the man who did speak of this mood of the world's end in his *Decline of the West*[3] made a significant and noticeable impression, and this frame of mind will become increasingly prevalent.

Actually, we do not need to speak of the end of the world. It has already ended in the sense that humanity can no longer find the spirit based on nature; it is a matter of realizing that we live in a spiritual world. Humanity's error of not knowing that we live in a spiritual world has brought misfortune over us. It causes wars to be bloodier and bloodier. It is becoming increasingly evident that human beings act as if possessed. Indeed, they are possessed by the evil forces who confuse them, for their speech no longer expressed the inherent content of their *I*. They are as though possessed by a psychosis. This psychosis is much talked about but little understood.

What the first Christians meant by the end of the world, and what they understood by it, did take place.

The new age is here, but it must be recognized. People must realize that when the human being perceives, he does perceive as an angel, and when he becomes conscious of his own self, he becomes self-aware as an archangel. The significant point is that <u>the spiritual world has already descended and human beings must become conscious of it.</u> Many have thought that they take the Gospel seriously. Yet, although the Gospels clearly say that all things that were made, hence, all things under consideration should not be explained based on their earthly forces but originated through the Logos, people professed the Father God. He should be acknowledged as one with the Christ but as that aspect of the Trinity that was active until the earth was formed, whereas the actual ruler of the earth is the Christ, the Logos.

These matters could hardly be comprehended anymore in the ninth century when Scotus Erigena was active. This is why, on the one hand, his book about the divisions of nature is so great and significant. On the other hand, as I told you yesterday, this is why it is chaotic as well. This is why you only begin to find your way in it when you view it from the spiritual scientific viewpoint as we have done yesterday and today.

Well, as I said, in the fourth chapter, Erigena speaks of the uncreated entity that is not creating. If we understand the true meaning of what Scotus Erigena describes here, namely, the resting deity in which everything unites, then the necessary step has been taken. The world that is described in the preceding three chapters has come to an end. The world of the resting Godhead, the noncreated and noncreating being, is here.

Insofar as it is nature, the earth is declining. I have often called attention to the fact that this is the case by indicating that even geologists say nowadays that by and large, nothing new originates anymore on the earth. Certainly, as an aftereffect, plants develop, and so forth, plants, animals, and human propagate. But the earth as a whole has turned into something other than what it was. It is becoming fragmentized; it is splitting. The earth as a whole is already in a state of disintegration as far as its mineral kingdom is concerned.

The great geologist, Süess, [4] expressed this in his work *The Countenance of the Earth* (*Das Antlitz der Erde*) by saying that we walk around on the corroding crust of the earth. He points to certain regions on earth where this corrosion is evident. He stresses that in the past this was different. This is what the world view and conception of life in the first Christian centuries referred to, though not based on facts of nature but on the moral facts of humanity's evolution.

Indeed, it is true that since the beginning of the fifteenth century we live even more in the resting Godhead than did Scotus Erigena. This Godhead awaits our attainment of Imagination and Inspiration through our own efforts. Then we will be able to recognize the world around us as a spiritual world. We will perceive that we are indeed in a spiritual world that has thrown off the earthly one. This deity awaits our realization that we are living after the end of the world and that we have arrived in the New Jerusalem.

It is indeed a strange spiritual destiny for human beings that they dwell in the spiritual world and neither know it nor wish to know it. There is no substance in any of the interpretations aiming at representing true Christianity as mixed up with some half-baked conceptions of an end of the world, which, after all, did not occur and was only meant symbolically, and so on.

What we find in the writings of Christianity must be comprehended in its true meaning. It must be grasped in the right way. There must be clarity concerning the fact that the early Christian views referred to a world that had already changed after the fourth century A.D.

The teachings in the first Christian centuries stood in awe of the abundant wisdom of paganism, and the Christian Church Fathers attempted to connect it with the secret of Golgotha. Matters were actually viewed the way I described it today. Yet, it was not believed that mankind could understand them offhand. This is why the secrets of ancient time were preserved in dogmas meant only to be believed, not to be understood. The dogmas are by no means superstition or untruth. The dogmas are true, but they must be comprehended in the right way. They can only be understood, however, if this comprehension is sought for with the faculty that has developed since the beginning of the fifteenth century.

When Scotus Erigena lived, human reason was still a force. Scotus Erigena still sensed that the angel within him comprehended. After all, this human intellect was still a force in the best minds of that period. Since the middle of the fifteenth century, we have only the shadow of this reason, this intellect. Since that time, we have developed the consciousness soul. Yet we still retain the shadow of the intellect. When a person develops his concepts today, he is indeed far from having any idea that an angel is comprehending something within him. He simply thinks: I am figuring something out concerning the things I have experienced. He certainly does not talk about the presence of a spiritual being that is perceiving, much less of a still higher spiritual being, which he is by virtue of his self-awareness. The faculty with which we try to know things is only the shadow of the intellect that had developed for the Greeks, for example for Plato and Aristotle, and even for the Romans and that had still been alive for Scotus Erigena in the ninth century A.D.

But this is the point, my dear friends. We no longer need to be misled by the intellect; this insight can help us to progress. Today, people follow a shadow, the reasoning or intellect within them. They allow themselves to be misled by it instead of striving for Imagination, Inspiration, and Intuition, which in turn would lead once again into the spiritual world that actually surrounds us. It is really beneficial that the intellect has become like a shadow. Initially, we established external natural science with this shadowlike intellect. On the basis of this intellect we have to work further, and God rests so as to allow us to work. The fourth stage is completely here today. We just have to become conscious of it. If we do not become aware of this fact, nothing can develop further on earth. For what the earth has received as a legacy is gone; it is no more. New things must be inaugurated.

An individual such as Spengler beholds the fragments of the old civilizations. After all, they were prepared in sufficient numbers. In the ninth, tenth, and eleventh centuries, the mood of the imminent end of the world prevailed. Then came the Crusades. They really accomplished nothing new, for people sought in the material realm something that should have been sought in the spirit. Now, because the Crusades had brought no results, the Renaissance came, so to speak, to the rescue of mankind. Greek culture was again disseminated in what prevails today as education. Greek culture was present again but not as something new. The mathematical and mechanistic concepts of external nature developed since the beginning of the fifteenth century were the only new elements. But the ruins of antiquity were there, too, and they are crammed into our young people in the secondary schools. They then form the basis of civilization. Oswald Spengler encountered these fragments of the Renaissance. Like erratic blocks, they float on the sea that is intent on producing something more. Yet if you merely look upon these floating ice blocks, you behold the decline. For what has been retained from the past is characterized by a mood of decline, and nobody can galvanize our modern education. It is perishing. Out of the spirit, through primal creation, a different civilization must be created for the fourth stage is here.

This is how Scotus Erigena must be understood, who brought along his wisdom—already difficult to understand for him, I would say—from the Irish isle, from the mysteries that had been cultivated in Ireland. This is how we must interpret Scotus Erigena's work. Thus, not only the primal knowledge that can be attained through spiritual science, but also the documents of former times express this meaning if we are willing really to understand them, if we are willing finally to free ourselves from the Alexandrianism of the modern philosophic science that calls itself philology. For we must admit that the way things are handled today, we do not see much of either philology or philosophy. If we observe the methods of cramming and the way examinations are conducted in our educational institutions, very little is present of *philo*, of love. That has to emerge from a different direction, but we are in need of it once again.

It was my intention, first of all, to present the figure of Scotus Erigena to you. Secondly, I wanted to point out that the ways to properly grasp the buried primordial wisdom have yet to be sought. Nowadays people pay no attention to the fact that the Gospel of St. John clearly states that the Logos is the creative principle, not the Father God.

LECTURE XVII
Dornach, June 5, 1921

In the course of the last few days we had occasion to refer once again to the turning point in Western civilization in the fourth century A.D. with the example of John Scotus Erigena. In the present, when so many things are supposed to change, it is particularly important to understand clearly what really happened then to the human soul constitution. For it is a fact that we too are living in an extraordinarily significant moment in humanity's evolution; it is necessary for us to pay heed to the signs of the times and to listen to the voices of the spiritual world, so that out of the chaos of the present we may find a path into the future.

In the fourth century A.D., changes took place in the souls of those belonging to the leading nations and tribes, just as in our century changes in part have begun to develop, in part will still occur. And in John Scotus Erigena we have observed a personality who in a certain way was influenced by the aftereffects of humanity's world view prior to the fourth century A.D.

We shall now call to mind other things that also make evident this change of character. As far as can be done in a more outward manner, we will consider from this standpoint how the study of nature developed, in particular people's views of health and illness. We shall confine ourselves, first of all, to historical times. When we ask what the views concerning nature, particularly human nature in connection with health and illness were, and look back into the early Egyptian period, we can for the first time speak of any similarity between these ancient views and ours now. Yet, in regard to health, illness, and their natural causes, these ancient Egyptians held opinions still differing significantly from ours. The reason was that they thought of their relationship with nature quite differently from the way we think of it today. The ancient Egyptians certainly were not fully aware that they were gradually separating from the earth. They pictured their own bodies — and they naturally started by considering what we call "body" in an intimate connection with the forces of the earth. We have already mentioned in the last lecture how such a concept arises, how it is that the human being pictures himself in a certain sense closely bound inwardly to the earth through his body. I referred to the ancient soul forces in order to illustrate this. It was altogether clear to the ancient Egyptians that they had to see themselves as part of the earth, similarly to how the plants must be seen as belonging to the earth. Just as it is possible to trace the course of the sap or at least the earth's forces in plants more or less visibly, so people in ancient Egypt experienced the working of certain forces that, at the same time, held sway in the earth. Therefore, the human body was seen as belonging to the earth.

This could only be done because a view of the earth prevailed that was quite different from the view prevalent nowadays. The ancient Egyptians would never have thought of representing the earth as a mineral body the way we do it today. In a sense, they pictured the earth as a mighty organic being, a being not organized in quite the same way as an animal or man, but still, in a certain respect, an organism; and they considered the earth's masses of rock as a skeleton of sorts. They imagined that processes took place in the earth that simply extended into the human body.

The ancient Egyptians experienced a certain sensation when they mummified the human corpse after it had been discarded by the soul, when they tried to preserve the shape of the human body by mummification. In the formative forces proceeding from the earth and forming the human body, they beheld something like the will of the earth. They were trying to give permanent expression to this will of the earth. These Egyptians held views concerning the soul that seem somewhat alien to a person of today. We shall now try to characterize them.

It must be emphasized that when we go back to early Egyptian times, and even more so to the ancient Persian and Indian epochs, we find that, based on instinctive old wisdom, the doctrine of reincarnation—the return of the essential human entity in successive earth lives—was widespread. We are mistaken, however, in assuming that these ancient people were of the opinion that what we know as soul today is what always returns. Especially the Egyptian concept demonstrates that such a view did not exist. Instead, it must be pictured like this: The soul-spiritual being of man lives in spiritual worlds between death and a new birth. When the time approaches for this being to descend to the physical earth, it works formatively in the human body, in what comes through heredity from the successive generations. On the other hand, these ancient people did not think that what they bore in their consciousness during life between birth and death was the actual psycho-spiritual being that lives between death and a new birth and then shapes the human corporeality between birth and death. No, these people of antiquity pictured things differently. They said: When I find myself in the waking state from morning until evening, I know absolutely nothing of the soul-spiritual matters that are also my own affairs as a human being. I must wait until my own true being, which worked on me when I entered into earthly existence through birth, appears to me in half-sleep or in image-filled sleep, as was the case in these ancient times.

Thus, the ancient human being was aware that in his waking state he was not meant to experience his actual soul being; instead, he was to look upon his true soul entity as upon an external picture, something that came over him when he passed into the frequently described dreamlike, clairvoyant conditions. In a certain sense, the human being in former times experienced his own being as something that appeared to him like an archangel or angel. Only beginning in ancient Egypt, people started to think of this inner human essence as belonging directly to the soul.

If we try to characterize how the ancient Egyptians pictured this, we have to say the following. They thought: In a dream image, my soul-spiritual being appears to me in its condition between death and a new birth. It shapes the body for its use. When I look at the form of the body, I see how this soul-spirit being has worked like an artist on this body. I see much more of an expression of my soul-spiritual being in my body than if I look within. For that reason I shall preserve this body. As a mummy, its form shall be retained, for in it is contained the work the soul has done on the body between the last death and this birth. That is what I retain when I embalm the body and in the mummy preserve the image on which the soul-spiritual being has worked for centuries.

By contrast, the ancient Egyptians considered the experiences of the human being in the waking state between birth and death differently: This is really like a flame kindled within me, but it has very little to do with my true *I*. My *I* remains more or less outside my soul experiences in the waking state between birth and death. These soul experiences are actually a temporal, passing flame, enkindled in my body through my higher soul being. In death, they are extinguished once again. Only then does my true soul-spirit being shine forth, and I dwell in it until the new birth.

It is true that the ancient Egyptians imagined that in the life between birth and death they did not properly attain to an experience of the soul element. They viewed it as something that stood above them, enkindled their temporal soul element and extinguished it again; they saw it as something that took from the earth the earth's dust to form the body. In the mummy, they then tried to preserve this bodily form.

The ancient Egyptians really placed no special value on the soul element that experiences itself in the waking state between birth and death, for they looked beyond this soul nature to a quite different soul-spirit essence, which ever and again forms new bodies and passes through the period between death and a new birth. Thus, they beheld the interplay of forces between the higher human element and the earth. They really directed their attention to the earth, for to them, the earth was also the house of Osiris. Inner consciousness was something they overlooked.

The development of Greek culture, which began in the eighth century B.C., consisted precisely in man's placing an ever increasing value on this soul element that lights up between birth and death, something the ancient Egyptian still viewed as enkindled and subsequently dying flame. To the Greeks, this soul element became valuable. But they still had the feeling that in death something like an extinction of this soul element took place. This gave rise to the famous Greek saying I have characterized often from this viewpoint: "Better a beggar on earth than a king in the realm of shades." This saying was coined by the Greeks as they looked upon the soul element. To them, the latter became important, whereas it had been less significant for the ancient Egyptians. This development is connected with the view of health and illness held by the ancient Egyptians.

They thought that this soul-spiritual element, which does not really enter properly into human consciousness between birth and death, builds up the human body out of the earth elements, out of the water, the air, the solid substances of the earth, and the warmth. And since the ancient Egyptians believed that this human body was formed out of the earth, they set great store by keeping it pure. During the golden age of Egyptian culture, maintaining the body in a pure state was therefore something that was especially cultivated. The Egyptians thought very highly of this body. Hence, they felt that when the body became ill, its connection with the earth was in some way disturbed, in particular its relationship to the earth's water, and this relationship had to be restored. Therefore, there were hosts of physicians in Egypt who studied the relationship of the earthly elements to the human body. Their concern was to maintain people's health and, when it was disturbed, to restore it by means of water cures and climatic treatments. Already in the heyday of Egyptian civilization, specialized physicians were at work, and their activity was principally directed at the task of bringing the human body into the proper relation with the earth's elements.

Beginning with the eighth century B.C., particularly in Greek civilization, this changed. Now, the consciously experienced soul element became really important. People did not see it anymore in as close a connection with the earth as people in ancient Egypt had done. For the ancient Egyptians, the human body was in a sense something plantlike that grew out of the earth. For the Greeks, the psycho-spiritual element was the factor that held together the earth elements; they were more concerned with the way these elements in the body were held together by man's soul and spirit. On this basis developed the scientific views of Greece. We find them especially well expressed by Hippocrates, the famous Greek physician and contemporary of Phidias, Socrates, and Plato.[1] This view of the importance of the human soul element, which becomes conscious of itself between birth and death, is already clearly developed in Hippocrates, who lived in the fourth century B.C.

We would be very much mistaken, however, if we believed that this soul-spiritual element lived in Greek consciousness in the same way we experience it in our consciousness today. Just reflect on how poor, how abstractly poor this thing is that modern man calls his soul! When people speak of thinking, feeling, and willing, they picture them as quite nebulous formations. It is something that no longer affects the human being substantially. It had a substantial effect on the Greeks, for they had an awareness that this psycho-spiritual being actually holds together the elements of the body and causes their interplay. They did not have in mind an abstract soul element as people do today. They had in mind a full, rich system of forces that gives shape above all to the fluid element, bestowing on it the human form. The Egyptians felt: The soul-spirit being that finds its way from death to a new birth gives form to this fluid element. The Greeks felt: What I experience consciously as my soul element, this is what shapes the water; it has a need for air and then develops the circulatory organs in that form. It causes the conditions of warmth in the body and also deposits salt and other earthly substances in the body.

The Greeks actually did not picture the soul separately from the body. They imagined it molding the fluid body, bringing about the presence of air through inhaling and exhaling. They pictured the soul causing the conditions of warmth in the body, the body's warming and cooling processes, the breathing and movement of the fluids, the permeation of the fluids with the solid ingredients—actually representing only about 8% of the human body. The Greeks pictured all this in full vitality. They attached special importance to the shaping of the fluids. They imagined that in turn a fourfold influence was at work in these fluids due to the forces active in the four elements, earth, water, air, and warmth. This is how the Greeks pictured it.

In winter, human beings must shut themselves off from the outer world to a certain extent, they cannot live in intimate contact with it. They must rely on themselves. In winter, above all the head and its fluids make themselves felt. There the part of the fluids that is most waterlike works inwardly in the human being. In other words, for the Greeks this was phlegm or mucus. They believed all that is mucous in the human organism to be soul-permeated and particularly active in winter. Then came spring, and the Greeks found that the blood made itself felt through greater activity; the blood received greater stimulation than in winter. This is a predominantly sanguine time for human beings, emphasis is placed on what is centralized in the arteries leading to the heart and is active in the movement of fluids. In winter, it is the movement of the phlegm in the head, hence, this is the reason why the human being is then particularly inclined to any number of diseases of the mucous fluids. In spring, the blood circulation is especially stimulated.

The Greeks pictured all this in such a way that matter was not separated from the soul aspects. In a sense, blood and phlegm were half soullike, and the soul itself with its forces was something half physical in moving the fluids.

When summer approached, the Greeks imagined that the activity of bile (they called it yellow gall), which has its center in the liver, is particularly aroused. The Greeks still had a special view of what this is like in the human being. For the most part, people have lost this view. They no longer see how, in spring, the skin is colored by the blood's stimulation. They no longer notice the peculiar yellow tinge coming from the liver where this so-called yellow bile has its center. In the rosy flush of spring and the yellowish tinge of summer, the Greeks saw activities of the soul.

When autumn came, they said: Now, the fluids having their center in the spleen, the fluids of black bile, are particularly active. In this way, the Greeks pictured in the human being movements and effects of fluids that were directly under the influence of the soul. Unlike the Egyptians, the Greeks considered the human body by itself, apart from the whole of the earth. Thus, they came closer to the inner soul configuration of the human being as it is expressed between birth and death.

As this civilization progressed further, however, particularly as the Western element, the Latin-Roman element, gained ground, this view, which we find especially in Hippocrates who based his medical science on it, was to a certain extent lost. Hippocrates held that the soul-spiritual nature of man manifesting between birth and death causes these mixtures and separations of the fluids. When these do not proceed as the soul-spiritual influence intends them to go, the human being encounters illness. The soul-spiritual element actually always strives to make the activities of the fluids run their normal course. This is why the physician has the special task of studying the soul-spirit nature and the effect of its forces on the activities of the fluids in addition to observing the illness. If the activity of the physical body somehow tends to cause an abnormal mixture of fluids, then the soul element intervenes. It intervenes to the point of a crisis, when the outcome in the struggle between corporeal and soul-spiritual elements hangs in the balance. The physician must guide matters in such a way that this crisis occurs. Then, at some point in the body it will be evident that the bad fluid combination is trying to come out, to escape. Then it is the physician's task to intervene in a proper way in this crisis, which he has introduced in the first place, by removing the fluids that have accumulated in the way described above and that are resisting the influence of the soul-spiritual element. The physician accomplishes this either by means of purging or by bloodletting at the right moment.

Hippocrates' manner of healing was of a quite special kind and connected with this view of the human being.

It is interesting that such a view existed that pictured an intimate relationship between the soul-spirit element as expressed between birth and death and the system of body fluids. Things changed, however, when the Latin-Roman influence continued this development.

This Roman element had less inclination for a full comprehension of the form and the system of fluids. This can be clearly seen in the case of the physician Galen[2] who lived in the second century A.D. The system of fluids that Hippocrates saw was no longer so transparent to Galen. You really have to picture it like this: Today, you watch how a retort in a chemistry laboratory is heated by a flame underneath, and you see the product of the substances inside. For Hippocrates, the effect of the soul-spiritual element in the fluids of the body was just as transparent. What took place in the human being was to him visible in a sensory-supersensory way. The Romans, on the other hand, no longer had a sense for this vivid view. They no longer considered the soul-spiritual element that dwells in man in its connection to the body. They turned their glance in a more abstract, spiritual direction. They only understood how the soul-spiritual being can experience this spirit within itself between birth and death.

The Greeks looked at the body, saw the soul-spiritual in the mixing and separating of the fluids and, to them, the sensory view in its clarity and vividness was the main thing. To the Romans, the essential thing was what a man felt himself to be, the feeling of self within the soul. To the Greeks, the view of how phlegm, blood, yellow, and black bile intermingle, how they are, in a manner of speaking, an expression of the earthly elements of air, fire, water, earth in the human being became something they saw as a work of art. Whereas the Egyptians contemplated the mummy, the Greeks looked upon the living work of art. The Romans had no sense for this, but they had an awareness for taking a stand in life, for developing inner consciousness, for allowing the spirit to speak, not for looking at the body but for making the spirit speak out of the soul between birth and death.

This is connected with the fact that at the height of Egyptian civilization, four branches of knowledge were especially cultivated in their ancient form: geometry, astrology, arithmetic, and music. In contemplating the heavenly element that formed the human body out of the earth, the Egyptians imagined that this body is molded in its spatial form according to the law of geometry; it is subject to the influences of the stars according to the laws of astrology. It is involved in activity from within according to the laws of arithmetic and is inwardly built up harmoniously according to the laws of music—music here conceived not merely as musical tone elements but as something that lives in harmonies in general. In the human being. as a product of the earth, in this mummified man, the Egyptians saw the result of geometry, astrology, arithmetic, and music. The Greeks lost sight of this. The Greeks replaced the lifeless, mummified element, which can be comprehended by means of geometry, astrology, arithmetic, and music, with the living soul element, the inner forming, the artistic self-development of the human body.

This is why we note in Greek culture a certain decline of geometry as it had existed among the Egyptians. It now became a mere science, no longer a revelation The same happened with astrology and arithmetic. At most, the inner harmony that forms the basis of all living things remains in the Greek concept of music.

Then, when the Latin element came to the fore, the Romans, as I said, pictured this soul-spiritual being as it

332

is between birth and death together with the inner spirit now expressing itself not as something that could inwardly be seen but inwardly experienced, taking its stand in the world through grammar, through dialectics, and through rhetoric. Therefore, during the time when Greek culture was passing over into Latin culture, these three disciplines flourished. In grammar, man was represented as spirit through the word; in rhetoric, the human being was represented through the beauty and forming of the word; in dialectics, the soul was represented through the forming of thought. Arithmetic, geometry, astrology, and music continued to exist, but only as ancient legacies turned science. These disciplines, which in ancient Egypt had been very much alive, became abstract sciences. By contrast, the arts attached to man—grammar, rhetoric, dialectics—took on new life.

There is a great difference between the way a person thought of a triangle in ancient Egypt prior to Euclid and the way people thought of it after Euclid's time. The abstract triangle was not experienced in earlier times the way it was conceived later on. Euclid signified the decadence of Egyptian arithmetic and geometry. In Egypt, people felt universal forces when they envisaged a triangle. The triangle was a being. Now, all this became science, while dialectics, grammar and rhetoric became alive.

Schools were now established in accordance with the following thinking: Those people who want to be educated have to develop the spiritual potential in their already existent soul-spiritual human nature. As the first stage of instruction, they must master grammar, rhetoric, and dialectics. Then, they have to go through what remains only as a traditional legacy but forms the subjects of higher education: geometry, astrology, arithmetic, and music. These then were the seven liberal arts, even throughout the Middle Ages: grammar, rhetoric, dialectics, geometry, astrology, arithmetic, and music. The arts that came more to the fore were grammar, rhetoric, and dialectics; the arts that were more in the background, conceived by the ancient Egyptians in a living manner as they stood on a relationship to the earth, were the subjects of higher learning.

This was the essential development between the eighth century B.C. and the fourth century A.D. Look at Greece in the fourth century or in the third or fifth centuries. Look at modern Italy. You find everywhere in full bloom this knowledge of the human being as a work of art, as a product of the soul-spiritual element, of life of the spirit through dialectics, rhetoric, and grammar. Julian Apostate[3] was educated in approximately this way in the Athenian school of philosophers. This is how he saw the human being.

Into this age burst the beginning of Christianity. But by then all this knowledge was in a certain sense already fading. In the fourth century it had been in its prime, and we have heard that by John Scotus Erigena's time only a mere tradition of it existed. What lived in the Greeks based on the view I have just characterized, then was transmitted to Plato and Aristotle who expressed it philosophically. When the fourth century B.C. drew near, however, people understood Plato and Aristotle less and less. At most people could accept the logical, abstract parts of their teachings. People were engrossed in grammar, rhetoric, dialectics. Arithmetic, geometry, astrology, and music had turned into sciences. People increasingly found their way into a sort of abstract element, into an element where something that had formerly been alive was now to exist only as tradition. As the centuries passed, it became still more a tradition. Those who were educated in the Latin tongue retained in a more or less ossified state grammar, rhetoric, and dialectics. Formerly a person would have laughed if he had been asked whether his thinking referred to something real. He would have laughed, for he would have said: I engage in dialectics; I do not cultivate the art of concepts in order to engage in anything unreal. For there, the spiritual reality lives in me. As I engage in grammar, the Logos speaks in me. As I engage in rhetoric, it is the cosmic sun that sends its influences into me.

This consciousness of being connected with the world was lost more and more. Everything became abstract soul experiences, a development that was completed by Scotus Erigena's time. The ideas that had been retained from earlier times—from Plato and Aristotle—were only comprehended more or less logically. People ceased to find any living element in them.

When the Emperor Constantine[4] made Rome the ruling power under the pretext that he wished to establish the dominion of Christianity, everything became entirely abstract. It became so abstract that a person like Julian Apostate, who had been educated in the Athenian school of philosophy, was silenced. With an aching heart, he looked at what Constantine had done in the way of ossifying concepts and ancient living ideas, and Julian Apostate resolved to preserve this life that had still been evident to him in the Athenian schools of philosophers.

Later on, Justinian ruled from Byzantium, from Constantinople, which had been founded by Constantine.[5] He abolished the last vestiges of these Athenian philosophers' schools that still possessed an echo of living human knowledge. Therefore, the seven wise Athenians—Athenians they were not, they were a quite international group, men from Damascus, Syrians, and others gathered from all over the world—had to flee on order of Justinian. These seven wise men fled to Asia, to the king of the Persians, [6] where philosophers had had to escape to already earlier when Zeno, the Isaurian, [7] had dispersed a similar academy. Thus we see how this knowledge, the best of which could no longer be comprehended in Europe, the living experience that had existed in Greece, had to seek refuge in Asia.

What was later propagated in Europe as Greek culture was really only its shadow. Goethe allowed it to influence him and as a thoroughly lively human being, he was seized with such longing that he wished he could escape from what had been offered to him as the shadow of Greek culture. He traveled to the south in order to experience at least the aftereffects.

In Asia, people who were capable of doing so received of Plato and Aristotle what had been brought across to them. This is why during the sixth century Aristotle's work was translated based on the Asian-Arabic spirit. This gave Aristotle's philosophy a different form.

What had in fact been attempted here? The attempt had been made to take what the Greeks had experienced as the relationship between the soul-spiritual element and the body's system of fluids, what they had seen in full physical and soul-spiritual clarity and formative force, and to raise it up into the region where the ego could be fully comprehended. From this originated the form of science tinged with Arabism, which was especially cultivated in the academy of Gondishapur[8] throughout the whole declining age of the fourth post-Atlantean epoch. This form of science was brought in later centuries by Avicenna[9] and Averroes[10] by way of

Spain into Europe and eventually exerted a great influence on people such as Roger Bacon[11] and others. It was, however, a completely new element that the academy of Gondishapur meant to bestow on mankind in a manner that could not endure by way of the translation of Aristotle and certain mystery wisdom teachings, which then continued in directions of which we shall talk another time.

Through Avicenna and Averroes, something was introduced that was to enter human civilization with the beginning of the fifteenth century, namely, the struggle for the consciousness soul. After all, the Greeks had only attained to the intellectual or rational soul. What Avicenna and Averroes brought across, what Aristotelianism had turned into in Asia, so to speak, struggles with the comprehension of the human *I*, which, in a completely different way, has to struggle upward through the Germanic tribes from below to above—I have described this in the public lectures here during the course.[12] In Asia, on the other hand, the *I* was received like a revelation from above as a mystery wisdom. This gave rise to the view that for so long provoked such weighty disputes in Europe, namely, that man's ego is not actually an independent entity but is basically one with the divine universal being. The aim was to take hold of the ego. The *I* was supposed to be contained in what the Greek beheld as the being of body, soul, and spirit.

Yet, people could not harmonize the above with the *I*. This is the reason for Avicenna's conception that what constitutes the individual soul originates with birth and ends with death. As we have seen, the Greeks struggled with this idea. The Egyptians viewed it only in this way—the individual soul is enkindled at birth, extinguished at death. People were still wrestling with this conception when they considered the actual soul element between birth and death, the true soul element. The *I*, on the other hand, could not be transitory in this manner. Therefore, Avicenna said: Actually, the ego is the same in all human beings. It is basically a ray from the Godhead which returns again into the Godhead when the human being dies. It is real, but not individually real. A pneumatic pantheism came about, as if the ego had no independent existence but was only a ray of the deity streaming between birth and death into what the Greeks viewed as the soul-spiritual nature. In a manner of speaking, the transitory soul element of man is ensouled with the eternal element through the ray of the Godhead between birth and death. This is how people imagined it.

This shows to some extent how people of that age struggled with the approach of the *I*, the consciousness of the ego, the consciousness soul. This is what occurred in the span of time between the eighth century B.C. and the fifteenth century A.D., the middle of which is the fourth century A.D. People were placed in a condition where the concrete experience, which still dwelled in the mixing and the separating fluids and beheld the soul element in the corporeal being, was replaced. A purely abstract state of mind, directed more toward man's inner being, replaced this vivid element of perception.

It is indeed possible to say that until the fourth century A.D., Greek culture predominated in Romanism. Romanism only became dominant when it had already declined. In a sense, Rome was predestined to exert its activity only in its dead element, in its dead Latin language, in which it then prepared the way for what entered human evolution in the fifteenth century. This is how the course of civilization must be observed. For, once again, we are now faced with having to seek the way toward knowing of the approach of spiritual revelations from the higher worlds. Once again, we must learn to struggle, just as people struggled then.

We must be clear about the fact that what we possess as natural science came to us by way of the Arabs. The knowledge we have acquired through our sciences must be lifted up to Imagination, Inspiration, and Intuition. In a certain sense, however, we must also steel our faculties by means of observing the things of the past, so that we acquire the strength to attain what we need for the future. This is the mission of anthroposophical spiritual science. We must recall this again and again, my dear friends. We should acquire quite vivid perceptions of how differently the Greeks thought about soul and corporeal aspects. It would have sounded ridiculous to them if one had listed seventy-two or seventy-six chemical elements. They perceived the living effect of the elements outside and of the fluids within.

We live within the elements. Insofar as the body is permeated by the soul, the human being with his body lives within the four elements the Greeks spoke about. We have arrived at the point where we have lost sight of the human being, because we can no longer view him in the above manner and focus only on what chemistry teaches today in the way of abstract elements.

NOTES

Lecture I

[1]See Rudolf Steiner, *An Outline of Occult Science*, Anthroposophic Press, Spring Valley, NY, 1972.

[2]See lecture of March 21, 1921 (in GA 324), where a more detailed description is given, also in regard to the conclusions.

[3]Meeting of the Giordano-Bruno Society in Berlin: Date and title of this lecture could not be ascertained. Concerning this society, see Rudolf Steiner, *The Course of My Life*, chapter XXIX; Anthroposophic Press, NY, 1970.

[4]Johann Friedrich Herbart, 1776-1841; German philosopher, psychologist and educator.

[5]Moritz Benedikt, 1835-1920; Criminal psychologist. See Moritz Benedikt, *Aus meinem Leben. Erinnerungen und Eroerterungen*; Vienna 1906, vol. III, p. 315.

Lecture II

[1]Reference to lectures of the Second Course of the School for Spiritual Science.

[2]The threefold human organism was first mentioned by Rudolf Steiner in *Von Seelenraetseln*, GA 21. (*The Case for Anthroposophy*)

[3]Concerning Imagination, Inspiration, and Intuition, three forms of higher perception, see Rudolf Steiner, *An Outline of Occult Science*, chapter: "Knowledge of the Higher Worlds"; Anthroposophic Press, Spring Valley, NY, 1972.

Lecture III

[1]The participants of the second course of the School for Spiritual Science.

[2]Anaxagoras, around 500-428 B.C., Greek philosopher. See Rudolf Steiner, *The Riddles of Philosophy*, Anthroposophic Press, New York, 1973.

341

[3] A retired Major General, Gerold von Gleich emerged as an opponent of Rudolf Steiner in 1921/22 with his lectures that also appeared as brochures and contained an abundance of untruths and distortions of facts.

[4] Origen, around A.D. 185-254, Greek Church writer. Compare also the lecture of June 2, 1921 (Lecture XV in this volume) and note 4 to Lecture XV.

[5] Scotus Erigena, around A.D. 810-877, Irish philosopher and theologian at the court of Charles the Bald in Paris. See Rudolf Steiner, *The Riddles of Philosophy*.

[6] *De divisione naturae*. See the detailed discussion of this work in the lectures of June 2 and June 3, 1921, in this volume (Lectures XV and XVI).

[7] It could not be ascertained which one among the numerous theologians who were active opponents of Rudolf Steiner at that time was being referred to.

Lecture IV

[1] Aurelius Augustinus, A.D. 354-430, Church Father and philosopher. See Rudolf Steiner, *Christianity as Mystical Fact and the Mysteries of Antiquity*, Rudolf Steiner Press, London, 1972.

[2] Hippocrates, 460-377 B.C., founder of Greek medicine. Explained illnesses as results of faulty mixture of four body fluids: blood, yellow bile, phlegm, and black bile.

[3] Mithras: Persian-Indian cult of Mithras, the god of light and sun, spread through Europe in first century B.C. by Roman troops. Celebrations in underground caves, knew baptism, communion, celebration of birthday of the god on December 25.

[4] Arianism, teachings of the presbyter Arius of Alexandria (died A.D. 336), who rejected the idea that Christ's being was identical with the being of God the Father.

[5] Ulfilas (Wulfila in Germanic), A.D. 311-383, missionary to the West-Goths in the Balcan region; founder of Arianic-Germanic Christendom, who translated the Bible into Gothic.

[6] Dionysius the Areopagite, member of the Areopagus in Athens, around A.D. 500. Converted by Paul (Acts 17:34). Connected Christianity with neo-Platonic philosophy. Also compare with Lecture XV of June 2, 1921, in this volume.

7Constantine I., the Great, A.D. 286 or 287-337. Roman emperor from 306 to 337, made Christianity the state religion in 324.

8Justinian I, A.D. 483-565, Byzantine emperor from A.D. 527-565, builder of the Hagia Sophia in Constantinople. In A.D. 529, he closed the Platonic Academy of Athens.

9Basilius Valentinus, born around 1394, alchemist of the fifteenth century. His collected writings were first published in Hamburg by W. S. Lange in 1677.

10Theophrastus Bombastus Paracelsus of Hohenheim, 1493-1541. Concerning this great Swiss doctor and philosopher, see Rudolph Steiner: *Eleven European Mystics*, Rudolf Steiner Publications, New York, 1971.

11Jacob Boehme, 1575-1624, concerning the mysticism of the master shoemaker, see above book.

Lecture V

1Stoicism—philosophy and spiritual view of the Stoa (founded around 300 B.C. by Zeno).

Epicureanism—teaching by Epicurus in the Philosophers' School of Athens, founded by him in 306 B.C.

Both philosophical systems are mainly directed towards practical life, seeking "happiness" in it. The latter is understood to be a rational, moderate striving for self-control and spiritualization without negating nature. (The debauchery of the Epicureans belongs to a later age.)

2Concerning the reasons for this development, see also Rudolf Steiner, *The Mission of the Individual Folk Souls in Relation to Teutonic Mythology*, Rudolf Steiner Press, London, 1970; lecture of June 12, 1910.

3Homer, *Odyssey*, Song XI.

4See Friedrich Nietzsche, *Die Philosophie im tragischen Zeitalter der Griechen*, 1874.

5Thales of Milet, around 625-545 B.C.

6See Note 2, lecture III.

7Heraclitus of Ephesus, around 535-475 B.C., Philosopher of the age preceding Socrates.

8Rudolf Steiner, *The Riddles of Philosophy*, Anthroposophic Press, New York, 1973.

[9]Titurel, founder of the Grail-dynasty (grandfather of Herzeloide and great-grandfather of Parsifal) who erected the Temple of the Grail within 30 years. See Albrecht von Scharffenberg, who, continuing in the manner of Wolfram von Eschenbach, wrote "Juengerer Titurel" between 1270 and 1280.

[10]Scholasticism: medieval philosophy attempting to justify Christian faith through reason. Based itself on Aristotelian philosophy.

[11]Wolfram von Eschenbach, around 1170-1220, Medieval epic writer. Poet of *Parsifal* (1210), a novel in verses, as well as *Willehalm* and a fragment, *Titurel*.

[12]Gottfried of Bouillon, around 1060-1100, leader of the first Crusade in 1096.

[13]Peter of Amiens, around 1050-1115, Augustine prior who moved through France and summoned people to the Crusade; later, he joined Gottfried of Bouillon.

[14]See Rudolf Steiner: *Gesammelte Aufsaetze zur Kulturgeschichte*, Bibl. #31, 1966. Not translated.

[15]*An Outline of Occult Science*, chapter VI: "The Present and Future of Cosmic and Human Evolution. "

Lecture VI

[1]*Heliand*, (meaning "Heiland" or "Savior"), ancient Saxon poetical Gospel work from around A.D. 830.

[2]Reference to the overall tendency of descriptions of Jesus at the end of the 19th and beginning of the 20th centuries.

[3]Vladimir Soloviev, 1853-1900, Russian philosopher and poet.

[4]Reference to the first Waldorf School, established in Stuttgart in 1919, and the first Goetheanum.

[5]Gleich completed his lecture of April 6, 1921, in Stuttgart with a quote from a song by Martin Luther. On the day before, a Jesuit, Sorel, had recommended that people attend this lecture.

Lecture VII

[1]This refers to a petition by the German government, sent to the President of the United States, "to assume the mediation in regard to the question of reparations and to determine

the sum which Germany is supposed to pay to the allied powers. "At the same time, it included "the urgent request to bring about agreement among the Allies for such a mediation. The undersigned solemnly declare that the German government is ready and willing without restriction or reservations to pay the allied powers that amount of reparation deemed fitting and suitable by the President of the United States after a thorough investigation." (News report of the Wolf Agency on April 22, 1921. Evening edition of *Nationalzeitung Basel,* April 22, 1921.)

[2] See lecture of April 2 in this volume (Lecture I)

[3] Friedrich Nietzsche, 1844-1900. See Rudolf Steiner, *Friedrich Nietzsche, Fighter for Freedom* (RSE 473); Rudolf Steiner Publications, New Jersey, 1960.

[4] Aeschylus, 525-456 B.C.; Sophocles, 496-406 B.C. The first famous poets of tragedy in the flowering of Greek culture.

[5] Socrates, 470-399 B.C., Greek philosopher, teacher of Plato and the main discussion-partner in the latter's dialogues.

[6] Richard Wagner, 1813-1883, German opera composer. Composed *Ring of the Nibelungs.*

[7] Ulrich von Wilamowitz-Moellendorf, 1848-1931, professor of classic philology, at the end in Berlin. Author of *Zukunftsphilologie. Eine Erwiderung auf Friedrich Nietzsches "Geburt der Tragoedie"* ("Philology of the Future. A Rebuttal of Friedrich Nietzsche's 'Birth of Tragedy'"), Berlin, 1872.

[8] *Unzeitgemaesse Betrachtungen* by Friedrich Nietzsche, written between 1873 and 1876. They contain: 1. David Strauss, der Bekenner und der Schriftsteller ("David Strauss, Confessor and Writer"); 2. Vom Nutzen und Nachteil der Historie fuer das Leben ("The Use and Abuse of History for Life"); 3. Schopenhauer als Erzieher ("Schopenhauer as Educator"); 4. Richard Wagner in Bayreuth. Friedrich Nietzsche, Works in 3 Volumes, published by Karl Schlechta. Munich 1954-56, vol. 1, p. 135-434.

[9] David Friedrich Strauss, 1818-1874, theologian and author. *Der alte und der neue Glaube. Ein Bekenntnis* ("The Old and the New Faith. A Confession"), Leipzig 1872.

[10] Karl von Rotteck, 1775-1840. *Allgemeine Geschichte* ("General History"), 6 volumes, 1813-1818.

[11] Lujo Brentano, 1844-1931, political economist.

[12] Friedrich Nietzsche, *Richard Wagner in Bayreuth*, texts and outlines, 1872-1876; Complete works, vol. X, published by C. G. Naumann, Leipzig, 1896, p. 395-425.

[13] Arthur Schopenhauer, 1788-1860, German philosopher.

[14] Friedrich von Savigny, 1779-1861, historian of law.

[15] Leopold von Ranke, 1795-1886, historian.

[16] Francois de Voltaire (actually d'Arouet), 1694-1778, French philosopher of the Enlightenment.

[17] Nietzsche's Works vol. VIII, published by C. G. Naumann, Leipzig 1896, p. 355/56. The Poem, "Vereinsamt' ("Desolate") is followed by the poem, "Antwort" ("Reply"), to which reference is made here. It goes:

> Dass Gott erbarm'!
> *Der* meint, ich sehnte mich zurueck
> Ins deutsche Warm,
> Ins dumpfe deutsche Stubenglueck!

> Mein Freund, was hier
> Mich hemmt und haelt, ist *dein* Verstand
> Mitleid mit *dir*!
> Mitleid mit deutschem Quer-Verstand!

> (May God have pity!
> *He* thinks I long to return
> To German warmth,
> Into dull German happiness of mundane homes!

> My friend, what hampers, holds me here
> Is *your* reason,
> Pity for *you*!
> Pity for German perverse reason!)

[18] See Friedrich Nietzsche: *Also sprach Zarathustra* (*Thus Spoke Zarathustra*), 1882; Edition: Schlechta vol. II, p. 177-562.

[19] Adolf von Harnack, 1851-1930, Protestant theologian. *Das Wesen des Christentums* ("The Nature of Christianity"). Sixteen Lectures at the University of Berlin, Leipzig, 1910.

[20] *Der Antichrist. Fluch auf das Christentum* ("The Antichrist. Curse on Christianity"), 1888 Edition: Schlechta vol. II, p. 1161-1236.

[21]Franz Overbeck, 1837-1905. *Ueber die Christlichkeit unserer heutigen Theologie* ("Concerning the Christian Nature of Modern Theology"), 1873.

[22]See in *Also sprach Zarathustra*, part II. Edition: Schlechta vol. II, p. 382.

[23]See lecture of April 17, 1921 in this volume (Lecture VI).

[24]The name of this magazine could not be determined.

[25]See Rudolf Steiner's Mystery Drama, *The Soul's Awakening*, in *Four Mystery Plays*, Steiner Book Centre, Toronto, 1973.

Lecture VIII

[1]Rudolf Steiner: *Theosophy: An Introduction to the Supersensible Knowledge of the World and the Destination of Man.* Rudolf Steiner Press, London, 1973. RSE 592.

[2]"Il Sposalizio", Pinacoteca di Brera, Milano. Raphael, 1483-1520, Italian painter.

Lecture IX

[1]Johannes Scotus Erigena, A.D. 810-877, Irish philosopher of scholasticism in Paris.

[2]Council of 869: See Johannes Geyer, "Ein Konzilbeschluss und seine kulturgeschichtlichen Folgen" in *Die Drei*, vol. X (1922) and Alfred Schuetze, "Das Konzil 869 zu Konstantinopel und die Verleugnung des Geistes" in *Die Christengemeinschaft*, vol. I and II.

[3]Soma drink (Sanscrit): The fermented juice of the soma plant, a leafless vine (*sarcostemma acidum*), mixed with milk or barley, whose intoxicating and enthusing power was worshipped as the God, "Soma." Concerning the occult significance of "Soma" see also H. P. Blavatsky, *The Secret Doctrine*, vol. I and II.

[4]Eucharist-Dispute: The dogma of the Transubstantiation, the transformation of bread and wine into the body and blood of Christ (Fourth Lateran Council, A.D. 1215), was rejected by the Reformation.

[5]Johannes Hus: around 1370-1415, early Czech reformer from Bohemia, banned by the Church in 1410 and burned as a heretic in 1415.

[6]Gottfried Wilhelm Leibnitz, 1646-1716, German philosopher.

[7]"Die Tat"—Monthly Magazine for the Future of German Culture. VIII, 1921, vol. 1.

[8]Oswald Spengler, 1880-1936, German philosopher of culture.

Lecture X

[1]"Bolshevism" in pamphlets of *Stimmen der Zeit* ("Voices of the Times"), 6, 3rd edition Freiburg i. Br., 1919 by Bernhard Duhr, S. J. (1852-1930), historian.

[2]Charles Darwin, 1809-1882, natural scientist.

[3]Karl Marx, 1818-1883.

[4]Gustav Theodor Fechner, 1801-1887, natural scientist and philosopher.

[5]Gustav Robert Kirchhoff, 1824-1887, physicist.

[6]Robert Wilhelm Bunsen, 1811-1899, chemist.

Lecture XI

[1]Francois de Voltaire (actually d'Arouet), 1694-1778, French philosopher of the Enlightenment.

[2]Jean Jacques Rousseau, 1712-1778, French philosopher and pedagogue.

[3]Congress of Verona: Congress of the "Holy Alliance" (1822) to which all the European powers belonged with the exception of England and the Vatican. Under Metternich, it pursued a clearly reactionary course.

[4]Johann Gottlieb Fichte, 1762-1814, German philosopher.

[5]Hermann Grimm, 1828-1901, German art historian and literary critic.

Lecture XII

[1]Joseph-Marie Comte de Maistre, 1753-1821, French diplomat and political theoretician.

[2]Augustine, 354-430, neo-Platonist, Church Father. Converted to Christianity in 387, Bishop of North Africa. Wrote *City of God, Confessions,* among other books.

[3]"Considerations sur la France," London, 1796; "Essai sur le principe generateur des constitutions politiques," Petersburg, 1810; "Du pape," Lyon, 1819.

[4]Plutarch, around A.D. 125, from Chaironea. Greek philosopher and historian of the Roman-Hellenistic age.

[5]Joseph de Maistre, *Les soirees de St. Petersbourg*, 1821, or "Twilight Conversations in St. Petersburg, Discourses About the Reign of Divine Providence in Temporal Matters," with an appendix: "Explanations Concerning the Sacrifices."

[6]Ignatius of Loyola, 1491-1556, founder of the Jesuit Order, canonized in 1622.

[7]Alfonso Maria di Liguori, 1696-1787, founder of the Congregation of the Most Holy Redeemer, canonized in 1839.

[8]Francis Xaverius, 1506-1552, Jesuit; missionary to India and Japan.

[9]John Locke, 1632-1704, English philosopher of the Enlightenment.

[10]Jaques Benigne Bossuet, 1627-1704, French theologian and Church politician.

[11]Voltaire, actually Francois-Marie Arouet, 1694-1778, French theologian and philosopher of the Enlightenment.

[12]Madame De Sevigné's remark concerning an Italian writer: See de Maistre's *Les soirees de St. Petersbourg*, vol. 1, p. 413. Concerning his discourse about Locke, see the whole sixth conversation in *Les Soirees*, vol. 1, p. 337-430.

[13]Jonathan Swift, 1667-1745, Dublin, English writer and satirist.

[14]See note 5.

[15]Leon Gambetta, 1838-1882, French statesman and republican. Remark from a speech on May 4, 1877.

[16]Commune: Socialistic-Communistic community council that ruled over Paris for several months following the armistice of 1871 with Germany. The movement was bloodily defeated in May of 1871.

[17]Boulangism: George Boulanger, 1837-1891, French general and monarchist.

[18]Alfred Dreyfuss, 1859-1935, French officer, banished in 1894 for alleged high treason, pardoned in 1899. The Dreyfuss affair gave rise to consolidation of the political Left in France.

[19]Richard Cobden, 1804-1865, and John Bright, 1811-1889, adherents of free trade, brought about abolition of the grain tariff, which, along with other factors, brought about England's industrial advancement.

[20] Herbert, Earl of Oxford and Asquith, 1852-1928, liberal British Prime Minister in 1914; Edward Grey, 1862-1923, British Foreign Minister in 1914, belonging to the imperialistic faction of the Liberals.

[21] Benjamin Disraeli, Earl of Beaconsfield, 1804-1881, British Prime Minister from 1868 until 1880.

[22] Baron George Cuvier, 1769-1832, and Geoffroy de St.-Hilaire, 1772-1844, French natural scientists. See *Eckermann's Conversations with Goethe,* part 3, conversation of August 2, 1830 (the quote is not verbatim).

[23] August Weissmann, 1834-1914, zoologist.

[24] Ernst Haeckel, 1834-1919, natural scientist.

Lecture XIV

[1] Lectures of May 6, 7, and 8, 1921 in *Colour,* RSE 623, Rudolf Steiner Press, London, 1977.

Lecture XV

[1] Johannes Scotus Erigena, 810-877, Irish philosopher of scholasticism in Paris.

[2] Charles the Bald, 828-877, king of the Franconians, emperor from 875-877.

[3] Dionysius the Areopagite: connected Christianity with neo-Platonic philosophy. Had strong influence on medieval mysticism.

[4] Origen, around 185-254, Greek Church Father in Alexandria, later presbyter in Caesarea; basis of his philosophical theology: *De principiis* ("Peri archon"). Under Justinian I, during the fifth ecumenical council in Constantinople in 553, his teachings were condemned as heretical.

[5] After the Church had forbidden the reading of Scotus Erigena's texts, all editions were ordered burned in 1225.

[6] These words are reported by Plato in *Timaios,* 22 B.C.

Lecture XVI

[1] Publius Cornelius Tacitus, around A.D. 55 until 120, Roman historian and consul. His work, *De origine et situ germanorum,* is the oldest surviving source concerning the geography and ethnography of the Germanic peoples.

[2]Contained in *Die Naturwissenschaft und die weltgeschichtliche Entwicklung der Menschheit seit dem Altertum,* six lectures, 1921. GA 325, 1969.

[3]Oswald Spengler, 1880-1936, philosopher of history and culture.

[4]Eduard Suess, 1831-1914, geologist. *Das Antlitz der Erde,* 3 vol., 1885-1909.

Lecture XVII

[1]Hippocrates, 460-377 B.C., known already in antiquity as the greatest physician.

Phidias, 500-435 B.C., Greek sculptor in Athens, master of classical style.

Plato, 427-347 B.C., Greek philosopher, pupil of Socrates.

Socrates, 470-399 B.C., moral philosopher in Athens, developed Socratic dialog to teach his students to think for themselves.

[2]Galen, A.D. 129-199, outstanding physician in the days of the Roman emperors; personal physician to Marc Aurel. In his writings, he tried to compile all medical knowledge of antiquity.

[3]Julian Apostate, A.D. 332-363, nephew of Constantine the Great, Roman emperor from 361-363.

[4]Constantine I., the Great, 288-337, Roman Emperor from 306-337. Made Christianity the state religion in 324.

[5]Justinian I, see note 8, Lecture IV.

[6]"...to the king of the Persians...": Chosrau Nurshivan (king from A.D. 531-580) invited the sages from all over the world, particularly those versed in medicine, to Persia. He is frequently considered the founder of the academy of Gondishapur.

[7]Zeno the Isaurian, A.D. 426-491, Byzantine emperor from 474-491, closed the school of philosophers in Edessa in 487.

[8]Gondishapur (Djundaisabur), city founded by the king of the Sassanides, Shapur I (242-272). It was the cultural center of the kingdom for a long period.

[9]Ibn Sina Avicenna, 980-1037, Persian philosopher and physician, author of over 100 books.

[10] Ibn Roshd Averroes, 1126-1198, Arabian philosopher and universal scientist. Physician from Cordova. Following Aristotelianism, he attempted to combine philosophy and faith. His rational faith led to his banishment.

[11] Roger Bacon, around 1216-1294, English Franciscan, called doctor mirabilis on account of his comprehensive knowledge. He included natural scientific perceptions in his theological manner of thought.

[12] See note 2 to Lecture XVI.

For Further Reading

Write for a free catalog listing hundreds of titles by Rudolf Steiner and related authors.

In the U.S.A.:

Anthroposophic Press
Bell's Pond, Star Route
Hudson, NY 12534

In Great Britain:

Rudolf Steiner Press
38 Museum Street
London, WC1A 1LP